B/LUC
TS0840695X

)6

Five Up

By the same author:

The Sport of Prince's
Reflections of a Golfer

Flying Colours
The Epic Story of Douglas Bader

Wings of War
Airmen of All Nations tell their Stories (1939-45)

Out of the Blue
The Rôle of Luck in Air Warfare (1917-66)

John Jacobs' Impact on Golf
The Man and his Methods

Thanks for the Memory
Unforgettable Characters in Air Warfare (1939-45)

Glorious Summer
The Story of the Battle of Britain
(With Air Vice-Marshal J. E. 'Johnnie' Johnson, CB, CBE, DSO, DFC)

FIVE UP

A Chronicle of Five Lives

LADDIE LUCAS

WINGHAM PRESS—CANTERBURY

To Jill

First published in Great Britain in 1978 by
Sidgwick and Jackson Limited
Copyright © 1978 P. B. Lucas

ISBN 1 873454 04 X

Dust Jacket Drawings: John Moutray
This revised edition published 1991 by
Wingham Press, Seymour Place, 28 High Street, Wingham, Kent CT3 1AB
Typeset by Rowan Typesetters, Birchington, Kent
Printed by Short Run Press Limited,
Bittern Road, Sowton Industrial Estate, Exeter EX2 7LW.

Acknowledgements

A LIFETIME'S habit, learned early on in Fleet Street (and sometimes mocked at by one's friends), of keeping recorded notes, diaries, quotes, cuttings, photographs, scrap-books and the rest, has conferred many advantages over the years. But never have its benefits been more gratefully appreciated than in the composition of the pages which follow.

This process has not, however, avoided the need to check and check again much of the detail, as, for instance, in the closely woven story of 249 Squadron's contribution to the great air battles for Malta.

Here, as in confirming certain strange wartime events in Fighter Command, I have been signally blessed by the ready help I have received from Group Captain E. B. Haslam and his patient staff at Air Historical Branch (R.A.F.), to whom my many thanks are due.

I am also indebted to two old friends, who, before their recent and untimely deaths, offered valuable help. First, W. A. Douglas, who, in his native City of Edinburgh's 603 Squadron, served with us at Takali throughout those sunny Mediterranean days of 1942, and who later, as the commanding officer of 611, brought to the Coltishall wing, of which I was then the leader, all those special qualities which had first been recognized in him as a young pilot officer in the pre-war Royal Auxiliary Air Force.

Similarly, I remember now the help I received from Wing Commander Johnny Plagis, a stalwart comrade in arms, who headed the splendid Rhodesian contingent in 249 and left his imperishable stamp upon both the Malta battles and, later, the operations of Fighter Command.

I must also record my debt to Madeline Hanes, who typed the manuscript in her spare time—as, indeed, I must thank my brother, Ian, whose years with Northcliffe and Reuters at once cast him in the role of a discerning and encouraging critic of the text and particularly of the references to our golden golfing days at Sandwich in the decade or so after the First World War.

Thanks are further due to the following for permission to quote: Neville Spearman Ltd., publishers, for a quotation from *Aces High* by Christopher Shore and Clive Williams; Cassell & Collier Macmillan Publishers Ltd., for quotations from *Hinge of Fate* and *The Gathering Storm,* both by Winston Churchill; to *The Times* for an excerpt from an article by Bernard Darwin which appeared on 23 November 1934; to the *Daily Express* for an excerpt from an article which I wrote on 23 May 1942.

Finally, to all those friends, acquaintances, characters and heroes who have made the copy for the story, I offer my salute. Life in such company could never have been dull.

Contents

List of Plates

1

Royal and fairly Ancient

Chapter One
The land of make-believe

EVERY DAY was a sunny day at Prince's, Sandwich, in the lovely summers of the early 1920s, just after the First World War. This was the first and original Prince's, the creation of my father and Sir Harry Mallaby-Deeley.

Here was for me, in my childhood, a Land of Make-believe. The larks sang to us from the heavens. Heat waves danced jauntily across the glistening waters of Pegwell Bay. Beyond, the cliffs of Ramsgate, grey and secure, nestled low in the sea, just as they must have done over 1,400 years before when St Augustine landed with his followers at Ebbsfleet.

The country was wealthy in those halcyon days and the great fortunes were still intact. In the front seat of the Rolls-Royces, symbols of the times, sat liveried footmen, upright and disciplined, beside the chauffeurs. The footman's first duty on arrival at the club was to dismount quickly, place a footstool beside the rear passenger door and, with a light and respectful hand ready at the elbow, assist her ladyship graciously to earth on the first stage of the morning round of golf. A faintly submissive and respectful nod of the head finished the procedure off in style, as his lordship, following suit, put foot to turf.

The distinctive smell of Turkish cigarettes . . . the commanding figures in their spotless, cream silk shirts, white flannel trousers (pressed to a razor's edge) and white buckskin shoes . . . the occasional straw hat with its slightly faded Marylebone Cricket Club ribbon, and the equally faded I. Zingari tie (secured by gold pin) to complement it . . . all these little incidentals seemed to form a natural, yet discerning, part of the daily scene.

The girls (I don't know why, at the age of seven or so, I noticed these things), neat in their immaculate white pleated dresses, with hats or bandeaux (Nancy Astor, I recall, always wore a purple-coloured veil, which made her face a mystery), seemed, by comparison, quite soberly attired. God knows what my father would have said if some of these modern pro-ettes from the U.S. ladies' PGA tour, with their abbreviated and close-fitting coverings, had suddenly descended upon this preserve of high society.

If, after the morning round, the players stayed to lunch, watched over by the stern and dutiful Parsons, the steward, they were met with a cold table of infinite variety and quality, the like of which I was not to see again until, nearly two decades later, a year before the Second World War, I sampled the seafood they served at the Sunday lunches at the Seminole in Palm Beach, hard by the Florida coast, one of the loveliest places in all the world to play golf.

Everyone seemed to come, at one time or another, to Prince's in the 1920s. The then Prince of Wales and his brother, the Duke of Kent; members of the aristocracy; golfing members of the social clubs of London—White's, Buck's, the Bath Club, the Turf, the Junior Carlton; the Services' golfing societies; the Parliamentary Ladies'; the bankers, the newspaper barons, the politicians.

I retain to this day the clearest picture of my father wrestling each evening after tea, during the long parliamentary recess, with the way-ward game of the ever-spruce and well-dressed Captain David Margesson, who was later to become Chief Whip of the Tory Party. He believed he helped Margesson with his golf not because of any improvement in method—that, he said, would have been impossible—but because of the tranquillizing effect he was able to have upon the embryo Chief Whip's temper.

My father was much sought after as a teacher. He was more adept at the art than many a professional. He had the advantage of the games player's eye for style—and fault. He had himself played rugby football for Cambridge against Oxford and a lot of good cricket at the university without actually gaining a second Blue. He had, moreover, taught himself to play golf well enough to win the first Norfolk Amateur Championship ever played—at Royal Norwich in 1894—and to repeat the performance four years later at Sheringham.

To his games-playing ability he added a proficiency with a shotgun which, in his native Norfolk, some of the older ones still talked about when I was sent to Coltishall to command the fighter wing in wartime.

I remember shooting one day at Wroxham and the rather elderly next-door gun to me saying that he had often shot with my father. There was none better, he said, at high pheasants on a windy November day.

Lord Northcliffe, then moving upwards to the pinnacle of his dominion over Fleet Street, was a frequent visitor. Like others among the national figures of the time who came to Prince's, he found in my father not only a formidable personality with a determined and decisive character, who would stand no nonsense whatever— particularly from those who might have thought themselves immune—but also those qualities of trust, humanity and understanding which endeared him to many. He was a patient and discreet listener to the troubles of the mighty. But there is no denying it, he was an autocrat, running Prince's exactly to his taste, without the aid of committees or any other persons or bodies. Under his single, benevolent direction, I haven't a doubt that it was a happy place where people enjoyed their golf. They always seemed to come back for more.

Northcliffe spent the weekends and holidays at his Sandgate Castle close by the North Foreland. He would motor over to Sandwich each day, bringing with him the professional from the local club. In the back of his open coupé—the 'dicky' it used to be called—sat his boy caddie in splendid isolation, the bags of clubs propped up beside him. His lordship's initial act each morning was to go into the club and bring out a glass of milk for the boy. Another distinguished figure I well recollect seeing in frequent and interested conversation with my father was Baron Emile d'Erlanger, the head of the merchant bank which for long carried the family name. Emile d'Erlanger always had time for a word of encouragement for a small boy. Now and then, if I happened to have a club in my hand near the eighteenth green when he was finishing his round, he would throw me the ball he had been using, adding in that familiar and very un-English accent: 'Now see if you can hit *that* one.'

Long after my father's death, when I was working on the Sunday Express, I often used to stay with Emile d'Erlanger at his little cottage at Hythe in Kent. I can still smell the honeysuckle which grew in profusion around the front door. 'I like simple, humble things,' he used to say. 'I hate pretentiousness.'

*   *   *

Of all the families who came regularly to Prince's during the long summer holidays, the Astors and the Slazengers seemed most of all to dominate the scene.

Not surprisingly, the children's tennis parties which the Slazengers gave at their seaside house overlooking the fifth hole at St George's were highly organized affairs. The prizes were specially coveted. Fortunately, the standard of play among the competitors was so abysmal that I was usually able to lay claim to a choice part of the spoils.

But it was the pick-up cricket games in the garden of Rest Harrow, the Astors' rambling house at Sandwich Bay, which really brought things to life. They were rumbustious affairs, splendidly typical of the Astors, with rules and standards of umpiring which certainly wouldn't have passed muster at Lord's. The bowling was as erratic as the hitting and my recollection is of balls flying all over the place, into bushes, against the house, occasionally through windows. No one seemed to mind.

I had two special cricketing advantages. My cousin, A. P. Lucas, the magical 'Cousin Alfred' to my family but 'Bunny' to everyone else, had played several times for England against Australia as well as for Cambridge and Essex. As a schoolboy at Uppingham he had gone stone deaf—the result, it was always alleged, of being boxed over the ears by an aggressive master. Yet, remarkably, this disability did not seem to impair his forward march in the game.

I recall, as a young journalist, being despatched to do an interview with the great Sir Pelham Warner. In his characteristically kindly way with the young, Plum Warner tried to put me at ease by asking if I was a relation of A. P. Lucas. When I said I was, he made a comment which is still firm in the memory. 'Lord Harris used to say that Bunny Lucas was the best runner between the wickets he ever saw. I suppose to compensate for his deafness he was more alert than the rest.'

Cousin Alfred came occasionally to see us at Prince's. When he did, he and my father would take me off to the wicket which we kept specially cut out between the eighteenth green and the old seventeenth tee.

I treasure the memory of these two, under a hot August sun, coats off, braces exposed, each wearing a light grey trilby hat, bowling round-arm to me with a seriousness which, in retrospect, was engaging. As I was put through my paces, I can hear Cousin Alfred repeating, quite sternly, not to me but to my father: 'Percy, you must make him use his feet; he must use his feet to get to the pitch of the ball; we'll never make a batsman of him if you let him stand there flat-footed.' It was, though I didn't realize it at the time, a heaven-sent lesson—rather like showing a small boy how to grip a golf club and stand to the ball. The rest of it doesn't matter very much.

Then there were the excursions from Prince's in our old T-model Ford, with its brass parts gleaming, to Canterbury during the Cricket Week in August. These were marvellous days on one of the prettiest grounds in all England. I used to sit in front on the grass with the other boys, mesmerized by my beloved Frank Woolley. He was left-handed and so was I. I felt, in my Land of Make-believe, that we had much in common.

In the dash for the pavilion as the players walked off the ground for the various intervals, I was always well up with the fastest boys. If I got Frank Woolley's and Tich Freeman's autographs once I must have had them a dozen times. They were my first real, live cricketing heroes.

So perhaps it wasn't so strange that the frivolities of the Astor's cricket parties went rather against the grain. I wanted them so much to be serious. But I knew I was on good ground when it came to the golf. My father used to detail me from time to time to play with the Astor boys—Michael and Jakie and, towards the end of our time at Prince's, with Bill, who was several years older. Here, I felt, I could call the tune.

There was, however, more to it than the golf. Their father, the 2nd Viscount, and mine always got along comfortably together. One day I was out on the course with my father when Lord Astor came over to speak to him. I could go to the exact spot now. It was close by the old sixth green near where the coastguard cottages stood and close to where I shot my first partridge. I can still remember his words. 'I've had a piece of luck,' he said, 'My horse has won the Oaks. I want to give your little boy a present. I want him to have £100. It might be a help one day.'

When, years later, in 1936, I was picked, as an undergraduate, to go with the British team to America for the Walker Cup match against the United States at Pine Valley, I drew the money out of my savings.

Because, after a long run of good golf, my form fell away, I did not play in the match itself. The visit was, thus, to bring me the first big disappointment of my life and the first real test in adversity. But the cash helped me to forget.

*   *   *

The putting greens at Prince's became a legend in the inter-war years. After his family, they were my father's first joy. He was a genius with grass and possessed some second sense as regards its quality and preservation. Self-taught, apart from a spell in earlier days at an agricultural college, he was a protagonist of unsophisticated dressings provided by nature, by animal life, and by the sands of the sea. He eschewed the artificial in favour of the natural.

After surviving the rigours of the First World War, the course became a battle-training ground in the Second. Those hallowed putting surfaces were actually used as targets for mortar fire. When someone broke the dreadful news to Lord Brabazon, an old friend of my father's, and a long-time member of the club, who was then a member of Churchill's War Cabinet, he exclaimed, aghast, 'My God, it's like throwing darts at a Rembrandt.'

The key to the broad appeal of the original Prince's, of which my father had been a principal architect, was that it provided such an appealing test for all classes of player. On the one hand, it was sufficiently sympathetic, at any rate from the medium and ladies' tees, to offer a tolerable challenge for the ordinary mortal without in any way seeming overwhelming. If it had its fierce features, these were such that the meek and lowly could circumvent them without loss of pride.

On the other hand, Prince's was a stern enough examination to enable the Royal and Ancient Golf Club of St Andrew's, the governing body of golf, in its wisdom, to take the Open Championship of 1932 there for the special benefit, as it turned out, of the wonderfully likable and ever-smiling Gene Sarazen, one of the finest and certainly one of the most genial of all the great American players. He had been a frequent visitor here and he was, by then, in any case, ready for victory.

Years afterwards, in company with my old partner Leonard

Crawley, Gene came to lunch at the Bath Club in London. We talked of Prince's and I told him of my father's involvement with it. We had reached the coffee and Gene, having listened attentively to the story, put his cigar down, thoughtfully and deliberately, on the ashtray in front of him.

'Then I want to tell you,' he said—and he spoke seriously as if he intended that I should understand he meant it—'your Dad built a magnificent golf course; in my judgment, the greatest championship golf course in the British Isles. You should be real proud of that.'

Spoken with such authority, and even allowing for the licence of poetry and prejudice, it was a stirring tribute. I thought how moved my father would have been to hear it. Alas, he had died comparatively early, when I was no more than eleven; and five years before Sarazen's seventy-two holes' total of 283 had lifted him to the summit of the golfing world.

*   *   *

As for pride in my father's achievement, Gene Sarazen need have had no doubt about that. As a young boy, I was always taken on Sundays to Matins at St Clement's church at Sandwich. After the Creed, the Lord's Prayer and the Collects, we came to the Prayer for the King's Majesty. As the vicar intoned the familiar words—'O Lord, our heavenly father, high and mighty, king of kings, lord of lords, the only ruler of princes . . .'—I was utterly convinced he had but one person in mind.

My father.

Chapter Two
Through my bedroom window

NINETEEN TWENTY-TWO was a vintage year for British golf—and for Sandwich.

The Ladies' Championship came to Prince's and confirmed, beyond doubt, that in Joyce Wethered, Britain had found a golfer of almost unbelievable promise.

The Open Championship was played at St George's, and the incomparable Walter Hagen won for the first time. By his flamboyance and his life style ("I don't want to be a millionaire, I only want to live like one"), and by the daringly bold quality of his golf, he was to open the way for the widely publicized players who were to follow—for Henry Cotton, Arnold Palmer, Jack Nicklaus and the rest of the modern masters.

These were stirring times for a small boy of seven.

One morning, a few days before the championship started at St George's, I was looking out of my bedroom window with my father when a dream became real.

On to the first tee in front of us walked four arresting figures with their caddies. The qualifying rounds for the Open were being played at Prince's and Walter Hagen, startlingly attired in many colours, Jim Barnes, Jock Hutchison and Harry Vardon were going out together to have a look at the course. What talent was there!

Barnes had just won the United States' championship and within a couple of years was to add ours to his portfolio. Jock Hutchison was the reigning British champion, having come over from Chicago the previous year to beat Joyce Wethered's brother, Roger, in a famous replay at St Andrews. Harry Vardon—my father's idol, and a good deal older than the others—had already won our championship six times and, but for the war years, would probably have won another. Twenty years now separated him from his first and only victory on

American soil. As for Hagen, he had already twice won the United
States' title and was now on the threshold of international greatness.

Parental permission having been granted, I was off downstairs and
out of the house as quickly as my young legs would take me. Away we
went down the first fairway; just these four magnetic men, their
caddies, and me—a small boy, cock-a-hoop and quite alone with his
heroes. Strangely, it wasn't so much the golf as the bearing and
presence of these wonderful figures that absorbed me.

No one took any notice of me till we got close to the eighteenth
green. By then I was trudging wearily along. It had been a long way
round. Jim Barnes—I can see that figure now, a human stringbean of a
man, his tousled hair all over the place walked over to me. He seemed
so full of purpose I was afraid lest I had made some mistake.

'Son,' he said, 'have you got any clubs?' I nodded assent.

'Then I'll see you on the first tee' (pointing to it) 'at five this
evening. Bring your clubs with you.'

Promptly at five, this rangy and disturbingly tall man appeared from
the clubhouse with two boxes of new—yes, new—balls under his arm.
Each one had his name, 'Jim Barnes', stamped on it. He took me to
the front, ladies' teeing ground.

'I want you to tee these balls up and hit them hard. Each one that
finishes on the fairway you can keep.'

Recognizing that such a chance wouldn't come again, I spurned the
driver and went for safety, extracting from my bag a favourite little
spoon. Abe Mitchell had had it made for me in his shop at the North
Foreland, second prize in the local juvenile competition, beaten,
dammit, by three shots by Henry Longhurst, of whom the
distinguished golf correspondent of the *Daily Mail*, Endersby Howard,
wrote the next day: 'Longhurst, a sturdy little fellow, embarked upon
his task with all due circumspection . . .'

Modesty prevents me from disclosing the result of this primary
examination in accuracy. Suffice it to say that if no ball had reached
the fairway, I have no doubt Barnes would still have given me the lot.
They made a welcome change from the large Silver King 'Green Dot'
floaters with which, hitherto, my father in his innate wisdom, had
always compelled me to play.

A quarter of a century later, almost to the month, when the British
team, of which I was then captain, was in America for the Walker Cup

match, I met Jim Barnes again at Winged Foot, outside New York. Fred Robson, one of the most splendid characters of British professional golf, who had come over with us as coach to the side, was with me.

I reminded Barnes of the incident at Prince's. Sadly, he had long since forgotten all about it. 'Never mind, Jim,' said Fred, who had a knack of putting people at ease, 'who knows, but for your little encouragement our captain might not have been here today.'

*   *   *

The incidents come tumbling over one another. One day I saw a four-ball game which included Arthur Havers, who, within a year, was to win the championship at Troon—the last British player to do so until 1934 when, at St George's, Henry Cotton broke the run of United States' successes—and Abe Mitchell.

At the short fourteenth on the original course, Havers hit a beautifully flighted medium iron towards the target. It pitched on the top left-hand side of the green, and, with its slight fade, broke right, and, miracle of miracles, rolled gently down into the cup, the first hole-in-one I had seen.

By one of those curious quirks of fortune, I was playing a year or two later at Prince's with my father and one of my sisters when we came to the third, an exceptionally good one-shot hole of 154 yards. After my father and sister had driven, I hit my ball in the direction of the green using my trusted little Abe Mitchell spoon which I have recently given to Prince's for the juniors to play for annually in open competition.

The first two balls were quickly found but mine was nowhere to be seen. Having hunted everywhere, my father, in a final acknowledgment to providence, looked in the hole. He bent down and picked the ball out. 'They'll never believe it,' he exclaimed.

As I was nine years old at the time, there was inevitably speculation about whether this was a record for the 'youngest' hole-in-one. Within a year or two the *Golfer's Handbook* left the world in no doubt. A similar feat had been accomplished in California by some little perisher aged seven. Now the same source tells us that the mantle has passed to Tommy Moore, who at six years, one month and seven days—never mind the minutes—on 8 March 1968, achieved an ace at the 145-yards fourth hole at Woodbrier, Martinsville, West Virginia. My name has long since disappeared from the lists.

* * *

After my father died and we went to live in Hertfordshire, my brother used to take me back to Prince's each August for a fortnight's golf. I was at Stowe then and playing cricket and rugger for the school. Games, in those adolescent years, were my life.

Fortuitously, another summer visitor to Sandwich was Sir Ernest Holderness, one of the best of all Britain's amateur golfers in the inter-war years. He was in the habit of taking one of the coastguard cottages behind the old sixth green for his family's annual holiday.

Holderness, after coming down from Oxford, had won the 1931 Amateur Championship twice in three years just after the First World War. He had also captured the Oxford and Cambridge Golfing Society's President's Putter at Rye in each of the first four years the tournament was played. A fifth victory came a few years later, an extraordinary record for one who was then on the way to becoming a senior and distinguished civil servant at the Home Office and who, necessarily, had little time to play.

Every morning during this August period he would ask us to play with him. Usually it was just the three of us, Sir Ernest, my brother and myself; very occasionally some illustrious individual would come in to make a fourth. We always played off the furthest back tees on those rounds and all the putts had to be holed out. This was a serious exercise and was not to be treated as anything else. There was little conversation.

Holderness carried his nine or ten clubs (the woods all had steel shafts but the rusty iron heads had hickory sticks in them) in an old 'drain pipe' bag, and mostly, he went round in 70, 71 or 72. If he holed more putts than usual, or if the weather was very still, it might be 68. If the wind blew hard, it could be 74. He hit all his shots the same shape, as if giving them 'no option'; but he could move the ball either way in a wind at will. His form never seemed to vary.

He was spare of physique, so in his prime he never had quite the potential of the strongest players of the day; but as a striker and as a precision robot, discharging a golf ball day in and day out, from tee to

target, I only saw one other British amateur who was his equal—
R. J. White, with whom I later played for England.

Ernest Holderness was a shy and reserved man, but he was always
ready to hold out an uninhibited hand to a young and enthusiastic
player who wanted to learn. Often, after our morning round, he would
say, 'I will be in the cottage after tea if you want to come and hit some
balls with me.' And for a priceless hour or so, with no one else within
sight, we would fire ball after ball, taking it in turns to hit. It was all
made the easier for me because I used to get the impression he was
enjoying it just as much as I was.

In 1933, immediately after our last summer stint at Prince's, during
which the same absorbing daily routine was observed, I went north
with my brother to Carnoustie to captain the English boys' team
against the Scots and to play in the Boys' Championship.

It was my fifth and last attempt to win this tournament and I wanted
greatly to succeed. By now the Scots boys had established a definite
ascendency over us. Most of them could play golf all through the
summer, whereas at Stowe, where I had just finished the first of my
two seasons as captain of the cricket XI, we weren't allowed to touch
a golf club for the three months of the summer term—not, that is, if
you were also a cricketer. We were thus at a disadvantage, having no
more than three weeks in August in which to lift our game.

After the first round or two at Carnoustie, I began to feel I could
win. Here was a man-size course, a real scholarship test. If I could
survive the short, eighteen-hole encounters, and reach the final, I
thought it unlikely that on such a golf course I would be beaten over
thirty-six holes. All came right in the end. After I had won Ernest
Holderness wrote me a touching letter, full of feeling and
encouragement. He knew, I think, what a void my father's early and
untimely death had left in my life, and during those summer visits to
Prince's he had tried, in a golfing sense, to answer a need. I got the
feeling that my humble triumph in Scotland had brought him as much
delight as if it had belonged to his own son.

*   *   *

Prince's was fertile territory for a budding Cambridge patriot. Here
Cambridge University played Oxford six times between 1912 and the

outbreak of the Second World War, and only once failed to win. For
me, the contest of 1922 was memorable not because of the agonizing
narrowness of the Cambridge victory, but because of a single
downwind drive I saw Cyril Tolley hit, before the match itself, at the
old eleventh, a fine dog-legged hole to the left, over a range of hills
which used to be called the Himalayas. For ordinary mortals, the hole
that day was a drive and what we then called a mashie-niblick; today a
No. 8.

Cyril, whose lovely, round, fluid swing had already won him an
Amateur Championship and was, before long, to win him another—as
well as, remarkably, two French Opens at La Boulie against the cream
of the British and European professionals—was as long a driver then
as anyone else in the land. And, perhaps, longer.

The picture of the stroke is still sharp in the mind. It was hit dead
centre, right off the 'meat'. As Fred Robson, the great teacher, would
have said, you could 'taste it'. The ball came swinging in from the
right, borne on the wings of a strong tail wind blowing in from the
north-east across Pegwell Bay, to fit exactly the shape of the left-hand
dog-leg. It finished just to the right of the green, and level with the
pin, *408 yards away*. In fifty subsequent years, I never saw its like
again even from Nicklaus.

Cyril did not actually take part in that encounter but, during it, I
recollect my father, prophetically, saying to me: 'Perhaps, one day,
you will play in this match.' Fifteen years later, in my last year at
Cambridge, when I was captain of the team, it was our turn to select
the venue for the match against Oxford. I picked Prince's .

It was nice to win on home ground. Bernard Darwin gave me a
generous mention afterwards: 'With his victory over Mitchell-
Innes at Prince's, Lucas has now played top for Cambridge in each
of his three undergraduate years, and won each time. It is
something which, I think, has not been done before; and when the
names of his two other adversaries—Pennink and Duncan—are
placed beside his latest victim, it makes a record which I doubt will
ever be equalled.'

But none of us, in that match, ever drove a ball anywhere near the
old eleventh green.

*   *   *

Manston, the forward airfield in East Kent during the Second World War, to which we often moved to fly the sweeps over France, held a commanding view across the marshes to the golf club away to the south. For me nostalgia was never very far away. It seemed weird and unreal to be flying with the Royal Air Force no more than a few miles from the course which had been my home. Looking down on the place from a Spitfire aroused in me a sense of protection, rather like a dog defending his house against all comers.

Coming back one day from an escort mission to Lille, in northern France, I was hit, in circumstances best left unsaid, fair and square in the engine and starboard wing by a German Messerschmitt 109. At around 17,000 or 18,000 feet over Le Touquet, with smoke in the cockpit and the Rolls-Royce Merlin sounding disagreeably rough, things weren't promising. Ahead the Straits of Dover, sparkling in the clear September sunlight, had to be crossed. Halfway across, as the white cliffs began to beckon persuasively from the other side of the water, the engine called it a day.

As I was turning over the possibilities—and the impossibilities— away in the distance the outline of the Guilford Hotel, grey, tall and stark, standing guard over Sandwich Bay, came into view. A moment later I saw the clubhouse at Prince's. This was quite sufficient to dispel any nasty thoughts about bailing out. I felt I might just have the height, if I stretched the glide, to try to force-land somewhere around the first, second, fourth and twelfth fairways of the old course. Local knowledge, I knew, would be on my side.

After a few traumatic minutes, it became clear that I should have enough height at least to reach the coast; 2,000 feet over Deal seemed sufficient to give my plan a chance. Keeping the clubhouse as a marker, I aimed the Spitfire for Prince's. True to all known form, I missed not only the first, but the second, fourth, twelfth, eighth and ninth fairways, and the whole course, as well—in that order. The aircraft came to rest smoothly, and without incident, on its belly, out of bounds in the marsh at the back of the old ninth green, just short of the River Stour and no more than two or three miles from Manston. I noticed it was close to the bank where we often used to stand and flight duck on a winter's evening.

I undid my straps, got up in the cockpit and looked round.

As far as I could see, the whole of Prince's—fairways, greens, everything—was overgrown. Unless you knew it as I did, you would hardly have recognized the place.

What a damned shame, I thought, after all that had gone before.

Chapter Three
Then—and now—a hero

IT WAS the autumn of 1937 and Henry Cotton had just won his second Open Championship, this time in the face of the might of the United States' Ryder Cup team, with Nelson and Snead in it for the first time, one of the strongest American sides ever to come to Britain. His closing seventy-one at Carnoustie, under the whip and in atrocious conditions, had been as fine a round of championship golf as I, or anyone else, had ever seen.

He was now at the summit of his career, and still only thirty.

He drove a big red Mercedes, he wore suits made by Hawes and Curtis and silk shirts and cashmere pullovers fashioned by Izod, and he lived in a style hitherto unknown to British professional golf.

He was sustained, in many ways, by the wealthy and highly perceptive South American who became his wife. He and his friends called her Toots. It is arguable whether he could have achieved what he did without her. As he made his way down the fifteenth fairway in the last round of the 1934 Open at St George's, having apparently regained his winning stride after some terrible initial excursions, he turned to her as she walked beside him and said: 'Toots, I can't go on. I can't go on. My legs have gone.' What she said in reply doesn't matter now. But it had the effect she intended.

He was a controversial figure, surrounded by controversy, not least because he was an unconventional man who did unconventional things. He rather enjoyed playing it that way. Because, at the time, he was better at his job than anyone else in Britain (and probably the world), and because he was frequently involved in arguments, he was page one news.

He was content only with the best, and had driven himself mercilessly to attain it. He was always concerned for his health and went to exceptional lengths to build up his strength and fitness. He

27

was fastidious to a point about food—principally, I think, because early on he hadn't bothered about diet and had paid the resultant penalty.

He had a fertile and agile business brain, talked well and thought originally. He spoke fluent French with a strange, rather high, nasal accent. He wrote all his own copy for the newspapers. There was a colloquial simplicity about his writing and a personality with it, which could readily be recognized.

People used to make a fuss about his so-called 'public school education'—he was at Alleyn's School at Dulwich—but he never played it up himself. What he did go on at length about was being the reluctant bag-carrier for the cricket XI. He never, curiously, gave me the impression of being what is called 'a natural games player'; indeed, I don't think he was one. But he made himself, by ability, application, industry, intellect and, if the truth be told, guts, into a marvellous golf player. He may well have been, in his prime, the most precise *striker* of the lot, Hogan, Nelson, Snead and Nicklaus included. I've seen them all and I believe he was. But that's a stupid argument. All I'm concerned with is what I think—prejudice, licence, blind faith, hero worship, all thrown in.

Years later, he and I were on the bill at the annual dinner of the Professional Golfers' Association (his trade union) at Grosvenor House in London, a massive affair with 1,200 or 1,300 present. Brabazon of Tara and Bruce of Melbourne were also on the toast list. As I was following him, I telephoned him a couple of days beforehand and asked what he was going to say—a dark practice, not unknown to political science. 'I've no idea, boy,' he said. 'I'll pick up a few points from Brab and Bruce and put something together when I feel the mood. I like doing it that way.'

In the event, when he got up, he pulled out of his pocket several sheets of closely typewritten notes and proceeded to launch into a vehement, spirited and well-prepared attack on some of the methods and practices of his union. It caused great umbrage. For me it was a visitation from heaven—not least because I was fully expecting it and, anyway, had just been listening, that very afternoon, to Aneurin Bevan doing the same thing to his own front bench in the House of Commons.

There were plenty of people who were ready to run him down,

usually because they were jealous of him. Or didn't know him. Or both. He had his enemies and his detractors. Sometimes, let's face it, with reason. But, equally, he had his defenders and his friends who would have been willing to face a firing squad in support of him. I confess I was one among this number. I still am, despite the passage of time—and the advance of discretion and judgment.

He charged, for those days, heavily—particularly when he knew the customer could pay—because he had a proper pride in his ability and reckoned that what he was offering was unique and should be paid for. When the reverse was the case, and a young pupil was short of cash, he went light on his fees, or didn't charge anything at all. He remembered he had come up a harder way than some and that money had once been tight.

When I took the Cambridge team to Ashridge to play with him and be coached by him every day for a fortnight, he charged us each a fiver for the two weeks—no more. But he expected the twelve impecunious undergraduates to turn up each day—which they did, without fail.

He was at his very best at this time, in the late 1930s. People have forgotten now how good he was then. I haven't; nor have those who understand the game and who knew him at first hand in those years. He could flight and manoeuvre a golf ball with exquisite control, generally because he knew more about it than his contemporaries, British or American. He would say that golf should be played with the hands, but he had one of the best 'arm swings' in the game and his set-up to the ball never varied. He would tell you you should be able to hit a golf ball standing any way—on one leg or two, or even on the run provided your hands were trained. But it makes life easier if you can find the right set-up day in and day out. He stood *consistently* better to the ball, Fred Robson once told me, than anyone else he had seen, unless it was Ernest Holderness.

He went to the United States early in his career to see what there was there to learn. He concluded there wasn't much that he couldn't find out for himself. He played a lot with Tommy Armour, the Scot, who had himself settled in America and who, despite the loss of an eye, won both the United States and the British championships. Armour told me one day, when we were playing together at Boca Raton in Florida, that there was nothing about the young visitor's game in those earlier days which suggested that it might take him to the top—unless it was his blind determination to get there.

When he had reached his peak at Carnoustie, no offer would tempt him to the United States. If they wanted to take him they must come here to try. There was no point then in going to America. The money was here. The pound sterling could look five dollars straight in the eye. And our Open was the most coveted championship on earth. Jones and Hagen and Sarazen had already given it their seal.

When, after the war, he went back to the United States in the winter before his third, and last, Open victory—at Muirfield—it was simply to train, to eat good food, and to lift his game in preparation for one more assault on the peak. Whenever he was out at work on a practice ground, the American professionals would gather round and sit silently watching him hit. They said nothing, but inside they must have felt his like might not pass that way again. The fact that he won a tournament during his stay is purely incidental. . . .

The autumn, then, of 1937 . . . and here he is, once more the confirmed Open champion. Ashridge, his club in Hertfordshire, is holding a dinner for him in the big room of the Dorchester Hotel in London. It is a sparkling evening, splashed about with colour and ceremonial, a coming together of the golfing forces, an occasion on which, in the future, it will be nice to look back and say, 'I was there.'

His health is proposed by one of the best three or four in the after-dinner business—by the Hon. and Gallant Gentleman, the Member for the Wallasey Division of Cheshire, close to the heart of the textile country, Lieutenant-Colonel J. T. C. Moore-Brabazon, holder of the Military Cross, not yet a cabinet minister, not yet ennobled, and still with a few holes left to play before election to the captaincy of the Royal and Ancient Golf Club of St Andrews.

The Master of Ceremonies tees up the introduction . . . Then the pause, as the speaker, large, balding head thrust forward, stooping slightly and round-shouldered, eyes looking over the top of half-moon spectacles, notes (very full notes) held in the right hand, casually masked by the dinner menu, Turkish cigarette being puffed through a long, tortoiseshell and gold holder . . . The long pause, as the speaker, highly practised in the art, waits—timing, as usual, perfect—for the company to settle and silence to prevail.

And then the familiar, slightly cracking, metallic voice, with its acute enunciation, penetrates the room, confident and positive. 'It is, I suppose, only right [pause] that a Member of Parliament, whose constituency borders on Merseyside and Liverpool [pause], should be asked to get up on his hind legs [pause] and talk about—Cotton.

'Ladies and gentlemen, as Henry Longhurst was the first to call him, the Maestro.'

In golf, there was only one—my good friend, Henry Cotton.

Chapter Four
Diagnosing the Patient

> ... that we but teach
> Bloody instructions, which, being taught, return
> To plague the inventor; ...
> (*Macbeth,* Act 1, Scene VII.)

WHEN ONE looks back over the last fifty years of golf and contemplates the distance we have travelled along the instructional road—with its truths and falsehoods, its orders and counter-orders, its secrets and exposures, its sense and nonsense, its parables and realities—it is then that one begins to see the extent and depth of the morass we have come through if, indeed, we have come through it.

Some victims have, inevitably, been lost along the way. Others are still missing, presumed killed. And then there are the prisoners who, although they may not know it, can hardly expect to be accorded the usual civilities of golf's Geneva Convention.

Someone once asked Longhurst, just before he put his clubs up in the loft for good, how his game was progressing. 'Sunk without trace,' was the reply—and he wasn't the only one. Thousands upon thousands of conflicting words have been offered and written under the guise of 'instruction'. For every ten unimpeachable authorities who used to tell us to 'hit late', another ten can now be found proclaiming that a golf ball should be 'hit early'.

For every person who contends that golf is a right-handed game played with the left hand, or a left-handed game played with the right hand, there is always someone else who will claim that the opposite is the truth.

For each advocate of the belief that the true path of the golf swing is from inside to out, there is an opponent who will say, not so, the swing plane is from inside to inside.

For each professor who alleges that golf is 75 per cent hands and 25 per cent the rest, at least one graduate will be found to advance the thesis that the accent should really be on the legs rather like Byron Nelson says.

For every protagonist of the 'head down and slow back' theory, you will now find a swelling band of patrons who adhere to the principle that the head should be kept up and the rhythm to the player's natural speed. 'Head down and slow back and you'll keep me in business for ever.' The journal of the Professional Golfers' Association of America once picked out and splashed these words as a headline for an article. They belong to John Jacobs, perhaps the best teacher of them all.

The problem the poor golfing citizen has to face is that, possibly without knowing it, the majority of the professors (yes, yes, we know the exceptions) tell us not how they *play* golf, but how they themselves *feel* we ought to play. And between that, and what we actually *need* to be told, there lies, I fear, a gaping divide. It is this abyss which separates the few exceptional teachers—a dozen or so in the world— from the rest who do their best for us, sustained happily by the knowledge that, in golf, as in life, hope will always spring eternal.

*   *   *

Two teachers of golf, in my extensive book, select themselves for mention. And the arresting fact is that, in technique, they have, or had, much in common with each other.

Although, blessedly, we were allowed to continue to enjoy his company for some years after the Second World War, Fred Robson really belonged to the inter-war years. Addington, his last club, became the Harley Street where all, in the end, were obliged to repair. To walk slowly with him from his shop, over to the long second hole on the Old Course, with the tall fir on the right, was to feel at once a sympathetic humanity which is given only to the few who mix humility and gentleness with greatness.

I once sent a friend to him, quite a respectable player, whose principal fault, as he himself well knew, was a total inability to relax when addressing, or swinging at a golf ball. After a few minutes with the driver, Fred stopped him. 'There's nothing much wrong with you, Mr X,' he said. 'All we've got to do with you is to break down them adhesions.'

Sometimes he had recourse to aids which were, to say the least, bizarre. There was a serious-minded and purposeful New Zealander who played in the Cambridge side with me in the 1930s named Ian Ewen. We were in the same college and close friends. He was having a struggle to find a place in the team against Oxford so I sent him off to see Fred. Every fortnight, unbeknown to his tutor, he motored down to Addington, and although his game improved perceptibly during the season the victories he so badly needed eluded him. His prospects, as the university match drew nearer, looked poor.

One evening, Ian came into my rooms holding a bottle of black medicine. 'Fred's given me this,' he said, without the semblance of a smile. 'He thinks I get a bit jumpy before these matches and that's the trouble; he calls it "his settling medicine". Says some of the pros take it during the tournaments. I have to take two tablespoons half an hour before I go out.'

Ian Ewen won most of his last matches in the Lent Term including, finally, his foursome and single against Oxford.

When next I saw Fred I tackled him about this mixture. 'What was that stuff you gave Mr Ewen, Fred?' I asked. 'It certainly did the trick.'

'Oh,' he replied, with a chuckle, 'that's just a little tonic Dr Flaherty makes up for me for one or two of my pupils who don't seem to be able to settle.'

'Yes, Fred,' I persisted, 'but what's *in* it?'

'Don't you tell Mr Ewen or any of the others,' he said, 'but it's liquorice, topped up with black treacle with just a dash or two of water.'

But he wasn't always so understanding with his clients. There is the immortal tale of that biting day in February, with a searing east wind blowing sleet showers across the Old Course, when Fred was seen to be having unusual difficulty with a pupil who was cutting every ball away to the right. Try as he would, he could do nothing to stop those dreadful bananas curving away on the wind. When it was over, the next man asked him what the trouble was. 'Oh,' said Fred, 'that's my late commanding officer in wartime. I've given him a slice such as will last him for the rest of his days.'

Fred Robson was more than a golfing psychiatrist, however. He had a simple basic approach to the game, and to its teaching, which those of us who had the good fortune to sample it will never forget. In his own way, and in his own time, he was alone. And quite extraordinarily successful. He believed in two governing principles; and he stuck to them throughout his teaching life.

He contended, first, that a man has to make do with what he's got. There is no way he can be given a new swing, a new method. It is a question of making the best of what is already there.

Second, he held that if a reasonably proficient player went off his game, eight times out of ten it was because his set-up to the ball—his stance, his address, his 'make-up', as he put it—was out of alignment.

Time and again you would see Fred stop a man when he was about to hit. Marking the positions precisely with peg tees, he would put first his right, then his left, foot, with delicate care, exactly where his pupil's feet had been. When he had sized the resultant position up for himself he'd look up at the pupil and, with a broadening grin, exclaim: 'Mr X, you can't hit it from there; you're getting in your own way.' And after a few minor adjustments a 'new' man would walk out of the surgery.

Fred was all for a golfer who had been 'off' having a go at the ball. There was to be no holding back, no 'hitting it quietly'. A man must hit his full weight, and never mind where the ball goes. 'Go on, Mr Lucas,' he once said to me, 'hit it. The worst you can do is miss it.'

His reading of a man's golfing mind was uncanny. I have always (perhaps unfairly) doubted the teacher who has never himself known what it is to stand on the last tee in a tournament with a par four to win, and then, with a series of quite passable strokes, takes six—for no better reason than that there was never a chance, in the circumstances, of doing better.

Fred, with a second and a couple of fourths, had once or twice had the Open almost within his grasp; but the way always seemed to be blocked in the end either by Jones or by Hagen. He knew better than most the games that nerves could play.

The evening before the first post-war Walker Cup match against America, I asked him to come out with me to a secluded spot on the New Course at St Andrews, when no one would be about, and watch me hit some shots. I was uneasy about the morrow, and Fred knew it.

When we got to the spot we could only muster, between the two of us and the caddie, one chipped, wooden peg tee. Every time Fred tried to tee the ball up (he would never allow you to tee it up yourself) it fell off.

After about twenty minutes of this balancing exercise, his inexhaustible patience began to give. As yet another ball fell off, he straightened up and gave that endearing little chuckle.

'Tomorrow morning, Mr Lucas,' he said, 'in the foursome with Mr Crawley, you'll need a peg tee so big as will take a coconut.'

Then there was the time when we were all at Ganton, in Yorkshire, playing in the English championship. Fred was usually present on these occasions to lend a helping hand.

As the week wore on, it became clear that if Gerald Micklem and I both got through we would meet on Thursday afternoon. On Thursday morning I had an easy match but Gerald, who was another devotee of Fred's, then had a very tight game with Charles Pretzlik which, begging Charles's pardon, he would normally have expected to win with a little to spare. It went to the extra hole before the favourite prevailed.

Walking back to the clubhouse someone asked Fred what had gone wrong with Micklem. 'There's nothing wrong with Mr Micklem, sir,' he replied. 'Mr Micklem's trouble was that he was playing this afternoon's match this morning.'

If you stood well back behind Fred Robson as he peeped through the crowd at a 'pupil' struggling away in a tournament, you could see him living every shot. He had a little habit, when he got anxious about someone, of swivelling his right foot around on the turf. I pulled his leg about it once.

'I know, Mr Lucas,' he said, 'I get so excited watching my pupils in a championship that I rub a blister on my big toe by the middle of the week.'

Here, then, was one of the gems of professional golf. Everyone loved old Fred. That, in a way, was his problem. Whether he was playing for himself, or watching a pupil, he got himself fully involved; but the shafts of winning humour and that little chuckle were never far away.

I once showed him three pairs of brightly coloured, thick, woollen socks (never wear thin ones in great heat) which my wife had given me to take to America. They had just come back from one of those appalling four-hour laundries which used to abound in the United States. They were shrunk to nothing and quite unwearable.

'Whatever will my wife say, Fred?' I pleaded.

'Never mind, Mr Lucas,' he said, 'they'll make a lovely set of new covers for your woods!'

*   *   *

In a sense, John Jacobs picked up Fred's mantle, dusted it off, and then created something quite fresh out of it for himself.

Twice a Ryder Cup captain with a notable international playing record of his own, Jacobs' rise as an instructor-extraordinary in the last four decades is one of the exceptional stories of British golf. But, of course, it goes far beyond teaching, for rather like Henry Cotton before him, John has introduced into his golfing life an unusual business (and corporate) acumen which is the product of a clear and practical Yorkshire mind.

Having been associated with him for nearly thirty years in company life, and having been a member of Sandy Lodge during his eleven years as the professional there after his successful sojourn in Egypt, I speak with a close knowledge of the subject.

It is a measure of the man's ability that whereas British teachers (apart from the early Scottish expatriates) never cut much ice in the United States, Jacobs built a reputation there as the pioneer which still takes him across the Atlantic for protracted spells at his Practical Golf Schools. He is the first of the truly international coaches to emerge from latter-day British golf. Beginning in the late '60s and early '70s, it is an astonishing story.

Apart from his work in America, he has for more than a quarter of a century been travelling regularly to Spain and other Continental and Scandinavian countries, preaching his gospel of the golf swing principally to the young up-and-coming professionals and assistants, but also to the amateurs in the international teams—women as well as men.

Unlike some, he is reticent about these things (he can afford to be), but, knowing the facts, I haven't a doubt that the remarkable rise of Spain as an international golfing force owes much to the periodical visits which John has been paying to Madrid and elsewhere, at the behest of the Spanish golf authorities, since the early 1960s.

One could reveal names of British, American, European, Australian and South African professionals—world names—who, at one time or another, without saying much about it, have sought him out. But if I did I should earn no thanks from him—nor, I guess, from some (though not all) of them—for, although things have changed markedly of late, professional golf and tournament golf is a strange world where credit is not readily given.

It is a truism to say that none of Jacobs' attributes would have been invested with the same authority and status had they not rested—just as Fred Robson's did—upon a playing record of national and international worth. Like Robson, Jacobs has known what it is to be 'out in the middle', alone with his golf ball and God, with the searchlight beating fiercely down.

Where, then, lie the abilities which have raised him to the pinnacle?

First, in a flair for almost instant, positive diagnosis. Second, in the total rejection of inessentials and the selection only of fundamentals in striking at the root cause of a weakness. And, third, in the use of graphic phrases to convey a mind-picture of his meaning. 'Hit the ball', he once said to me, when rhythm had escaped on the wind, 'hit the ball, not the air in the backswing.' And again, when the shots were floating high and ineffectually, 'use your legs; use your legs to drive the ball forward. Make use of the bottom half of your body. That'll give the ball a better flight and more penetration . . . *The top half is too active—the bottom half too inactive.*'

To watch Jacobs give a lesson—for the sophisticated as well as for the average player—is to recognize at once the skill of the exceptional practitioner. A few easy exchanges with the patient; maybe a pleasantry or two; no note taken of the golfing pains which are described; no questioning of the ailments which specially bring him (or her) to consult the master. It is a strictly 'without prejudice' approach, but always one senses on Jacobs' part an impatience to get to see the *shape* of the customer's shots—*the shape of the flight of the ball.*

'Let's see you try a few with the 4 iron. Take the target (naming it) and hit for that.'

The order is familiar. It is spoken from behind the player, for, unlike Robson or, for that matter, Tommy Armour and others in their time, Jacobs never teaches from the side. He stands well back, keeping the pupil on a direct line between himself and the target. From this rear vantage point, his acute eye is easily able to absorb the player's alignment, the plane of his swing and the resultant flightpath of the ball. The flight of the ball . . . Ah! This lies at the bottom of it all. It is the key which unlocks the door to all diagnosis. Here will be seen the symptoms which lead to the reason for the disease . . . and to the remedial prescription which will soon follow.

John picked a ball out of a basket one day when I was hitting some shots for him, and held it up between his forefinger and thumb. 'This is your best pro,' he said. 'This is what tells you what to look for. The ball is your best instructor.'

The patient hits half a dozen shots—probably quite well. Maybe, with a 4 iron, they fly left of target. Jacobs stops the action.

'With that club, you're hitting all those balls left of target. Tell me,' he asks, in prophetic interrogation, 'with the driver do you hit most of your shots straight right, or maybe right of the target with a swing to the right at the end? I expect you do.'

The face of the pupil takes on the look of the incredulous Watson as Holmes uncovers another mystery in the Baker Street chambers.

The diagnosis is complete; the antidote follows—simple and short. As with Robson, the player's set-up to the ball comes in for special attention.

Ten or fifteen minutes sees the exercise through, tidy and complete. The rest is a restatement of the judgment. Jacobs rounds it off. 'It'll take you two or three weekends to get the feel of that, and then you should be hitting the ball a much better shape . . .'

The surgery door closes.

A knock and another patient enters. The same process follows. This man can play a bit—five or six handicap. A few shots, this time with a 6 iron, and then on to the woods. Every ball finishes left of target.

'Good players,' says John, by way of lifting morale, 'hook the ball. How long have you been playing like that?'

'Three years,' retorts the customer.

'Three wasted years,' muses Jacobs.

He takes the club from the player's hands and tells him to stand behind.

A few crisp and direct sentences (not all of them complimentary), and a couple of simple demonstrations, and the diagnosis is laid out bare, in pieces on the ground.

The prescription is soon written; quite different ingredients are employed from those dispensed to the last man. There is no stereotyped, repetitive formula in Jacobs' teaching. He'll go down a line of half a dozen players, high-class or modest, and spend five minutes with each of them, and you will find six different diagnoses and six different prescriptions emerging. There's no self-perpetuating dogma.

As the customer takes his leave, John recapitulates, and then adds some cautionary words. 'Play that way for a few months and then watch that you're not overdoing it . . . Exaggeration is the curse of golf instruction. People overdo what they're told. That's why you must learn from the flight of the ball. The flight of the ball—that's the key. The shape of your shots will tell you everything. Always watch the way the ball is beginning to move.'

*   *   *

Fred Robson's lifetime spanned six decades of the game; John Jacobs is very much 'in play' after five. The generations are different and so are the personalities and the humour. Particularly the humour. Fred was apt to favour the human and philosophical approach; John, with his strong Yorkshire slant, tends to go straight to the point.

An Oxford undergraduate, with a poor golfing method, but with a good opinion of his game, went to Sandy Lodge one day with two of his team mates for a lesson. Quickly sizing him up, John asked him what was his best recent round.

'Seventy-three in the last Medal,' came the confident reply.

'Then I expect you had a good day with your putter.' The rejoinder touched a fragile nerve.

Years ago, when he was first giving my wife a lesson, he established early on that the only other person she had ever had any instruction from was the author. Things didn't go too well, and progress was slow. A touch of impatience intruded.

'It's a great pity,' he said, as he teed up another ball, 'that your husband ever tried to teach you to play golf. If he hadn't, we wouldn't be in all this mess now.'

Yes, the generations, the personalities, the temperaments, are different. Yet the unmistakable similarities remain . . . Two teachers, each in his own way just possibly unique. And each a lasting credit to the game.

Chapter Five
Kinder to shoot the lot

IN THE Golf Foundation, of which I have the honour to be a past president, we had a motto—'Play golf, the game of a lifetime'—for this is, indeed, what golf can provide. Learn young and you have a friend and an ally for life—an agreeable companion in the good times, a stalwart and understanding friend in the bad.

It can take you, if you are fortunate, to some of the loveliest places on earth. It can bring you friends early on who will stick for ever. It teaches hard disciplines the hard way, but it's none the worse for that. After all, as Alec Douglas-Home once reminded a few of us: 'Life without rules would be intolerable.'

It is a game which offers temptations and, in so doing, tests the higher qualities. It is a champion of the cause of the humble, for golf can, literally at a stroke, transport you from the Fields of Elysium into the Slough of Despond. It is the great leveller and one of the few games—indeed, perhaps, the only game—in which, with the aid of a strange handicapping system, the poor and the mediocre players can mingle happily with the good.

There was never a game like it for giving one up and then, unpredictably, taking one back on board again. The times one has said: 'That's it. Never again. I've finished with it now, once and for all.'

Henry Longhurst recounts the tale of a round he once played with Valentine Castlerosse at Walton Heath. His lordship came to the last hole after a very bad day. Another execrable stroke disappeared into the heather. Castlerosse threw his club helplessly to the ground.

'Caddie,' he commanded with aristocratic disdain, 'pick that up, have the clubs destroyed and leave the course.'

Walton Heath has, if one may interject, always claimed its characters. It is, after all, a character-making golf course. In all the

41

first seventy-three years of its distinguished history it only had two professionals, James Braid and Harry Busson.

I recall the last round I ever played with James on the Old Course, if only for one incident the like of which he, in three score years and more of golf (including five Open Championship wins and three seconds, all within ten years—what a record!) could hardly before have witnessed.

It was a quiet Sunday afternoon fourball. In addition to James and myself, my brother-in-law, Douglas Bader, and the chairman of the News of the World Group (who then owned the club), Sir William Carr, himself an old Cambridge player, were in the game. An interested onlooker was E. J. Robertson, who at the time was still chairman of Beaverbrook Newspapers. I remember he had lunched with us beforehand.

Bill Carr, James and I had all driven. It was now Bader's turn. With his two tin legs he had played, extraordinarily, for years to a single-figure handicap. But such were his physical circumstances that once he started to swing, he was, one might say, 'committed'. There was no stopping the club at the top.

In front of the first tee on the Old Course at Walton there runs a road. Traffic, not all of which is golf-trained, passes along it frequently. As Douglas started his backswing, a large Harrods' van, going apace, came round the bend and straight across the line of fire, its driver oblivious to the danger.

Shouts of 'hold it . . . wait . . . HOLD IT . . .' were to no avail.

Bader's ball hit the van, with a crack which could be heard right across the heath, slap bang in the middle of the 'O' of Harrods. The driver, who claimed that he had heard nothing like it since the advance with Montgomery's 8th Army down the Western Desert, jumped out to find a dent the size of his fist in the side of the van.

The ever-resourceful Robertson, placator of all rows, stepped immediately into the breach. Taking a visiting card and pen from his pocket he asked the driver the name of his transport manager. Writing it on the back of his card, Robbie added a rider. 'If you don't believe the driver's story kindly ask Sir Richard Burbidge [then chairman of Harrods'] to telephone me.'

*   *   *

St Andrews, 1947: the Walker Cup v. U.S.A. Driving from the 17th tee in the 36-holes singles. R. D. (Dick) Chapman beat me by 4 and 3.

'He could just have been, in his prime, the greatest *striker* of the lot—Hogan, Nelson, Snead, Nicklaus, included. I've seen them all and I believe he was. But it's a stupid argument. . . .'
One of the classic action pictures in golf. Henry Cotton—the 'maestro'—in the mid-1930s.

'After the first round or two at Carnoustie, I began to feel I could win. Here was a man's size course, a real scholarship test.'
The Boys' Championship August 1933. *(Above)*

On the new practice ground at Worlington during my freshman's year at Cambridge, May 1935. A month later, despite an appalling eight at the short 13th in the final round I was the leading British Amateur in the Open at Muirfield. I had to live with the eight for months. Still, I took comfort in knowing a number of eminent professors were below me. . . .
(Left)

Putting on the 18th green at St Andrews in the foursomes of the Walker Cup v. U.S.A., 1947. Leonard Crawley and I beat M. H. (Bud) Ward and S. L. (Smiley) Quick by 5 and 4 at the 32nd hole.

OFFICIAL PROGRAM
1949 WALKER CUP MATCH
WINGED FOOT GOLF CLUB
MAMARONECK · NEW YORK

THE CAPTAINS OF THE TEAMS
GREAT BRITAIN: LADDIE LUCAS · UNITED STATES: FRANCIS OUIMET

PAIRINGS AND STARTING TIMES ON BACK COVER

British captain in 1949 at Winged Foot, New York. Francis Ouimet, one of the great figures of American golf, a man of supreme gentleness and modesty, was my opposite number in the U.S. Walker Cup Team.

WALKER CUP MATCH

SATURDAY, AUGUST 20, 1949

SINGLES: 36 HOLES, MATCH PLAY

GREAT BRITAIN VERSUS UNITED STATES

STARTING TIMES		CADDIE NO.	PLAYER	RESULTS	POINTS	CADDIE NO.	PLAYER	RESULTS	POINTS
A.M.	P.M.								
8:30	1:30	10	RONALD WHITE	4+3	1	20	WILLIAM P. TURNESA		0
8:45	1:45	5	S. MAX McCREADY		0	19	FRANK STRANAHAN	6+5	1
9:00	2:00	1	JAMES BRUEN, JR.		0	18	ROBERT H. RIEGEL	5+4	1
9:15	2:15	2	JOSEPH B. CARR		0	14	JOHN W. DAWSON	5+3	1
9:30	2:30	3	R. CECIL EWING		0	13	CHARLES R. COE	1 hole	1
9:45	2:45	9	KENNETH THOM		0	11	RAYMOND E. BILLOWS	2+1	1
10:00	3:00	8	ARTHUR H. PEROWNE		0	15	CHARLES R. KOCSIS	4+2	1
10:15	3:15	6	GERALD H. MICKLEM		0	17	JAMES B. McHALE, JR.	5+4	1
			TOTAL POINTS		1		TOTAL POINTS		7

WINNERS ARE CREDITED ONE POINT. HALVED MATCHES SCORE NOTHING

Other members of the two teams, with their Caddie numbers, are:

GREAT BRITAIN		UNITED STATES	
4	PERCY B. LUCAS	12	STANLEY E. BISHOP
7	ERNEST B. MILLWARD	16	BRUCE N. McCORMICK

WINGED FOOT'S WEST COURSE

OUT

HOLE	1	2	3	4	5	6	7	8	9		
YARDS	460	383	226	415	521	335	175	454	515	3,484	YARDS
PAR	4	4	3	4	5	4	3	4	5	36	

IN

HOLE	10	11	12	13	14	15	16	17	18		
YARDS	200	390	500	220	389	405	465	456	430	3,455	YARDS
PAR	3	4	5	3	4	4	5	4	4	36	
								TOTAL	6,939	YARDS	

RESULTS OF FRIDAY'S FOURSOME MATCHES

GREAT BRITAIN TEAM	POINTS	UNITED STATES TEAM	POINTS
CARR & WHITE, 3 & 2	1	TURNESA & BILLOWS	0
BRUEN & McCREADY	0	STRANAHAN & KOCSIS, 2 & 1	1
EWING & MICKLEM	0	BISHOP & RIEGEL, 9 & 7	1
THOM & PEROWNE	0	DAWSON & McCORMICK, 8 & 7	1
TOTAL POINTS	1	TOTAL POINTS	3

RECAPITULATION

GREAT BRITAIN	POINTS	UNITED STATES	POINTS
FOURSOMES	1	FOURSOMES	3
SINGLES	1	SINGLES	7
GRAND TOTAL	2	GRAND TOTAL	10

The result was a heavy disappointment, but I consoled myself with those lines of Grantland Rice, the splendid American sports writer:
'For when the one great scorer comes to write against your name,
He writes not that you won or lost but how you played the game.'

Critch (Brigadier-General A. C. Critchley) holed the putts
which counted. We were at the Seminole, Palm Beach, Florida,
in February, 1938.

Dead-End Kid (aged six) with Cecil Leitch, four times British
ladies' champion. We played seven holes at Prince's after tea,
July, 1922.

I count it among my blessings that on a very few cherished occasions I was old enough and young enough to be able to play a round or two not only with James Braid but also with John Henry Taylor and Harry Vardon who, together, made up golf's Great Triumvirate.

The first round with Harry Vardon at his home club, South Herts., in North London, was a memorable affair. It took place on a warm August day in 1930—19 August to be precise—six years before he died. I hadn't yet passed my fifteenth birthday.

Vardon, who was then sixty-one, had been very unwell, as, sadly, he often was towards the end of his life. He hadn't, on his own admission, touched a golf club for eight weeks. As we started out on our fourball, with Vardon dressed in plus-fours, a light pullover and white, starched, 'butcher boy' collar, it was on the understanding that he wouldn't go more than ten or twelve holes with us.

He played the first nine holes that day in twenty-nine strokes without a two in it. Transparently elated and stimulated, he was encouraged, probably wrongly, to go on and finish the round. Tiring fast and breathless, he completed the second nine in 38 for a total of 67 before slumping exhausted into an armchair in the clubhouse with a whisky and soda, of appropriately dark colour, in his hand.

Strangely, my recollection of Vardon that day is not primarily of his twenty-nine strokes for the first nine holes, astonishing though that was in the circumstances, but of the *shape* of his shots. They weren't just hit straight in the sense that you and I mean straight—coming up from left or right and finishing in the middle of the fairway or dropping relentlessly round the flag stick.

The shots which Vardon hit that day—and on the few other occasions I was lucky enough to get a game with him—came closer than any others I personally ever saw to meeting Euclid's definition of a straight line. I'm not saying they were hit better than anyone else's—at his age that couldn't be—but I do contend that they flew straighter (without fade or draw) than anything I have seen since.

I plucked up courage afterwards to ask him how he got the ball to fly so straight in the air. His answer didn't help me then. 'If you had been brought up, as I was, on a gutty ball and hickory shafts (steel was only then just coming in) you would have learned how to do it. You couldn't mis-hit a gutty and get away with it like you can with this rubber-core ball.'

The other thing I remember he said to me about the game, not that day but later—was, according to most pundits at the time—and now—heresy. Gripping a driver and holding the shaft vertically upwards till his large hands were level with his face, he opened all his fingers, leaving only the forefinger and thumb of each hand gripping the club.

'There,' he said, holding on only with forefingers and thumbs, 'are the important things to grip with. These are the points where the pressure should come in the grip, not in the other fingers. Grip the club tight with the other fingers, particularly [in a right-handed player] with the last two fingers of the left hand, and you'll never swing properly. You won't hit a golf ball well that way.'

So there you have it. That's what the old master told me in the early thirties. And he didn't play so badly for a heretic.

*   *   *

It has been one of the strengths of golf that from the earliest days an excellent relationship has always existed between the professionals and the amateurs in the game. The Royal and Ancient Golf Club and the United States Golf Association have never fallen for the nonsense which has bedevilled and belittled some other sports and games—the Olympic Games in particular—where the two groups have been kept obstinately apart in a form of odious sporting apartheid. It is, of course, true that there used to be anachronistic attitudes to the professionals' use of the clubhouse and all that sort of thing, but there have never been any inhibitions about professionals and amateurs doing battle in open competition on the golf course; there, the two have always been completely free to fight it out together.

There can, indeed, be few more exhilarating challenges in sport than the chance the young amateur has of pitting his ability against the pick of the professional game in the Open Championship. There is everything to gain and little to lose.

To the end of my days I shall remember the 1935 Open at Muirfield, perhaps the most engaging of all Britain's championship tests, which I played in at the close of my freshman's year at Cambridge. In those days we played two qualifying rounds and the four rounds of the championship proper all in the same week. The final thirty-six holes were completed on Friday.

It was a stern test, but I have always felt more at home over four rounds of medal play than with any other form of competition. Eighteen-hole matches, with little time to catch an opponent's 32 or 33 to the turn, can be devilishly unsettling affairs. The long stretch over four rounds, or even two, with card and pencil, and with only yourself to blame, is more reassuring.

Seventy-five and 74 at Gullane qualified me safely for the championship. I then played the first thirty-six holes at Muirfield with Alfred Perry, the ultimate winner, hardly an orthodox striker. My 74 and 73, which left me, at halfway, three shots behind Alf, were encouraging. As rounds of golf they had compared well with his.

I went to bed on Thursday night thrilled to think I was to be playing the final rounds of the tournament with golf's alumni.

Moreover, it was comforting to be drawn on the last day with Hector Thomson: he was a fine Scots player, who was to win the Amateur Championship at St Andrews the following year before turning professional.

My third round of 72 was as good as I could properly expect. It gave me a fifty-four holes' total of 219, one shot in front of the American, Lawson Little, the reigning British and U.S. amateur champion, who was soon to turn professional and go on to win the Open Championship of his native land. We were comfortably ahead of the rest of the amateurs in the field.

Alf Perry's 67 on the last morning had spreadeagled the field and given him a clear lead as he went into the final lap. I remember looking at the scoreboard at lunchtime and seeing that I was only one shot behind my idol, Henry Cotton. I felt that I had a chance of finishing well up at the end. I was then lying equal seventh in the whole field.

Lawson Little was soon into his stride in the last round, playing his characteristically strong and aggressive game. His final 69 in the rising wind was a fine effort and remained untouched by any of the other leaders. I could hardly have expected to match that, but after going fairly steadily for twelve holes I missed the green at the short thirteenth, found a large and unfriendly footmark in a bunker beside the green, took a deplorable eight, and that was that.

It was a reverse which I had to live with for months. Still, in spite of that, I found it comforting to know that no other British amateur had matched my total and that a number of eminent professors were below me.

At nineteen, it had been a stimulating and salutary experience. Of one thing I was quite sure: for a young British amateur there could never be another golf tournament quite like the Open to play in.

*　　*　　*

It is, I believe, doubtful, to say the least, if the best of the young players in Britain today play golf any better than the best of them did forty years ago. What is undeniable is that there are a great many more who play well. I cannot think, for instance, that any boy of fourteen or fifteen today could play better than John Langley did at that age when he was a schoolboy at Stowe.

I remember very well playing a game with him and his father at Deal in August 1932 just before the Boys' Championship at Lytham. John was then fourteen and already manifestly adept as a player of games. He could hit a ball instinctively with anything, a cricket bat, a squash racket, a golf club or a broom handle and, such was his timing, he could catch it, eight times out of ten, fair and square off the meat. There wasn't another of his age at Stowe like him.

On this day, the wind was blowing strongly from the south-west over the course of the old Royal Cinque Ports club. Big, billowy clouds of white cotton wool (cumulus meant nothing to me then) chased one another across the blue heavens, casting shadows over the dry land. It was a lovely golfing day, warm and testing. Off the back tees, the long second nine into the wind made as searching an examination as you could find on any championship links.

John played the first, downwind half in 34 without the suggestion of a mistake in it. The last nine, with several of the long holes unreachable in two, he completed in 38. The Bobby Jones, 'Calamity Jane' putter he was then using saved a stroke here and there, but on the whole his 72, authoritative and controlled, was played almost as precisely as par demanded. It would not have been possible for a boy of fourteen to have hit the ball better.

At a time when there were a number of highly proficient amateur players about in the country, Langley, at sixteen, seventeen and eighteen, could hold his own with any of them. He won the Boys'

Championship at Balgownie the year after my win at Carnoustie. He was still at Stowe when he reached the final of the 1936 English Championship and still there when he received his invitation to play for Britain in the Walker Cup match against the United States at Pine Valley later that autumn.

I have watched a little of the Boys' Championship in recent times and although, nowadays, the best dozen or so play well—a few very well—I haven't seen one who played with the same precocious command and authority as John did at the same age all those years ago.

*   *   *

The Walker Cup matches between Britain and the United States have always been friendly and yet energetically contested affairs. They have done much to sustain the easy Anglo-American dialogue. Certainly no contest between the two great nations has provided, over what is now getting on for seven decades, a more diverse collection of characters.

My old partner, Leonard Crawley, must figure in any roll-call of personalities. His contribution to the series, spanning as it did some fifteen years, five of which were war years, is notable, not least when seen against the background of his extraordinary games-playing record. Dare I suggest, could it just possibly be, that Crawley was the outstanding all-rounder of them all—golf, cricket, rackets, lawn tennis, football and the rest? I would put Charles Fry a loser in the final against him with Ted Dexter only a pace or two away.

He was an England golfer continuously (except just at the end) for virtually a quarter of a century, and all this, together with his service for Britain in the Walker Cup, came *well after* the winter of 1925-26 when he toured the West Indies with the M.C.C.

When, in the summer of 1932, he had the distinction of being the only British winner in the singles of the Walker Cup match at the Country Club, Brookline, Massachusetts (he beat George Voigt one up), he had also been sounded by the M.C.C. about his availability as a possible candidate for the tour of Australia the coming winter.

The first time I played for England in the Home International matches—at Prestwick in 1936—Leonard was in the side. Cyril

Tolley, our captain, had asked us to assemble at Turnberry three days
early for practice. Crawley delayed his arrival at the hotel until late in
the day before the first match. This wasn't well received, the more so
when he offered, as his excuse, that he had been 'playing cricket for
Essex'. But, of course, he got away with it.

To play a foursome with Leonard on an international occasion was
an exceptional experience. He habitually enjoyed the services of a
highly capable caddie named Mullins. Finely-drilled, bronzed and
spruce, Mullins had everything buttoned up. His knowledge of the
Turf, and the betting processes which went with it, was extensive. If
anyone was giving shots away, no finger would ever be pointed at
Mullins. He was an asset to any partnership.

It used to be said that such was Crawley's confidence in his adviser
that once, having been given the line of a fifteen-foot putt, he stopped
at the last moment as he addressed the ball. 'Mullins,' he asked, 'did
you say it was a foot to the right or a foot to the left?'

Mullins was carrying Crawley's bag in the foursome we played
together in the 1947 Walker Cup match at St Andrews. We were
second off in the morning at, I think, 10.15. As Leonard (after some
argument) was going to drive our first ball, I took up station with
Mullins, and my own caddie, beside the tee box.

At 10.14, a minute before the off, there was still no sign of
Crawley. Then, just as anxiety was beginning to mount, out of the
clubhouse and down the stone steps he came, with magisterial timing
and at a deliberately measured pace. He was dressed breathtakingly in
Harris tweed, reddish-brown plus-fours, a canary pullover, sky-blue
stockings and snow-white buckskin shoes.

'Cor,' gasped Mullins, 'Dorothy Paget up.'

On the seventh green, with the crowd gathered round, it was my
putt and Mullins was holding the pin.

'What's that, Mullins,' I asked, 'a couple of inches right?'

He lifted his eyes to the heavens. 'Not bloody likely,' he said.
'Union rules up here.' And, pointing to my St Andrews caddie, he
stepped back with proper deference.

Of the fine competitors who have characterized the United States'
sides in the Walker Cup, none has become a more welcome visitor to
these shores, or a more fervent supporter of the Anglo-American
cause, than an enduring friend from Atlanta, Georgia, in the 'deep

South', the hometown of the immortal Bobby Jones. Banker, industrialist and now, in so-called retirement, purveyor of the public good, Charles R. Yates, a winner of the British Amateur Championship and a United States' captain, is a highly regarded figure on both sides of the Atlantic.

An accomplished player, cast in an historic mould, Charlie Yates is one of the selfless band of members who, each year, perform prodigies in staging the U.S. Masters' Tournament at Augusta. It was an honour for our family when he said he would be a godfather to our younger son.

We first met at Pine Valley in New Jersey in 1936, when the Walker Cup match was played on that delectable course. For forty years and more, that unmistakable Southern voice seems to have been reverberating round the world's telephone systems, for Charlie is an inveterate user of the instrument.

I heard it in strange places in wartime. At Trois Rivières in Quebec, a thousand or two miles away from Atlanta, when we were learning to fly with the Royal Canadian Air Force long before the U.S.A. entered the war. I heard it, too, at Coltishall, in Norfolk, thirty minutes before my Spitfire wing took off in support of one of the U.S. 8th Air Force's daylight Fortress raids into the heart of Germany. Charlie, then an officer serving in a destroyer in the Battle of the Atlantic, was calling from the U.S. Navy's headquarters in London.

There was never any question of asking 'who's speaking?'.

He was once walking down Piccadilly during one of his wartime visits to London when he passed a telephone kiosk. Someone was making a call. Back view, it looked for all the world like Harry Bentley, an old sparring partner of Charlie's and one of Britain's best-known Walker Cup golfers.

Yates tapped on the door. 'Hey, Harry,' he called.

Bentley didn't even bother to look round.

'That's all right, Charlie,' he said, unmoved, 'I'll be with you in just a minute'—and went on with his conversation.

*   *   *

Golf has, of course, been specially favoured over the years in the standard of writing and commentating by which it has been adorned.

Longhurst had his place yesterday; Bernard Darwin achieved immortality in the years before that.

For the young, Darwin, in his later years, presented a formidable personality. As an opponent on a golf course he played the game, as befitted one who had represented his country, with a spirit, a vigour and a purpose which left no doubt whatever that his principal aim was to win. If a rub of the green ran against him, it was essential to maintain a respectful silence as he questioned the Deity's intentions.

I saw it all one unforgettable day at Royston, in Hertfordshire, on one of the last occasions on which Bernardo played for the club ('poor little Royston') in the annual match against Cambridge ('its enemies').

Two up on me with two to play, his spirit was now rising visibly as he closed in for the kill. At the seventeenth, after two good drives, only one ball was visible on the fairway. It must have been a full fifty or sixty yards longer than any drive Darwin had hit that day—or probably any other day for several years. He walked straight to it, selected an iron and prepared to hit his second.

I had little doubt that it was my ball, nor had my caddie; but the thought of an undergraduate even suggesting to *The Times* correspondent that he might perhaps be playing the wrong ball was totally unacceptable. Supposing he was right?

He hit the ball confidently into the middle of the green. The *coup de grâce* was at hand.

Let Darwin's anonymous pen pick up the story.

> 'This part of the course seems unlucky for him. Years ago a young lady ran away with his ball, and was never seen again.
> This time both he and his caddie were too blind to tell one ball from another . . . and he played Lucas' ball and lost the hole. This was a *little unlucky* [my italics], as the 17th is a likely hole to halve.
> Lucas hit a great drive to the edge of the home green, and, after Darwin had just missed in the odd, holed a seven-foot putt for a 3 to halve a capital game.' (*The Times*, 23 November 1934).

What *The Times'* readers were never told was that, after the disaster at the seventeenth, all the way down the hill to the eighteenth green, their correspondent, in a torrent of words, kept invoking the Almighty, calling upon Him to declare His hand and say once and for all why it was that He always picked on His faithful disciple and never on his opponents.

Poor Bernardo. By the time he had reached the last green there was no known way for him to hole his putt for victory.

*   *   *

Perhaps once or twice in a lifetime, one strikes up an association which defies the years and is refreshed, from time to time, in diverse and unexpected ways. Absence doesn't affect it for, with reunion, the game is at once picked up where the players last left it.

With Henry Longhurst, whose writings and commentaries took his name across the world, I enjoyed such a friendship. It found its derivation in golf and then, in peace and in war, moved on, unexpectedly, to unusual fields of endeavour, to newspapers and to politics, with a pause now and then for a taste of some of the richer and less exacting joys of life.

A mind of rare agility; an eye which saw humour that was often unrecognized by others; an ability to go to the point of an argument and to penetrate and debunk anything which looked for a moment to be specious, pompous or false; the courage to insert the critic's knife—deeply—if it was deserved; willingness to try anything once and to stand in the other man's shoes to test his lot; a faculty for finding a phrase, consisting of a few short, simple words, to convey a picture. These were the attributes upon which his renown was built.

Soon after I joined the *Sunday Express* in pre-war days and had begun writing a weekly column on golf under my own name, I directed what I thought were some well-selected remarks at that much maligned being, the Average Golfer. This somewhat patronizing epithet recurred frequently in the piece.

The following Tuesday morning an envelope, sent anonymously to the Golf Correspondent of the *Sunday Express*, lay on my desk. Inside was a clipping of the previous Sunday's piece, with the offending words 'Average Golfer' ringed eight times within the 600 words. The hand written comment underneath left no doubt about its authorship. 'Give the little b - - - - r a chance.'

With the humour, and the occasional shaft of astringent wit, there always went a finely tuned perception of the feelings of others, especially when under pressure. Longhurst knew all about the frailty of man, which was what made him such a fair commentator.

On the eve of the first match against America after the war, the British Walker Cup team were sitting about in their hotel room overlooking the Old Course at St Andrews. It was after lunch, we had all finished our last practice, and now there was nothing else for it but to face that awful, agonizing wait for the next morning to dawn and action to begin. Some were asleep in armchairs, others were playing cards, one or two were just staring vacantly out of the window. Yawns betrayed the gathering tension. Longhurst put his head round the door. Momentarily he surveyed this motley crew.

'Kinder,' he said, 'to shoot the lot.'

*   *   *

After Longhurst and I had both unsuccessfully fought the election of 1945, and I had had to return to the Royal Air Force to play out my time in the Service, Henry came to stay with me at the fighter station at Bentwaters, in Suffolk, which I was then commanding.

Kindly neighbours allowed me to walk over their land with my dog and gun and take a companion with me. We were, moreover, no distance from the marshes of Orfordness where there were usually enough duck about to make the evening flight a rewarding exercise. All this, of course, was right down Longhurst's fairway.

But, as so often happens, the two or three days brought us little success. I doubt whether we had a worthwhile shot at a mallard between us. Some part of the blame had to be laid at the feet of a young and unsteady Irish setter puppy (he and Red II, his successor, became devoted companions of the family) which I had recently acquired. His performance in the field left much to be desired.

I heard Henry recounting our experiences—including the irregularities of the wayward puppy—to the faithful Crisp, my civilian batman. Crisp had retired from the Royal Marines after more than twenty years' service and was then living in Woodbridge, from where he commuted each day.

He was a batman in a million; there wasn't a job he couldn't do or a problem he couldn't solve. He made shoes and buttons shine as they had never shone before. There was no one better with a thimble, needle and thread. He allowed himself no deviation whatever from the path of respect and propriety.

He brought my customary cup of tea at 0730 hours the morning Henry was leaving. My clothes were laid out in the usual, immaculate way; uniform pressed, shoes glistening, socks turned inside out, tie and handkerchief ready to hand on the dressing table.

The routine complete, Crisp prepared to withdraw, as silently as he had entered. Halfway to the door he paused as if wanting to say something.

'What is it, Crisp?' I asked.

'Excuse me, sir,' he said, 'but your friend, Mr Longhurst, he really is a most comical gentleman.'

Chapter Six
Cameras on the game

I HAVE often thought that of all the political performances I witnessed during my time in the House of Commons, probably the most skilled were those tours de force with which, from time to time, Anthony Eden, as Foreign Secretary, used to entertain the Tory Party's Foreign Affairs Committee at its private meetings upstairs.

In twenty or twenty-five minutes, with no more than four or five cross-headings on a sheet of paper to guide him, he would take us round the world in a fluent recital of fact and impression with an understanding and a verve which were unmatched.

The reaction of the Quai d'Orsay to this; the significance of the Kremlin's rebuttal of that; the background to the hard Foster Dulles line with Peking; the effect upon the balance of power of the recent nuclear developments; Nasser's moves in the Middle East and the reasons behind them . . . For grip, comprehension and judgment, and an innate 'feel' for foreign affairs, there wasn't a minister, past or present, who could begin to equal Eden at this sort of exercise.

And always at the end, after circling the globe's troubled areas, the round-off would come, naturally and easily: 'And so, in this necessarily brief and hurried journey, I come back to where I began . . .'

A master on top of his job. It was, to a humble backbencher, a wonderfully impressive routine.

And so, extending, by leave, the metaphor, I come back to where it all began, to that golden morning at Sandwich, now some seventy years ago, when I looked out of my bedroom window and saw, 'live', the magic of Walter Hagen, Jim Barnes, Jock Hutchison and Harry Vardon. That moment, and the long walk round Prince's with them which followed, was a priceless opportunity for an aspiring young golfer. In those days, you had to be specially placed for that sort of thing to happen.

Now the experience is open to all. The televising of golf has pierced the barriers of privilege to an extent which, even yet, we may not fully comprehend. The great players of today—the heroes of today—are there for the young to see, literally, at the push of a button.

Nothing in my lifetime—the growth in the use of the motor car, the rise of the so-called affluent society, the social revolution in people's habits—nothing has made so decisive an impact on the game. Once the preserve of the few, the camera lens has opened the Royal and Ancient game to all.

Bred into Britain so many hundreds of years ago, golf seems to possess a magnetism for the young, just as it did for me all those summers ago. They have an intuitive feel for its intricacies and its mysteries; boys *and* girls now want to play. The problem, of course, is where? But here I like to think that the Sports Council, the Golf Foundation and others are pointing a way whereby the public and private sectors may provide the facilities.

What all this 'exposure' will mean to golf another fifty years from now, we must leave to the historians of the future to say. One thing is certain. When that point is reached, the young player of today will address his offspring of tomorrow, and, with truth, will be able to say: 'Play golf, son. It's the game of a lifetime.'

2

The Street called Fleet

Chapter Seven
Come, my friend, and sit down

STORNOWAY HOUSE, St James's; a Tuesday evening in late May 1938. The last shafts of sunlight were lifting from the park. It had been a warm, clear, blue day. Couples in shirtsleeves and gay dresses were still sitting about on the grass; others were leaving their offices to begin the journey home. To the young, war still seemed remote.

The butler answered the doorbell. I was greeted with a faintly welcoming 'Yes, you are expected. Come this way.'

Silently, as if by habit and ritual, I was led through an anteroom and into the library overlooking the park. I was put into a chair tucked away in a corner of the room.

The two men who were talking did not look up. The one dressed in a navy blue suit had a large head, a slightly bronzed face and, seemingly, a small body. He was slumped back, almost enveloped by the armchair in which he was sitting, surrounded by telephones and dictating machines; there were a lot more than one usually saw in those days. It was the first time I had ever seen that unmistakable face close to. I remember thinking that David Low's cartoons had got it just right. Behind, the french windows were open into the garden.

The other man was sitting alert and erect on the sofa, facing Lord Beaverbrook. Although he had his back to me I formed the impression that he was edgy. The ball wasn't running for him. Some long, complicated explanation, which patently carried little conviction, was followed by an unsettling, tell-tale silence. My heartbeats felt as if they would burst out of my chest.

A faintly grating Canadian accent, which I recognized at once from the imitations I had heard in the office, only confirmed my gathering apprehension. 'Tarmpson' (the words were measured and spaced for effect), 'Tarmpson . . . I gave you that story . . . a fortnight ago . . . and now the Nooze has gart it.'

The rejoinder was inaudible, and anyway superfluous.

My heart was now substantially out of control. If that was what Thompson (whoever he might be) was getting, whatever, I thought, would be coming to me?

'Come, my friend, and sit down.' The disarming friendliness of the invitation was comforting, almost reassuring. In the absence of any further direction there was clearly only one place to sit, and that was on the sofa exactly where the luckless Thompson had sat. I didn't dare to lean back.

'Do you know that man?' My negative reply was overtaken by the answer. 'That's Reginald Tarmpson, the editor of the *Evening Standard*.' God, the *editor* of the *Evening* . . . being spoken to like . . . 'Tarmpson, I gave you that story . . .' The words were still rattling round the room. The *editor* of the . . .

My incredulity and unease must have been transparent for the interrogation—and the unbroken commentary—was instantly switched. It was a testing moment for one who had not yet completed a year's employment with Express Newspapers.

'So you have come to work for my *Sunday Express*? Have you made a friend of Gordon yet? John Gordon is a great editor. He edits a great newspaper. He's a great journalist. Learn all you can from him; he'll help you.

'What do you think of the *Sunday Express*? It's my favourite newspaper. Have they told you that?'

The questions and comments came flooding out, but somehow they didn't seem to need, let alone demand, an answer—not, that is, until, as if to catch me off-guard, his lordship interjected, almost as an aside:

'What makes you think you can help my *Sunday Express*?'

It wasn't an easy one, but something plainly had to be done about it. I tried some rather hesitant, ineffectual stuff about having contributed with a small measure of success to the *Cambridge Review* during my time as an undergraduate.

Lord Beaverbrook snapped up the point at once. 'So you were at Cambridge? My son, Max, was at Cambridge. Do you know Max?' Having said yes, I did, he shifted the line of questioning again.

'Have your parents got money?'

I said no, my father had died when I was eleven and things had been quite a struggle for the family.

'Then you have to work for a living?' Yes, I replied, I would have to work for every penny of it.

'You start with a great advantage, my friend; a great advantage.'

It finished there. I had arrived at Stornoway House at 6 p.m. I noticed it was 6.40 as I left. Before we parted, Lord Beaverbrook shot another question which took me by surprise.

'Where are you dining tomorrow evening? I would like you to come and dine with me. Nye and Brendan are coming. Do you know Nye? Have you met Brendan? Anthony is probably coming, too. You've met Anthony, I expect? Max will be here.'

Nye Bevan . . . Brendan Bracken . . . Anthony Eden . . . For a young employee of less than a year's standing, a novice, a rank cub in the profession of journalism, the invitation was electrifying—and exhilarating.

'Come half an hour early at 7.30, I want to talk to you.'

The fact that between 7.30 and 8 p.m. the next evening Lord Beaverbrook asked me most of the same questions as on the previous day is immaterial.

He had touched a spark. The flame which sprang from it was to burn brightly down the years.

Make the young feel you're interested in them. Encourage them; let them have their head; give them chances; offer them responsibility— and do it early. Make them feel they matter to the organization. Take risks with them, if you like. If they fail, why, at that age they can always start again. Elsewhere.

Much was to flow from that first, unconventional meeting. Its impact was immediate. It endures to this day.

Chapter Eight
We were at the summit

I SHOULD be surprised if anyone who was able to spend, as I was, three years as a young employee on the editorial staff of Express Newspapers in those cataclysmic years from 1937 to 1940, when the papers—and Beaverbrook himself—were at, or near, their zenith, would deny that this was, in its own way, as fine an all-round education as one could hope to find at the outset of a working life when impressions cut deep.

It was probably fortunate for me that John Gordon, the editor of the *Sunday Express*, and I had one significant thing in common; we were both golfers.

I had written to him, while still an undergraduate, on the advice of my friend, Henry Longhurst, who was then the golf correspondent of Beaverbrook's *Evening Standard* and already outstanding in the trade. I said I was looking for a job and wondered whether he wanted a golf writer. Rather cheekily I added that I had noticed he hadn't got one.

To offer a specialist service was my obvious—indeed, I thought, my only—way into journalism and Fleet Street. The response was not unhopeful. 'Send me anything you have written,' he wrote.

A few unsigned pieces from the *Cambridge Review* were all I could muster. The comment which came back was characteristically objective. It was tempered with a shade of encouragement.

'I have read what you sent me. You write simple, plain English. At least I can understand it. Telephone me on Saturday morning, 250 words on the two finalists in this week's Amateur Golf Championship at Sandwich. If the copy is suitable, I'll use it.'

I woke in Cambridge the following Sunday morning, put on a dressing gown and ran—yes, ran—out of college and along Trumpington Street to where the paper seller always stood.

I could hardly bring myself to open the paper for fear of

61

disappointment. A glance—and there was the story, surprisingly on a news page, just as I had written it, under my own name. I must have read it a dozen times as I walked back along the pavement to Pembroke. I was thrilled by the turn of events.

Two or three days later a letter arrived from Gordon.

'You may have noticed,' he wrote, 'we used your piece on Sunday. If you will telephone my secretary I should like to see you.'

Two months short of my twenty-second birthday, I came down from the university on a Thursday. The next Tuesday morning I was at work, raw, anxious and nervous, in the great black glass building in Fleet Street. At £8 a week, I reckoned I was well paid.

*   *   *

We were a bold, brash, sometimes belligerent lot on the *Sunday Express* in those days. We had the confidence—I do not quite say the arrogance—which came from knowing that we were at the summit of our kind of Sunday journalism.

We were jealous of our all-round status as a family newspaper. To get beaten with a story by a competitor was for us (and probably still is, for all I know) the ultimate disaster. It was like scoring an own-goal. The craving for supremacy unquestionably stemmed from Beaverbrook at the top.

This motivating stimulus seemed to penetrate with undiminished strength right through the editorial side—through John Gordon and the two exceptionally able assistant editors, Brian Chapman, who came to 'the Sunday' from editing the *Daily Express* in Manchester, and Harold Barkworth; through the news and sports editors, Jack Garbutt and my immediate boss, W. R. G. Smith; right through the talented feature writers and columnists whom the paper had at its command—Peter Howard on politics, pungent, pugnacious and petulant; Stephen Watts on films, who could make up a page as well as he could write it; Nathaniel Gubbins, Sitting (splendidly) On The Fence each week; Valentine Castlerosse, who seemed to know—and did know—everyone, writing his Londoner's Log on page two in a prose style which set him apart; Bernard Harris on anything, as good a digger-out of a factual, intricate story as there was in Fleet Street; R. H. Naylor, Foretelling The Stars, with a weekly postbag that was the envy of all; Godfrey Winn being . . . well, Godfrey Winn; Jim Connolly on soccer, who contrived to have an open line to every football manager in the country and a ready-made story at the end of it—each was exceptional in his own way.

We felt we had an editorial team which could win—and did. And when we got down on to the 'stone' on a Saturday evening and saw the products of the week's and the day's work coming off the presses, as each edition went to bed, just the same spirit was to be found there among the compositors who set the type.

The 'comps' were a marvellously difficult bunch. Treat them wrongly, be off-hand with them, be unreasonably demanding in your ways, and woe betide you and all your works. But make friends of them, understand their problems and the preciseness of their job, and you had allies for life, for whom no deadline, no last-minute change, was impossible. They were the salt—and the pepper—of the earth.

I have only twice in my life met a similar spirit to the one we had in the *Sunday Express* in those glittering, colourful, pre-war days. One was in 249 Squadron in the Royal Air Force in the spring and summer of 1942 at the height of the Battle of Malta, when a handful of Spitfire pilots, outnumbered by eight or ten to one, were daily mixing it with the weight of Field Marshal Kesselring's Luftwaffe in Sicily. What an earthy, rugged, straight-talking amalgam of English, Scots, Australians, New Zealanders, Rhodesians, Canadians, South Africans and Americans they were. They beefed about everyone and everything—the flies, the food, the Maltese, the smells, the lack of aircraft—everything, that is, except the job they were sent out to the island to do. And did.

The other was in the Tory Party in Parliament in the eighteen months after Harold Macmillan had taken over the leadership from Sir Anthony Eden in January 1957. He lifted us up by the boot straps, welded the various factions together, and by sheer intellectual quality came to dominate the House of Commons.

For a new boy starting out in his early twenties, having previously spent a dozen relatively sheltered years being traditionally, expensively (and gratefully) educated, it was like jumping into an ice-cold bath before breakfast. It was rough getting into it; but, boy, when you were over the shock and had had a rub down, you felt like sprinting a couple of times round the block.

Chapter Nine
I shall print the story

THAT JOHN GORDON was, as Beaverbrook had put it, 'a great editor', few would trouble to deny. His record supported the contention. He had reached the top (for those times) the conventional way. Starting humbly in his native Aberdeen he had come to London, and via the *Evening News* and the *Sunday Express* he had conquered.

Gordon knew all the tricks of the business. His eye for the makings of a news story was acute. His ability, born of exact training, to take hold of a drab piece, lift the meat out of it, sharpen it up, and make it bite, was, for its author, on occasions, alarming. His habit of knocking out a headline after one edition and replacing it in the next with another, with all the characteristics of a gimlet, could be unnerving.

One Sunday, soon after I had been given a sports column to write across half the inside back page of the *Sunday Express*, I had the good (or ill) fortune to stumble on a story about a charity boxing tournament which had many of the ingredients dearest to Gordon's heart. There had been malpractice, pay-outs on the side, backhanders and the rest. Everyone, it seemed, had come out of it all right except the charity. In a word, it stank.

Not far removed from the trouble was a boxing writer of repute, now long-since deceased, whose authoritative views on the ancient art of pugilism were widely read. This was too near home for comfort.

My source of information was certain. The facts were complete and correct. The possibilities of exposure were—well—tempting. To a young journalist who had just got his toe on the ladder, they offered a chance 'to make a mark'. And holding down a sports column on a national newspaper in the late 1930s, with getting on for a couple of million unemployed outside, wasn't to be taken for granted.

I confided in W. R. G. Smith, the sports editor, an unemotional, understanding and conservative journalist who wasn't much given to

64

the peddling of dirt, no matter where it came from. He was a trusted ally, blunt when he had to tell me my copy was poor, but always ready with a good word when there was reason for it. A pillar of the pre-war Territorial Army, he inclined towards rectitude and prided himself, justifiably, on the fact that the sports pages of the *Sunday Express* bore his stamp.

I got the impression as I unfolded the story that Bill Smith wished he had never heard of it. 'I think,' he said with a bland detachment which hid some alarm, 'we should have a word with the editor; it's fairly inflammable stuff.'

To Gordon, of course, it was the red meat news stories are made of. He gave his instant decision. 'I shall print the story somewhere in the paper on Sunday even if it's not under Lucas's name. We have a duty to expose these bad things.'

I left the office earlier than usual on the Saturday evening, having seen the column passed by the lawyers and safely put to bed. I remember thinking the headline on it was rather less pungent than the piece itself. I found this, secretly, somewhat comforting.

I walked down Fleet Street and along Farringdon Street to the station with mixed feelings. Elation, because here was the scoop I needed to help me hold the job down. And apprehension, because I felt instinctively it would spell trouble—particularly among journalistic colleagues. Already there were mutterings about the speed of my advance since joining the *Sunday Express* in July 1937. This would certainly add a drop or two of paraffin to the embers.

It was the last edition of the paper which was delivered to our home at Rickmansworth on Sunday mornings in those days. I opened it at breakfast, unashamedly and immediately, at the inside back page. A new headline leaped out at me.

'THE WORST BOXING SCANDAL FOR YEARS'

Gordon had killed the original headline after the first edition (and after I had left the office) on the grounds that it was 'too soft for the story'. I doubt whether the introduction of his barbed alternative produced quite the result he expected. Or wanted.

When I got to the office on Tuesday morning (we always had Mondays off on the *Sunday Express*—a delicious experience when all your friends are working) a brief, clipped note, in the solicitor's familiar jargon, lay on my desk. It told me simply that a writ for libel would be issued against me and the newspaper and that the client would vigorously deny the allegations complained of in the article. These, it was claimed, were totally without foundation. The editor got a similar letter by the same post. It was, for me, a shaker.

Gordon sent for me. He was chuckling and pugnacious. 'Never mind this correspondence,' he said, 'provided the facts are right. An occasional one of these won't do you, or the paper, any harm. Mr Robertson wants to see you. Go to his office at once.'

E. J. Robertson was the executive head of Express Newspapers, Beaverbrook's right- and left-hand man, a Canadian of exceptional talent, humanity and kindliness and possessed of great skills in management. I had never spoken to him before, let alone been to his office. Dick Plummer, with whom I was later to serve in the House of Commons, albeit on opposite sides, was also in the room when I knocked.

Robertson's opening shot was not at all what I expected. 'I have been watching your column in 'the Sunday'; it's coming along well. John Gordon tells me he's pleased with your work. I liked the story on Sunday. Will the person who gave you the information—I take the facts to be correct—stick by you in a court of law?'

I had to say I expected he would but obviously I had to ask him. 'Then go away now and find out,' he said. 'Come back as soon as you've got the answer.'

My informant, not half as shattered as I was, was predictably solid. Yes, he would go into the witness box, if need be. No, there was no doubt whatever about the facts being correct.

Robertson's response was quiet and direct. 'Then we'll fight,' he said. 'Our lawyers here will take you to see the solicitors. If we have to brief Counsel, I would expect us to instruct Pat Hastings. We retain him for this kind of problem. Don't let this worry you. If you attack you must expect this sort of thing.'

I can't say the thought of trial by jury, with the prospect of Sir Patrick Hastings taking me through the events which led to the publication of the story, much appealed to my youthful mind. I began fervently to wish I had never touched the story.

Two or three unsettling months later the matter was mercifully disposed of, settled out of court. We did not pay out a penny and there

was no question of an apology. The defence had held firm. My relief
was intense, my confidence immeasurably strengthened. A subsequent
note from the company secretary told me that my salary had been
raised from £8 to £12 per week.

*   *   *

Throughout these immediate pre-war years John Gordon was, for me,
an interested, encouraging, yet exacting master. He could be very
forthright.

One week, admittedly to do a friend a good turn, I worked
unobtrusively into my column a reference to some new type of sports
equipment. A pull of the article, with the relevant paragraph ringed in
heavy black pencil, appeared on my desk. A note, in an all too familiar
hand, was added to it: 'See me about this. J.R.G.'

I guessed what was coming, but I hardly expected the potency of
the comment.

'If you're going on writing for me,' said Gordon, 'you must learn
that the things people want to read about themselves in newspapers
are advertisements and should be paid for. The things they don't want
to read about themselves are news. I am interested in news.'

Gordon was, at times, an irritating man. He wanted things done his
way and to his liking. If they weren't, his sarcasm could be
penetrating. He had no respect for persons. Beaverbrook was the only
man he looked up to.

I remember Valentine Castlerosse telephoning me one day at the
office and asking me to go and see him at Claridges. He was ill,
propped up in bed, in a room full of the most expensive flowers—
offerings from some of the gorgeous women whose photographs often
decorated his Londoner's Log, perhaps the most widely read and
arguably the best written column of the day.

'Tell me,' he enquired, 'how many times did John Gordon make
you rewrite your first column?'

'Three,' I replied.

'Lucky man,' said Valentine. 'He made me do mine seven times.'

When Lord Castlerosse's health worsened and he had temporarily
to stop writing, Gordon brought in C. B. Fry for a few weeks to fill the
top half of page two.

Charles Fry, one of the most remarkable of Britain's all-rounders, with a brilliantly versatile if eccentric mind, had been writing an original, and successful, daily column on cricket for the *Evening Standard* under the banner 'C. B. Fry says:—'.

Charles, a proud man, met his match in Gordon. After the third (vain) attempt at obtaining editorial satisfaction for his copy, he strode back across the news room, resplendent with monocle, spotted bow tie, light grey suit, black and white shoes and all, and sat down at my desk, nonplussed.

'Moral for life,' he said. 'Never argue; but never give in.'

Gordon was nothing if not controversial. Controversy had, for him, a mesmerizing appeal. Some of his own statements and ideas were monstrously and deliberately provocative.

The London Press Golfing Society (as it was then called) was running its annual foursomes tournament for pairs representing the national newspapers, the periodicals, the technical press and others. It was called the Sutton Salver.

John had commanded me to play with him for the *Sunday Express* in, I think, the last tournament before the war. It had gone on interminably, round after round, week after week. The nearer we got to the end, the keener John became to win. Victory would clearly have, for me, more than a passing significance for my future.

Now, after an agonizing series of exertions, we were in the final against the house of Newnes, playing over thirty-six holes of the Old Course at Addington.

As we sat with our opponents on the 2nd tee after lunch waiting for the players in front to move on, John delivered himself of one of those unlikely, characteristically dogmatic and confident assertions, designed specially to provoke.

Sir Frank Newnes had been going on about the allegedly 'successful campaign' which one of the national dailies, a sharp thorn in the side of the *Express*, was then running.

'Believe me,' said John, 'it'll get them nowhere. In thirty years of journalism I have seen newspapers with small circulations and great power turn into newspapers with great circulations and little power.'

Coming from the distinguished editor of one of them, it was rich stuff. I rather think we were eight up at the time.

Chapter Ten
Tides flow in the affairs of men

IT WAS late on Sunday evening when the telephone bell rang at home. Bill Smith, the sports editor, was on the line. I guessed he wanted a game of golf the next day—our day off on the *Sunday Express*. He lived close by at Chorley Wood, in Hertfordshire, and we sometimes played together on a Monday.

My guess was wrong.

'The *Evening Standard* have been on to me,' he said. 'They want you to cover the News of the World golf tournament at Stoke Poges for them this coming week. Henry Longhurst is ill and can't do it. I've spoken to John Gordon and he's agreeable. This is a good chance for you. Be there first thing tomorrow morning; but don't forget, I shall want your copy for 'the Sunday' on Friday morning just the same.'

I was at Stoke Poges at 8.30 the next morning. There was a message waiting for me to call the sports editor of the *Evening Standard* immediately.

The instructions were clear-cut but somewhat unsettling for someone who had never done any evening newspaper reporting before. They wanted 300 words telephoned at 10.30, the same again at 12.30, and 400 at 2.30. The last call, with 300 words and a new 'intro' to wind up the day, was to be no later than 3.30.

The *Standard* used to give a lot of space to golf in those days, and this was the principal professional tournament of the year. All the same, 1,300 or so words in one day, telephoned under 'deadline' conditions, was a formidable prospect. I remember sitting down alone in the clubhouse at Stoke to gather my thoughts, wondering what I had let myself in for, and, more important, what I was going to be able to say at 10.30 that would take 300 words. Play wouldn't have been going for much more than an hour.

A light hand touched my shoulder. It was Charles Macfarlane, the correspondent of the rival *Evening News*, a good and dependable friend.

'And what will you be doing here at this hour?' he asked in that lilting Scots accent, with a ring of inquisitive kindness about it. I explained my predicament. 'Aye,' mused Charlie, 'then you'd better stay round with me for a day or two, and I'll show you the road. Aye.'

For years afterwards, whenever I saw Charlie, those comforting words of help always came back to me. I really felt he was as anxious as I was that I shouldn't make a mess of it that week.

Midway through the tournament, just as I was getting used to the routine calls to the office, and even beginning to enjoy the work, the B.B.C. made contact. They wondered if I would do a broadcast for them for their evening sports programme on each of the last three days' play. I would have to go to the studio to do it, but they thought I would have enough time to get there after filing my last piece for the Standard, knock out a script to fill three or four minutes, and then go on the air.

I was surprised to find myself saying yes. Having done so I could hardly credit my temerity. I had never broadcast before and the arrangements in those days were very different from what they are today.

A couple of decades later when, for a few years, I sat on the General Advisory Council of the B.B.C. and took part in its various discussions, I used sometimes to ponder the extent of the journey which had been travelled since those first broadcasts for the Corporation so many years before.

They went rather well. Other assignments sprang from them. Here was one of those rare tides which flow in the affairs of men. It was certainly not of flood proportions, but it was running strongly enough to make me feel that, after the initial struggle, I was on my feet and moving forward.

My modest confidence was bolstered further by a letter which arrived about this time from the editor of *Golf Illustrated*, one Elliot Cockell, a stoutly built, well-groomed and rather autocratic man, who presided over one of the oldest of all Britain's golfing periodicals.

A few weeks earlier over lunch Cockell had broached the possibility of my doing for him a regular series of character studies of the golfing personalities of the day. The idea had appealed, not just because of the few extra pounds it would bring in but because I had begun to get a feel for 'human interest' stories, which I had quickly learned to be one of journalism's sure-fire certainties. I genuinely felt I would like to do it.

I had run the suggestion with Gordon. He had given me, I thought, a rather abrupt no. He didn't want me spending my time writing for periodicals; and, anyway, contributing to *Golf Illustrated* wouldn't help my journalistic career. I felt he was taking a fairly narrow line.

Cockell now returned to the issue with a formal, written offer. Would I be prepared to undertake to do a series? It would provide the chance, he said, to 'spread your wings'.

I remember telling my friend Brigadier-General A. C. Critchley, another remarkable Canadian who, like his compatriots Beaverbrook and E. J. Robertson, had succeeded notably in the maelstrom of British business, of the *Golf Illustrated* offer and Gordon's initial reaction. 'Ask him again,' said Critch, in his familiar, staccato manner. 'The hardest thing in business is to say no.'

*   *   *

As the scope of my work broadened the clouds of war were beginning to gather over Europe. Their reality had been brought sharply home to me by a strange interlude which came at the end of an idyllic six weeks' working and playing visit to Florida.

We had returned to New York City from Palm Beach or, more precisely, from nearby Boca Raton, to embark in the north German Lloyd's S.S. *Bremen*, a magnificently appointed liner, which offered all the accepted comforts and rather more beside.

We were to go aboard at midnight at Pier 84 on West 44th Street. After dinner at the Ritz Carlton we adjourned, well fed, to Madison Square Garden where, fortuitously, Tommy Farr, the Welsh heavyweight from Tonypandy, was fighting the colourful American, Max Baer, in a return of the contest which the two had earlier fought in London. I recall, and indeed reported at the time, that Farr had an angry-looking boil between his shoulder blades. I was concerned for the fitness of our man. A boil and 'peak condition' hardly seemed synonymous.

As we left the Garden, somewhat dejected after a British defeat, the newspaper headlines stopped us dead. The front pages of the two tabloids shouted the story in thick black type a couple of inches deep.

HITLER INVADES AUSTRIA

In an hour's time we were due to embark in a German ship bound for Southampton and Bremen. What if they gave Southampton a miss? The British contingent who, for the past two or three hours, had been happily entertained at the ringside were now, suddenly, apprehensive. Calls were made to the embassy in Washington seeking advice. The radio's highly dramatized news flashes were anxiously devoured.

Once aboard, there was nothing for it but to enjoy the voyage. The ship was full of well-heeled Germans returning from their highly publicized exhibition at the New York World's Fair. From the start their determination to be friendly and totally composed was transparent. A handsome and finely groomed countess in her early thirties, a sculptress of no mean repute, whose subjects, I remember, included the Führer himself and the world heavyweight champion, Max Schmeling, invited us to dine at her table. She gave us the full treatment. Herr Adolf, she claimed, was her friend. He was in full command. All would be well. I recall admiring his choice.

It was a strange, almost unreal Atlantic crossing, as rough as they come and devoid of any news whatever, save what we were allowed to read in the heavily censored *Ocean Times*. For all we knew, Europe might be erupting. Amid the fun and glamour it was all rather eerie.

Looking back now, our anxiety may have been misplaced. All I know is that, at the time, when the great ship hove to off Cherbourg and we disgorged into the tender which was to take us into Southampton, the relief was genuine. And totally shared.

I often wondered afterwards what happened to the countess.

*   *   *

Back in Fleet Street, I found encouragement in one of those little incidents which mean so much in one's forward march.

After six weeks away from the office, during which I had been sending copy back to the newspaper each week without much response from London, I was dubious about what I might find on my return. I was even ready for the sack.

It was, therefore, with some relief and not a little elation that on getting in on Saturday morning I found the last piece I had sent from Florida about the life and high times of the internationally known rich in Palm Beach—the forerunners of today's so-called 'jet set'—being used as a feature on one of the principal pages.

In the early evening I went down to 'the stone' as usual as the first edition was going to bed. Tom Blackburn, then the manager of 'the Sunday', and later to follow E. J. Robertson as the senior executive of the Beaverbrook group, was reading a pull of the page which carried my story.

I kept out of the way and busied myself with my task. A moment or two later a tap on my back told me to expect the worst. 'That's a good piece of yours from America,' said Tom. 'If you go on like this you'll have nothing to worry about here.' I left the office that night walking a couple of inches taller.

*   *   *

In my time with Beaverbrook there was little interchange between the editorial staffs of the *Sunday* and the *Daily Express*. Although we worked in the same building we lived apart. Each paper went its own way and developed its own personality and character. The one was as different from the other as Bomber Command of the Royal Air Force was from Fighter Command; and Oxford is from Cambridge.

Except on Saturdays, when bedlam was apt to reign, life on 'the Sunday' took a relatively even course. There was little of the bustle of daily journalism to disturb our ways. As the weeks went by, and I began to find my feet, with the work coming easily and enjoyably, I began to hanker for the excitement of the daily grind. Unfortunately the war intervened to prevent this.

However, I had earlier made friends with Trevor Wignall, a temperamental, effervescent, unpredictable and unrepentant Welshman, who dealt principally in the currency of controversy and who filled his Daily Sportlight (later the Daily Searchlight) in the *Daily Express* with a facility which, in my short time in Fleet Street, I personally never saw matched.

Trevor was always ready to offer the young a hand. Sometimes he would invite me to his office to witness the last stages of the daily process. It was a humbling performance to behold. On a normal afternoon he would wind the first sheet of paper into his typewriter at, maybe, 4 p.m., with the content and construction of the column already established in his mind. From the moment the opening paragraph was tapped out, the rest of the 1,200 words or so flowed on, relentlessly, fluently and without interruption. An hour and a half to two hours later, the exercise was complete—copy tidied up, desk cleared, carbons put away. Whatever anyone may have thought about Wignall's column—and there were many who detested it (but still read it)—it was a thoroughly professional job. And, remember, it was repeated five days a week, week after week, as gruelling and as exacting a task as any in Fleet Street.

Of course Wignall's methods were open to question. And sometimes to censure. If he knew something was white he felt a compelling desire to call it black. He was continually immersed in argument and debate. He revelled in it. Resignation was usually just round the corner. Trevor's sources of information were many, his 'exclusives' numerous. If he hadn't got a story to file, he allowed his extensive imagination to fill the gap. 'If you're stuck for a piece,' he once told me, 'remember the old trick. Lead the column with the words: "If I am to credit my information". After that you just let it run.'

With Trevor two and two could readily be made into five, and maybe six. Trouble came aplenty. He infuriated and he pleased. He inflamed passions and stimulated controversy. Intentionally. You could tell his writing a mile off. Like it or loathe it, it had a personality about it which was unmistakable. In his own way, he was a master of his craft.

Yet behind all this was a side of the man which few, except his closer friends, knew. For all his monstrosities and irregularities, there was a kindness, a sympathy, an understanding, about him which endeared. For a young, groping novice in Fleet Street, he reserved a place in his heart. It was the opposite of what his reading public thought of him. I had reason to be grateful for it.

*   *   *

Through Wignall I came, in my early days with Beaverbrook, to meet others among the alumni of the *Daily Express*. They towered over me from their pedestals. Occasionally, through these contacts, I got the chance to do an odd humble job for the paper. When I did, it was like pinching an apple from the orchard next door. Gordon didn't like his reporters shinning over the garden wall.

'Downstairs', where the *Daily Express* staff worked, became a term which, to us on 'the Sunday', implied alien territory. And when we went 'downstairs' ourselves on a Saturday to produce the paper for Sunday, the exercise took on some of the flavour of an armed reconnaissance. All that was missing on our return were the prisoners.

Although it could have been, in those early days and circumstances, little more than a headmaster-third former relationship, I received spasmodic if well-disguised encouragement from Arthur Christiansen, editor of the *Daily Express*, an operator of unquestioned class, who drove the newspaper forward with a verve, an enterprise and an enthusiasm which were infectious. Once in a while he would come into Wignall's room when I was there. Moreover, he, Trevor and I had an old and mutual friend in Jack Izod, debatably the best shirtmaker and clothier in the West End of London. To do me a good turn, Jack used sometimes to arrange lunch or dinner for the four of us, at which I was a quiet listener. The big talk of newspapers fascinated me. It was a privilege to be present.

Christiansen was the ultimate professional. He always seemed to be wound up tight and going flat out. Thoughts, ideas, suggestions, criticisms and comments came cascading from him. As a young man, having come to London from the north, he had had a phenomenal rise through 'the Sunday' to obtain the editorship of the *Daily Express* before he was thirty. This advance was built on ability, brilliance and courage—and a bit of luck.

A human powerhouse, Christiansen's output of work was immense. His flair oozed from the paper. He got close to his staff and communicated with them. He was with them, of them, and for them. He expected a great deal and got it. He boiled over very quickly. Under his direction the *Daily Express* became an exceptional production job. He was skilled in presentation and make-up and he inflicted strict rules on his reporters and sub-editors.

Chris disliked long sentences. 'Your column in "the Sunday," he once said to me early on before Gordon had started to get at it, 'rambles all over the place. Sharpen up the sentences. Use commas and full stops to break them up. Give them some air. You're choking them.

'And tell your story in the first couple of paragraphs, then build it up, giving it a good kick right at the end. You take too long to get to the point. I'm bored when I get there.'

And as if that wasn't enough, he added as an afterthought: 'And another thing. Don't let them put a "head" on the piece without a verb in it. Headlines without verbs can't live.'

Twenty years later, not long after I had become managing director of G.R.A. (The Greyhound Racing Association), Chris and his wife, Brenda, came to dinner. He had retired from the *Express* a year or two before, his heart scarred by a lifetime of pressure. He had just finished his autobiography. I asked him what he was going to call it.

'Strange you should ask that,' he replied. 'Believe it or not, I couldn't find a title for it, so I added a paragraph the other day to my weekly column in the *World's Press News*.

' "Here I am," I said, "I've been writing headlines all my life and now I can't find a title for my own book. £5 for the best idea on the back of a postcard." '

A couple of days later the winning postcard was on his desk.

'You've got it there in your last paragraph,' it ran. ' "Here I am, I've been writing headlines all my life and now . . ." "Headlines All My Life"—that's your title.'

'So that's what it's to be. "Headlines All My Life".'

'But Chris,' I said, plaintively, 'it hasn't got a verb in it.'

A broad, cherubic grin stretched gradually across his tanned face. He put a hand on my wife's arm.

'Jill,' he said, 'when they come out of a good stable, they never forget.'

Chapter Eleven
Pre-ordained prelude

WE WERE a small, tight-knit team on the sports desk of the *Sunday Express*, as different from one another as could be, and yet under Bill Smith we worked happily together. We had rows but there were few of them.

There were only four or five of us who worked full-time. Jim Connolly was our star and football was his business; but if a good or difficult general sports story came up he was the man who was put on to it. Our 'character', however, was a little Cockney sub-editor from the East End of London named Barney Hyams. He couldn't have stood much over five feet, but what he lacked in stature he made up for in stockiness. His head, rather like Lord Beaverbrook's, was too big for his body. He was always in his shirtsleeves, and two features in his rugged, worn face were striking. His mouth was outsize. And permanently in one corner of it was a cigarette which was always smoked down to the end. The marvel was it never burned his lips.

When Barney spoke the only concession he made to his audience was to shift the cigarette from one corner of his mouth to the other with a dexterity which defied imitation. He never left his listeners in any doubt about his meaning. When things weren't to his liking (and on Saturday evening around edition time they never were) he had ready to hand a selection of expletives which brooked no rejoinder.

Below a wide brow there was set the kindest pair of eyes I ever saw. Barney Hyams had spent most of the First World War in the trenches. He had known the hard life. He had no aspirations about advancement. All he asked was to be left to get on with his job. And to keep it.

It was quite a time before he sized me up. A public school and university education was not a recipe which immediately appealed to Barney. But by one of the stranger twists of human nature the two

extremes came together. Hyams lived in East Ham. 'East 'am' as he
would have it. He was a fervent supporter of West Ham Football Club.
No other team mattered. In the football season we used to run a
column on the sports page by John Wadham. Wadham was a fictitious
character who never existed. The job of his ghost was to take the
highlights of the day's league matches from the agency reports and
blend them together into a readable whole. Hyams often subbed the
stuff, and when it was my lot to write it, win or lose, I never failed to
include a paragraph about West Ham. It put me right with Barney.

When the time came for me to leave the paper to serve in the Royal
Air Force, Barney and I went out for a drink. I was dispirited to find
him ill at ease and uncomfortable, not at all like he usually was with
me. After a glass of beer we parted.

'Thanks Barney,' I said, 'you've been the hell of a help to me. I
wouldn't have got out of those awful scrapes without you.'

'That's all right, boy,' he replied. Then, after an embarrassed pause,
he looked up at me and added: 'I 'ope you come back, boy. I've been
'appy working with you.'

It was all he could do to say it. A tear in those kindly Cockney eyes
told me the rest. Barney Hyams was a man in five million.

*   *   *

My time in Fleet Street was now running out. The so-called 'phoney
war' of the winter of 1939-40, during which Gordon put me on to
reporting stories of Britain's war effort, was at an end. Hitler's panzer
divisions had cut through the Low Countries. The Allied armies had
fallen back to the Channel ports. France was on the point of collapse.
Churchill was bracing the British people for the aerial onslaught
which was soon to follow.

Those of us who had volunteered for the Royal Air Force at the
outbreak of war, and who had then been sent back to our civilian jobs
until there were aircraft for us to fly, now got our marching orders.

I left the office late on Saturday 15 June 1940. It was my last
evening with the *Sunday Express* and I had wanted to stay till the
second edition had been put to bed. As I walked alone along
Farringdon Street to the station I reflected not so much upon what life
might now hold, or whether I would ever see the office again, but

upon the events and experiences of the past three years since first I had set foot in the big black glass building which was the Express.

I can still remember vividly being seized of a compelling conviction that, whatever might now be going to happen, my few years with Beaverbrook had somehow been 'meant'. I felt they had been sent as some kind of pre-ordained prelude to the tests—and opportunities—which must come. One thing I knew for sure. No one could take them from me.

Chapter Twelve
So you finally made page one!

ONCE A journalist, they say, always a journalist. At heart, yes.

The translation, in three short days, from sports columnist of the *Sunday Express* on Saturday night, to Aircraftman 2nd Class, Lucas P. B., 911532, the next Tuesday morning, did not bring down the final curtain on my association with the *Express*.

At the height of the Battle of Malta, in those hot Mediterranean days of 1942, the irresistible urge to get something down on paper welled up again. The compulsion was stimulated by a desire to counter the heavily censored and slanted stories we had been reading of the fighting which was taking place in the daylight air over the island.

The chance came when I was sent back to Gibraltar for a few days, with two or three other combat-hardened pilots from the Squadron, to lead in a fresh consignment of Spitfires. We were to fly them off the Royal Navy's aircraft carrier Eagle, from a point roughly opposite Algiers, about 700 miles from Malta, and link up with other aircraft from the U.S. Navy's massive carrier *Wasp*, which was to steam down the Mediterranean with us.

In the blessed quiet of the Rock I put together a piece which, to avoid the censor, I persuaded a Catalina pilot, who was flying back to England, to take personally to Air Commodore (no longer Brigadier-General) Critchley, then the Air Officer Commanding, 52 Group, at his headquarters at Sunningdale.

A typewritten covering note, bearing no traces of authorship, simply carried the words: 'John, Chris or Robbie might perhaps be interested.' I guessed Critch would get my meaning. He knew Beaverbrook and the three people mentioned very well.

With that I flew back, satisfied and refreshed, to the island and to the daily grind of readiness at dawn.

Three or four weeks later a formidable-looking brown envelope, marked O.H.M.S., arrived for me in our mess in the holy city of Medina. I never knew who brought it. Tucked incongruously inside was a folded—and unexpectedly thin—copy of the *Daily Express*. It was dated Saturday, 23 May 1942. It had four pages, by comparison with the customary twenty-four we had known in peacetime.

I opened the paper just as eagerly as I had scoured the *Sunday Express* for my first story on that anxious Sunday morning in Cambridge five years before.

There, down the length of the first column on page one, was—my piece. Security demanded that it be unsigned, but it carried, distinctively, a three-sided rule round the headline:

AIR KNIGHT OF MALTA
WRITES HOME

BATTLE OF BRITAIN HAD NOTHING ON THIS

I flinched slightly at the intro: 'The Daily Express publishes below the first story from one of the gallant band of Spitfire pilots who are defending Malta. He sent it as a letter to a friend in Britain.'

Clipped to the front page was a brief note. 'So you finally made Page One!' It was signed 'C'.

Nearly fifty years on, the elation of that sunny, Maltese day remains strong. Not even the inhibitions aroused by the rough, unrounded style of the sentences can dispel the desire for reproduction:

> For a brief space I am out of the Battle of Malta. Thus, from this strangely-peaceful spot I can give you a disjointed and sketchy account.
>
> It has, of course, been an experience of the first order. I am inclined to think the Battle of Britain had nothing on the Battle of Malta. And when the story is told later it will surprise many.
>
> Up to the time I left, a few days ago, on a particular mission, our squadron had shot down 46$\frac{1}{2}$ for the loss of five pilots. The boys have been magnificent.
>
> Always the odds have weighed heavily against us; sometimes

it has been 10 to 1 against on fighters alone, and another 10 to 1 against on the bombers.

To me, the miracle has been the small losses. Our squadron, better equipped in experience than the others, has suffered least.

GERMANS NOT YELLOW

None would deny that the Hun has done a damned good job. His raids have been well organised. His flying, in general, belies the fact that he has inexperienced squadrons in Sicily.

These Germans are not yellow. They are not cowards and they are not poor pilots. It makes us wild to hear stupid propaganda tales to the contrary.

The fact is, our own boys have got to be a little bit better. If they're not they will be killed. And we're fighting this war to live, not, we hope, to die.

Most of the fellows we have lost have been those with the least experience, generally speaking. And here let it be said it would be a crime to send a pilot to Malta without battle experience.

It is not fair to him, and it's not fair to the other boys. The longer a fellow lasts the less likely it becomes that he'll be shot up, given reasonable fortune.

I learned as much in a week in Malta as I ever did in all the sweeps in England.

I would go back to the sweeps again with an entirely different outlook and with shocking confidence.

We have, for instance, hit on a particular formation which we have found to be the only possible one to fly. None would ever fly another way so long as he was alive and there were Huns to attack. And, curiously, the Hun is flying the same way, too!

The Malts have taken the blitzing damned well. They have shown courage and a will.

One little point as an instance. I had to make a crash landing in a cornfield—about the only one in the island. There were a few old men and women working in it.

When I plonked down my engine was on fire, but, given assistance, I reckoned we could put it out. These old Malts didn't run away; they got their sacks and kept filling them with earth and emptying them on the engine until the flames were out.

Then one old woman (they are, of course, all Roman Catholics), came up, put her hand on the port wing and made the Sign of the Cross on her chest. I think I never saw anything in my life which left a more indelible impression of sincere faith.

RAMMED A NAZI

The bombing has almost all been done with 87's and 88's, and it has all been dive-bombing—from about 12,000-14,000 down to 1,000-1,500 feet.

I repeat, these Huns aren't yellow. Sometimes the boys go up, have a sharp go-to with the bombers, and come back to find the airfield full of bomb craters. It's a bit of a problem getting a spot to land!

I have been very fortunate. I came out with my great friend in the R.A.F. We were at the I.T.W. at Cambridge together; we trained in Canada together; we went to the O.T.U. in England together, and then we went to the same squadron.

Finally we went to Malta together, and to the same squadron. And, of course, we never fly apart.

Incidentally, he rammed a 109 the other day and knocked its wing off. He force-landed back on the airfield. It shook him no end!

A week or two after I received the paper from Christiansen, a letter arrived for me from E. J. Robertson. It contained three sentences. 'Lord Beaverbrook has asked me to say he is stirred by the exploits of your squadron. We have paid £50 into your bank account in England. It could, perhaps, be useful just now.'

A few days later another letter came for me from Robbie. It was equally concise. 'Lord Beaverbrook tells me we haven't paid you enough. Another £50 has now been passed to your bank in England.'

Happily, I got the second letter at the end of a very good spell for the squadron. The duration of the party which followed posed yet again the thought: If Dawn comes can Readiness be far behind?

3

The Sky alone was
the Limit

Chapter Thirteen
Prelude to the storm

> Often do the spirits
> Of great events stride on before the events
> And in today already walks tomorrow.
> (Coleridge, *The Death of Wallenstein,* Act V, Scene 1)

A SIGNAL had come through to 66 Squadron from 10 Group headquarters of the Royal Air Force's Fighter Command asking for two pilots to volunteer for Burma. Both Raoul Daddo-Langlois and I had now been with 66 for six months, stationed most of the time at Perranporth in north Cornwall and housed comfortably in the Droskyn Castle Hotel overlooking the Atlantic Ocean and St Agnes' Head.

After completion of our flying training in Canada, on the first course of the great Empire and Commonwealth Air Training Scheme, this had been our initial experience of squadron life.

The operations in the Portreath sector had been singularly dull. Daily patrols over shipping convoys, plying their way round Land's End and the Lizard, bound for Plymouth, Southampton and other ports, interspersed with uneventful sweeps over Brittany in support of Bomber Command's attacks on the two German battle cruisers, *Scharnhorst* and *Gneisenau,* snuggling together in Brest, made a fairly unappetizing menu. My promotion to command 'A' Flight, after no more than four months with the squadron, had not really changed things. We felt in need of a move.

'Never volunteer for anything,' said the old sweats. Boredom, however, and an ignorant lust for action, defied advice. Raoul and I decided to put our names forward.

'Burma,' we cried, 'here we come.'

Two days later we were posted to Malta.

Paradoxically, our place of embarkation was not to be an airfield but Plymouth, from whence we were to be transported by Sunderland flying boat to Gibraltar and thence to Malta. Our train would leave Paddington on Friday, 13 February 1942—a propitious date on which to start an enterprise!

We were just ending our embarkation leave in London when, on the morning of 12 February, the news broke. The German Navy was attempting the impossible.

Taking advantage of darkness, surprise and a favourable forecast of low cloud and worsening weather to come, *Scharnhorst* and *Gneisenau*, and now *Prinz Eugen,* frequently claimed in those days to have been immobilized by bombing, had put to sea from Brest during the night and had been ploughing their way at speed north-east up the English Channel. Now the three warships were making a run for it through the Straits of Dover in one of the great epics of the war.

Fighter, Bomber and Coastal Commands of the Royal Air Force were erupting viciously in support of the Royal Navy in a blaze of activity such as we had not known in our time with 66. Indeed, we wondered what we might be missing . . . and whether this was merely the prelude to the real storm.

By the time the train had reached Plymouth the cruisers were safely at anchor in Kiel and Wilhelmshaven. In the ancient West Country seaport, the Royal Navy were hardly having a ball.

Four other pilots from 11 Group joined us in the old-fashioned quayside hotel where we were to foregather—a Canadian squadron leader, one Percival Stanley Turner, from the Tangmere wing, and three other pilot officers, Harry Fox and Bob Sergeant from England and Tex Putnam, a Canadian, born in the United States. I could see at once that Stan Turner, with experience of Dunkirk, the Battle of Britain and the sweeps over northern France behind him, thought little of this motley crew. Casually, and with some disdain, he flicked open my unbuttoned greatcoat and looked at the left breast of my tunic. A deprecating glance told me unmistakably that a flight lieutenant without a decoration wasn't worth a damn.

As the Sunderland thumped its way off the water and set course for a point well west of the Brittany peninsula, Turner passed an oblique comment on the Germans' astonishing dash through the Straits. 'At least, after all this,' he said, 'with all the Hun fighters up in the Pas de Calais and Holland, we shouldn't get bounced off Brest.'

We reached the Rock, and its circus of lights, in the evening, and after the inevitable visit to the bar at the Bristol turned in for our last quiet night's sleep for weeks.

The Sunderland pilot bided his time at Gibraltar until the next evening. Then, flying through darkness and one electric storm after another, we made our way eastwards down the Mediterranean, landing in Kalafrana Bay as the sun began to rise above the eastern horizon.

As we headed for the mess for breakfast the sirens began to wail. In a moment or two a section of five manifestly old Hurricane IIs passed overhead, strung out in V formation, labouring to gain height over the island. High up above them, eight Messerschmitt 109s, flying fast and purposefully in pairs in line abreast, swept southwards across the brightening sky, dominant and unchallenged. It was a different world from the Spitfires of Fighter Command and the sweeps over northern France.

Turner watched in silence, and gathering apprehension, as the Hurricanes disappeared into cloud. 'Good God,' he exclaimed, turned on his heel and strode on towards the mess.

*   *   *

Stan Turner's impact on the day fighter operations in Malta was immediate and lasting. And his achievement was the more remarkable in that he arrived on the island when our fortunes had reached their nadir.

The few Hurricane IIs which remained serviceable had seen better days. Their work-rate had been extraordinary, their results indisputable. In capable hands they still had, for a while, an effective part to play. But the brute fact had to be faced: tactically, and for speed, the Messerschmitt 109 Fs, with which Kesselring's squadrons in Sicily were equipped, had the measure of them. At altitude the discrepancy became increasingly marked. British propaganda claimed otherwise. The propagandists were mistaken in adopting this stance. It was unsupported by the facts. Even an inexperienced pilot officer, joining a squadron for the first time, knew this at once.

For aircrew arriving fresh from England, who for nearly a year had flown little else but Spitfire Vs against the German 109 Fs over France, the story became a laughing stock. Turner killed it stone dead.

He had the experience, the knowledge, the authority—and the sheer nerve—to do so.

Taking over 249 at Takali when things were close to their worst, he sized the situation up in a couple of days. He put the case bluntly to Group Captain A. B. Woodhall, the operations controller, with whom he had worked closely at Tangmere. Either we get Spitfire Vs on the island in days—not weeks—or we're done. Woodhall understood immediately. He did not need to have it explained further. He, in his turn, was equally forthright with the Air Officer Commanding, Air Vice-Marshal Hugh Pughe Lloyd, who knew the score anyway.

Under pressure—real pressure—Lloyd was, without doubt, the most accomplished field commander I personally saw in the Royal Air Force in wartime. He was fearless but he had judgment. He had himself been knocked about in the First World War so he saw things from the pilot's point of view. He also understood the wider, strategic issues. He didn't say a lot, but when he spoke the sentences bit. He chose his words deliberately and with care, particularly with the pilots and the groundcrews. He was firm and hard, but humanity was always close at hand. He never seemed disturbed, but complacency was not of his nature. He pushed people to the limit—and beyond; but he drove himself in exactly the same way. Above all, Lloyd didn't give a damn—except about the survival of Malta. As far as that was concerned, no personal consideration, no thought of what the consequences might mean for himself, was ever entertained. There wasn't a pilot at the height of the battle who wouldn't willingly have gone to the stake for him.

Hugh Pughe Lloyd put the picture, in all its simplicity, to the Air Staff in London. Thence to Churchill. This was February 1942. In March the first of the Spitfire Vs landed in Malta, flown in from the carrier *Eagle*, steaming at speed eastwards down the western Mediterranean. As the Prime Minister put it later, in another context: It was not the end. It was not even the beginning of the end. But it was, perhaps, the end of the beginning.

Stan Turner's other lasting accomplishment was to change the squadrons' style of flying on the island. The effect upon him of having seen, on his first morning, that section of five Hurricanes, clambering up in straggling V formation, with the 109s thousands of feet above, had been profound.

In the Tangmere wing under Wing Commander Douglas Bader, where so much success had been achieved for relatively so little loss, Turner had become accustomed to operating with individual sections of four aircraft, flying loosely together in line abreast. They called them 'finger fours' after the spread of the outstretched fingers of a hand.

The principle of line abreast was simple. The pilots of the two aircraft on the right would each look inwards to the left, having no thought for anything to their right. Conversely, the two pairs of eyes on the left would scan to the right, disregarding everything to the left. In this way four pairs of eyes traversed the whole sky. Reduced to its most elementary form, a pair of aircraft flying together in line abreast, with each pilot looking inwards at his mate, and crossing over on the turns, provided complete and sustained cover. Each pilot was utterly dependent upon the other for survival—and success. It made for reliance between comrades. It was the basis upon which command of the daylight air over Malta was won. Its immediate origin could be laid at Woodhall's and Turner's door. Further back, the copyright belonged, and still belongs, to Bader.

Within a week of Stan Turner's arrival, pairs and fours in line abreast had become the only battle formation flown on the island. Vs and line astern, which some of the wings in England, with the luxury of numbers to sustain them, had slavishly clung to, were out. With the odds we were dealing with in the Mediterranean, we couldn't afford them.

And, anyway, if, in those rugged days, we had tried leaving an Australian sergeant pilot out in the cold, flying in line astern as tail-end Charlie at the back, protecting some of the more senior and commissioned backsides in the front, I wouldn't have given too much for their owners' chances.

*   *   *

Apart from the change in the style of flying, the tactics employed in promoting the interceptions were radically overhauled. In this both Woodhall and Turner played a part.

No longer were the sections, even with the old Hurricanes, vectored straight on to approaching enemy aircraft, with the manoeuvring climb left to the leaders' own discretion. Instead, the few serviceable aircraft were got off the ground much earlier, as the raids began to move in from Sicily, sixty miles away. In place of a climb northwards towards the enemy—or, at best, sideways to the east or west—the instructions to the pilots were to use the extra time in gaining altitude to the south of the island, right away from the course of the attackers. It gave much more elbow room. Then, on the word from the ground controller, and keeping the sun at their back, the sections were brought in fast, building up speed as they lost the superior height they had won. It made the very most of such performance as the Hurricanes had left in them. The kills increased, the losses were reduced. By the time the Spitfire Vs arrived in strength the drill was automatic and universally acclaimed. The maximum advantage could then be gained.

*　　*　　*

Stan Turner only led 249 and the Takali wing for a couple of months or so before they took him off operations. His nervous system was already strung tight after two continuously hard operational years during which he had had no rest. Having come over, as a Canadian, to join the Royal Air Force before the war, he had had much more than his fill. I suspect he well knew it. The signs were there for all to see. He was leading faster and faster in the air. Too fast, in fact. He never took a day off. He was becoming more edgy all round, and he had started fidgeting about with details which didn't matter and which, anyway, could well have been left to the flight commanders to handle. Exhausted, he was now transferred to Headquarters.

But he had done the job which Lloyd and Woodhall had demanded of him. And much more besides. He had taken Malta's flying apart and given it a refit in readiness for the major battle which, with the big Spitfire reinforcements, was about to break. No one else on the island at the time could have done it. History should accord Turner a chapter to himself in the Malta story.

Chapter Fourteen
The Rock of Malta

IN EVERY story of endeavour there comes a moment when, in retrospect, we can stand back and say: 'That was it. That was the turning point.' A match, a race, a career, a battle, a campaign—at some point in the contest the crunch comes. A mistake is made. A thrust succeeds. All is suddenly changed, and there is an inevitability about the subsequent course of events which nothing can arrest. Relentlessly, inexorably, the last scenes are played out.

So, painfully, it was with the Malta story.

We were near enough to things in the air battle to recognize the truth. Instinct could be confirmed by fact. From our vantage point, we could easily see the ebb and flow of the tide. The island was too small a place to hide its secrets from us. We had the feel of it from week to week, from month to month.

The low point was 20-22 April 1942, the three days when hopes rose high and were then cruelly dashed. This was the juncture when, collectively, we came nearest to dying. And even, for the first time, *thought* we might die.

'During March and April,' wrote Churchill, 'all the heat was turned on Malta, and remorseless air attacks by day and night wore the island down and pressed it to the last gasp.' (*The Hinge of Fate* published by Cassells.)

Those April days were our 'last gasp'.

Control of the daylight air was what counted. The Germans possessed it to an increasing extent in the first four months of the year.

As 1942 wore on it was plain that the battle for the Western Desert would soon reach its climax. Rommel needed a safe passage for his Mediterranean conveys to victual the Afrika Korps for the final clash which must come. Malta stood between them and his army. The thorn

92

must, at all costs, be removed, or the pain, at least, be neutralized. Field Marshal Kesselring's Luftwaffe in Sicily, equipped to the standards of the Western Front, with a front-line strength of 600 aircraft, stepped up the pressure. Against this the home defence could put up no more than a handful or so of Spitfires with a few Hurricanes thrown in.

Heroic deeds were performed by the island's fighter, bomber—and strike pilots, by the toughened groundcrews who sustained them, and by the unutterable courage of the gunners who kept up a steel umbrella over the three airfields and Grand Harbour. But there was no blinking the fact: the enemy was on top.

Food and ammunition had dwindled alarmingly. These commodities could only be supplied by sea. The February convoy from Alexandria had had to turn back. The March attempt to run the gauntlet had met disaster. The serviceability of the few Spitfires which, that same month, had been loaded on to *Eagle* at Gibraltar and flown off the carrier again at a point just north of Algiers, 700 miles or so from Malta, had now fallen critically. In any case there hadn't been enough of them. A maximum fly-off of sixteen aircraft at each operation, which was all that *Eagle* could then manage, meant little more than a bucketful of water chucked into the Mediterranean.

But air superiority had somehow now to be achieved if the island was to survive. There was no other way. It was a formidable challenge.

The Prime Minister urged the President of the U.S.A. to allow the U.S. Navy's massive aircraft carrier, *Wasp*, to be brought into service. By reducing her own complement of aircraft to a single Grumman fighter squadron, she could take forty-eight Spitfires by comparison with *Eagle's* sixteen. As things stood, this was tactically an altogether more realistic proposition. Four dozen aircraft, all arriving in Malta at the same time, would be quite different from the single consignment of sixteen.

601 and 603 Squadrons went aboard *Wasp* at Greenock in the Clyde in circumstances of great secrecy. With forty-eight Spitfire Vcs, each carrying four 20-mm cannons and a ninety-gallon overload drop-tank under the belly, the great ship headed for the Straits of Gibraltar and the Mediterranean.

On 20 April the aircraft took off in a succession of flights and sections and set course for the island. Not one of the pilots had flown off a carrier before. Only one failed to reach his destination, apparently preferring the sanctuary of North Africa to the rigours of a life of bully beef, bitter, 'half-caste' bread, goat's butter, bouts of sand-fly fever and the recurrent local stomach malady known as 'Malta dog'.

The sight of these aeroplanes, three and a half hours later, roaring in over the hilltop citadel of Rabat and fanning out to land at Luqa and Takali, was a tonic for lowering Maltese morale. Hopes for the future rose again.

The German intelligence and reporting system along the western Mediterranean was always sharp. This time there was no doubt about its accuracy. Within an hour of the landings the first of a series of major dive-bombing attacks by Ju 88s and Ju 87s was launched against the airfields. These raids were driven home with the utmost resolution. The new aircraft were their target. It was plain for all to see.

No more than two or three days later, all save seven of the new Spitfires had been either destroyed or immobilized. The life-saving mission, upon which so much had rested, had failed. It seemed as if the blow might be mortal. If this could not succeed what would? It was a sombre moment in the deepening drama. The dawn for which all had waited had now proved false.

At this cataclysmic moment a new plan was born. It was clear to the pilots that this would be the last throw. If it failed, well, nothing would be left. This, then, was it.

The whole concept of the operation was dramatically broadened. On the one hand, the method of feeding in the new aircraft from the carriers had to be rethought. Experienced, battle-trained pilots would be flown back to Gibraltar to lead in the next lot of aeroplanes. And the size of the reinforcing exercise would be stepped up to maximum strength, with *Eagle* and *Wasp* working in unison. Sixteen plus forty-eight, which equals sixty-four new aircraft a time, must now be the goal.

On the other hand, the arrangements on the island for handling the arrivals had to be thoroughly overhauled. A repetition of the recent disaster could not be borne. The nub of the thing was to refuel and re-arm the aeroplanes in the minimum possible time on landing. The need to get the aircraft off the ground again before the enemy could

What the Flight Sergeants used to call 'the lowest form of animal life'. Pilot Officer, 66 Squadron, summer 1941, Perranporth, Cornwall.

The moment we could have done without.
Reinforcing Malta, May 1942. Spitfires prepare to take off from the aircraft
carrier, *Eagle*, north of Algiers. Malta is 700 miles away.

The battle for Malta reaches its climax. 249 Squadron at readiness, Takali, May
1942.

The Ju 87s and Ju 88s made three runs a day—breakfast, lunch and dinner—it was like a railway timetable. These 88s settled for lunch and picked Takali, May 1942.

249 and 603 get another 'confirmed'.
Wreckage of a Ju 88 shot down over Malta. The dead pilot went up in the flames.

George (Screwball) Beurling, Malta, 1942.

'... When I said all this those startlingly blue eyes peered incredulously at me as if to say that, after all his past experience ... in the Service, he didn't believe it. He was soon to find that a basis for ... mutual trust did exist. He never once let me down ...'

Squadron Leader, 1942. After being made C.O. of 249 Squadron in Malta, 1942, I became C.O. of 616 Squadron in 10 Group, 1943.

'"Boss", he said, preserving at least some reverence for his commanding officer, "I couldn't fault that one." It was the ultimate accolade.'
Sergeant George Beurling (*centre*) with 249, July, 1942.

'I sat in the corner of the empty carriage . . . as the train hurried south. My mind was tortured by thoughts of that fateful lunchtime meeting. . . . It haunts me still as I write.'
Squadron Leader the Hon. Michael Strutt, personal assistant to the Duke of Kent, who was killed in the early autumn of 1942 when the Sunderland flying boat in which he and His Royal Highness were travelling to Iceland, crashed into a Scottish hillside.

Pilot Officers! 66 Squadron, July 1941, Perranporth, Cornwall. On the right is Raoul Daddo-Langlois who became a flight commander in 249 in Malta in 1942 when I was C.O. Raoul was killed on the first day of the Sicilian landings, 10 July, 1943.

My last appointment in the Royal Air Force. Station Commander at Bentwaters, in Suffolk: autumn, 1945, aged 31.

BOOTH'S DRY GIN
MAXIMUM PRICES
23/4 per bottle, | bottle 11/9
Prices shown do not apply to Eire.

BLACK-OUT
ZERO HOUR TO-NIGHT UNTIL 5.12 A.M.
MOON 1.25 RISE 8 PM   MOON 3.22 SET 5 AM

Daily Exp

No. 13,100   Saturday, May 23, 1942

12th day of Russian push opens 12th month of Russian w

COSSACKS TAKE OVEI
FROM THE TANK

AIR KNIGHT OF MALTA
— WRITES HOME—

Battle of Britain had nothing on this

*T*HE *Daily Express* publishes below the first story from one of the gallant band of Spitfire pilots who are defending Malta. He sent it, as a letter, to a friend in Britain.

FOR a brief space I am out of the Battle of Malta. Thus, from this strangely-peaceful spot I can give you a disjointed and sketchy account.

It has, of course, been an experience of the first order. I am inclined to think the Battle of Britain had nothing on the Battle of Malta. And when the story is told later it will surprise many.

Up to the time I left, a few days ago, on a particular mission, our squadron had shot down 46½ for the loss of five pilots. The boys have been magnificent.

Always the odds have weighed heavily against us; sometimes it has been 10 to 1 against on fighters alone, and another 10 to 1 against on the bombers. To me, the miracle has been the small losses. Our squadron, better equipped in experience than the others, has suffered least.

Germans not yellow

None would deny that the Hun has done a damned good job. His raids have been well organised. His flying in general belies the fact that he has inexperienced squadrons in Sicily.

These Germans are not yellow. They are not cowards and they are not poor pilots. It makes us wild to hear stupid propaganda tales to the contrary.

The fact is, our own boys have got to be a little bit better. If they're not they will be killed. And we're fighting this war to live, not, we hope, to die.

Most of the fellows we have lost have been those with the least experience, generally speaking. And here let it be said it would be a crime to send a pilot to Malta without battle experience.

It is not fair to him, and it's not fair to the other boys. The longer a fellow lasts the less likely it becomes that he'll be shot up, given reasonable fortune.

I learned as much in a week in Malta as I ever did in all the sweeps in England.

I would go back to the sweeps again with an entirely different outlook and with shocking confidence.

The only way

We have, for instance, hit on a particular formation which we have found to be the only possible one to fly. None would ever fly another way so long as he was alive and there were Huns to attack. And, curiously, the Hun is flying the same way, too!

The Malta have taken the blitzing damned well. They have shown courage and a will

Sabres and tommy-guns roll Germans back

From her boundless reserves of man-power, Russia pours fresh troops into the Battle of Kharkov. In this radioed picture one of many streams of Red Army infantry is on the way to the front.

Express Staff Reporter E. D. MASTERMAN
STOCKHOLM, Saturday morning.

COSSACKS and infantrymen are leading Timoshenko's advance on Kharkov this morning. Because of the heavy losses on both sides the tank battle has burned itself out momentarily in most sectors.

Now, in the fields before Kharkov, the Cossack horsemen, some with tommy guns, some with automatic rifles, some with sabres, are shooting and slashing their way through German positions.

Front-line despatches from Soviet reporters say that the Russian advance continues unchecked.

You might call today Budenny's Day. Throughout the winter the famous Cossack marshal has been training his riders of the Steppes in the great hinterland of Russia, while Timoshenko has been holding off the Germans. Now Budenny sees his men in the vanguard of the offensive.

Budenny's Day is historic for two other reasons—it is the beginning of the twelfth month of the Battle of Russia and the twelfth day of the non-stop drive on Kharkov.

"Don't yield a step" was the cry of the embattled Soviet commanders a few months ago. Today it is: "Forward and westward, ever westward!"

CONSOLIDATING

Wastage in the tank battles has been high on both sides, but the Russians are confident that they have all the material and men they need to regroup their forces in a few days and renew the armoured assault.

The midnight Soviet communiqué, announcing the continuation of offensive battles in

[Map]
BERLIN CLAIMS CITY SHELLED
LENINGRAD
RUSSIANS ATTACK
MOSCOW
TANK BATTLE PAUSES

Morley Richards'
SATURDAY REVIEW

TIMO SCORES 4 POINTS

MARSHAL TIMOSHENKO has not won a decisive victory yet. But he has secured these gains:—

1. Von Bock's army for the invasion of the Caucasus oil area has been made to fight before it was ready and has been forced to disperse itself over a 120-mile front.

2. So tremendous has been the enemy loss in men and metal

'So you finally made Page One!' C.
My Piece on the Battle of Malta in the *Daily Express, 23 May 1942.*

Greats of the U.S. 8th Air Force
(*Above*) Incomparable Group leader. Colonel Don Blakeslee briefing the 4th Fighter Group before a daylight mission deep into Germany. Listening in the front are (*left to right*): Jim Clark, Bernard McGrattan and Jim Goodson.
(*Below*) The urbane Lieutenant-Colonel James A. Goodson, whom the War Department credited with thirty-two enemy aircraft destroyed. He flew Hurricanes with 43 Squadron R.A.F., Spitfires with the Eagle Squadrons and Thunderbolts and Mustangs with the 4th Fighter Group U.S.A.A.F. In peace, Jim headed up Goodyear, Hoover and then I.T.T. in Europe).

Don Gentile was another outstanding pilot in the U.S. 8th Fighter Command. Like Blakeslee and Goodson he was, before it, a U.S. Eagle Squadron volunteer with the Royal Air Force. Walt Disney designed the Eagles' motif seen here on the side of Don's P-51.

When General of the Army Dwight D. Eisenhower pinned the American D.S.C. on Gentile's and Blakeslee's tunics, he said at the investiture 'I feel a sense of humility being among a group of fighting men like this.'

attack was paramount. The turn-round had to be treated like a pit stop in the middle of an international Grand Prix road race when each second counts. Where possible, Malta-based pilots had to be ready to take over the new Spitfires and get them airborne. To achieve this end, pilots and groundcrews would be standing by in the sandbagged dispersal points at immediate readiness to act. Petrol and ammunition would be available in each aircraft pen. Such serviceable aircraft as remained on the island would be airborne to cover the landings.

At this point Wing Commander E. J. Gracie took over command of Takali. Here was an exceptional organizer with drive and purpose. Within days the spirit of the station, and the morale among groundcrews and pilots, had been transformed. Jumbo Gracie was the man we needed.

At dusk on 30 April a posse of the island's most experienced pilots, specially selected for the task, took off from Luqa in Hudsons of Transport Command and flew back to Gibraltar on the first stage of the critical, make-or-break operation.

The quiet of the Rock, the good food, the twinkling lights, the well-filled shops, the restful nights—all offered a heaven-sent antidote to the pounding and privations of the past hard weeks. This brief lull, with its blessed contrasts, coupled with the recuperative powers of young, fit men, prepared mind and body for the climacteric which was at hand.

*   *   *

There were now to be two quite separate reinforcing operations. Both were under the overall control of Wing Commander J. S. McLean, an officer of special calibre, who was based in Gibraltar. Crisp, plain-spoken and positive, his uncomplicated methods and instructions were tailored to the need. He did not underrate the hazards but his good sense and balance allowed them no more than their appropriate weight. If his familiar and frequent use of the phrase 'a piece of cake' did not take in the old hands from Malta, it certainly seemed to allay the worst apprehensions of those who were new to the game.

The hard-won lessons of the earlier reinforcing attempts had been properly learned. Now, early in May, all was made ready to enable *Eagle*, with her complement of sixteen aircraft, to sail from Gibraltar, join up with *Wasp*, and, with an impressive protective screen of cruisers and destroyers, steam briskly eastwards, and synchronize the first joint fly-off from the two ships.

Sixty-four Spitfire Vcs, led by practised hands, landed in Malta on 9 May, and immediately the turn-round plan became effective. So finely drilled and rehearsed had been the procedures that the exercise, which had been given a maximum limit of thirty minutes per aircraft, was being accomplished first in nine minutes and later in six.

Kesselring threw in nine raids that day. Each was met with a force utterly different from anything the Germans had experienced over Malta before. For a change, it was the enemy who was getting the bloody nose.

The crescendo of the first operation was reached the next day, 10 May, when the Royal Navy's minelaying cruiser *Welshman*, bringing in a life-saving cargo of ammunition for the island's gunners, was due to dock at first light after a thirty knots' dash through the Narrows.

Throughout the day the Luftwaffe maintained an all-out offensive against the island. But, once again, the unfamiliar strength of the defence drew fresh blood from the enemy's already patched-up and battered face. For the crews of the Ju 88s and 87s and the Me 109 pilots the party was over. The Spitfires, with their Rolls-Royce Merlin 45 engines and their four cannons, were now able to stay and mix it in a way which hitherto had been reserved only for special occasions. This was our tomorrow, and another day. For the German Air Force in Sicily: 'Never glad confident morning again!'

*   *   *

As *Wasp* left the Mediterranean after her second historic intervention in the Malta battle, Churchill sent her captain and crew a personal signal. 'Who said a wasp couldn't sting twice?'

'*Wasp* thanked me,' he wrote later, 'for my "gracious" message.' (*Hinge of Fate* published by Cassell.)

*   *   *

The second reinforcing operation took place nine days later, on 18 May. It was a similar success. The unexpected speed with which the

Royal Navy and the Royal Air Force had jointly worked to prepare *Eagle* for a repeat performance bore testimony to the extent and quality of the co-operation.

McLean entrusted the task of leading in the sixteen Spitfires from *Eagle* to Flight Lieutenant Robert Wendell McNair and to me. Buck McNair was to become one of the best-known Canadian officers of the war. He and I were now flight commanders of 249 Squadron. Each recognized the measure of responsibility which was being thrust upon him.

The carrier, with a substantial part of the British Mediterranean Fleet to screen her, had ploughed her way eastwards during the night. Two violent manoeuvres somewhat disturbed the equilibrium as a pair of intrepid U-boat commanders, operating in tandem, penetrated the protecting force of destroyers and cruisers to fire a couple of torpedoes at *Eagle*. Both missed, but a Catalina of the Royal Air Force, which had also been screening the Fleet, was shot down by French fighters from the North African coast. The uneasy thought remained that the Luftwaffe in Sardinia, on the small island of Pantelleria, and in Sicily, would now know, well in advance, that another major reinforcing operation was under way.

McLean warned us to be ready to fight it out, if need be, on the last stages of the run-in to Malta. Short of fuel, it would not exactly be the most propitious moment for combat.

We were up at first light on the second day to make ready for the take-off at a point fifty miles north of Algiers, some 700 miles west of Malta. The fleet, impressively comforting, was deployed to port and for'ard, with the destroyers busying themselves like a covey of young partridges scampering about on a lawn with the parent bird, head up and vigilant, surveying the scene.

Our flying time was to be around four hours at a height of 10,000 feet and at an indicated air speed of 165 m.p.h.

McLean's briefing was characteristically sharp and unemotional. He dealt only with essentials: 'After take-off climb immediately to 2,000 feet, switch on to the 90-gallon overload tank and switch off the main tanks. When the drop-tank runs out, switch back again to the main supply and jettison it.

'If by chance your overload tank doesn't work, two choices are open to you. Either gain height and bale out and the Royal Navy will pick you up; or, if you don't fancy that, then fly south into North Africa, force-land, destroy your aircraft, and push off back home.

'In no circumstances is anyone to try a landing back on the carrier.' Minutely prepared, the flight went off without a hitch.

*   *   *

The procedure on touching down at Takali and Luqa on 18 May was as finely balanced as it had been on the 9th. An average of six to eight minutes was all that the turn-round of each of the sixteen aircraft required. Once more, Field Marshal Kesselring tried the obvious and let loose his Ju 88s and 87s, with hordes of Me 109 Fs in support, against the airfields. This time the response was even more vicious than before. German aircraft casualties mounted sharply while those of the defenders markedly declined. The dive-bombing attacks, which for weeks had been pressed with vigour to the limit, now took on an understandable and undisguised hesitancy. The damage caused by the raids started to diminish.

For the first time in the long night's vigil, faint and tentative shafts of light seemed to be stabbing the sky. We hardly dared to express it but, deep down inside us, the conviction was taking hold that, come what might, we were over the worst and that this last fateful heave, upon which all had been staked, had drawn us back from the brink.

*   *   *

This was not, however, in any sense, to be Kesselring's Retreat from Moscow. Defeated—irrevocably defeated—he and his air force may have been in the great May battles for the daylight air, but he still held most of the cards.

Malta remained isolated and impoverished. Sooner rather than later, the island had to be revictualled. An early attempt had to be made to capitalize on her new-found defensive strength and run a convoy carrying food, fuel and ammunition through the Narrows from the west. Without this the Maltese nightmare could not be ended.

After an evident re-appraisal of the battle scene, the Luftwaffe now abandoned the truculence and insolence of the spring. In place of the regular-as-clockwork, three-or-four-times-a-day dive-bombing attacks, pressed right home to a low level and with cheeky intrusions by the l09s into the circuits of the airfields, they adopted the more conventional and classical forms of aerial warfare.

Higher level bombing, lulls interspersed with spasms of activity, use of dusk and dawn and darkness—all these well-tried tactics were now brought into play in a continuing attempt to keep the island on tenterhooks and the element of surprise present. The Italian presence in Sicily was noticeably strengthened.

Eagle made another run down the western Mediterranean in June. This time the reinforcing Spitfires met a differently deployed Luftwaffe. Two aircraft were lost to Axis fighters based on Pantelleria, a little under 200 miles from Malta, while two more were accounted for by Me 109s before they reached the island.

Then came the rough battles over the mid-summer convoy from Gibraltar, and new setbacks and disappointments had to be faced. Only two of the six merchantmen which had sailed through the Straits on 11 June finally reached the island. The convoy from the eastern Mediterranean, which had put to sea from Alexandria on the same day with eleven ships, fared even worse. Hammered by the Italian Navy and the German Air Force from Crete, it was eventually forced to turn back. Thus, out of the seventeen merchantmen which had set out for Malta, concurrently from west and east, only two reached their goal. We had done little better than in February and March.

Yet despite these reverses, and despite the prevailing weight of crisis, the realization grew that, now the critical air battle for the island had been fought and won, this fresh catastrophe was only postponing, albeit at dreadful cost, the dawn of liberation. We felt instinctively that, bad though things now were, the darkest hour had passed.

                    *   *   *

Behind the fluctuating swings of battle, an unpublicized but vital service was daily being maintained by a small but highly regarded arm of the Royal Air Force. Much depended in these crucial days upon the pictorial information which our photographic reconnaissance aircraft could provide of the movement and disposition of enemy forces—air, naval and ground—in Italy, Sicily and Sardinia.

Flying unarmed, sometimes at a monstrously low level, but more normally relying on great height and speed, and doubtful camouflage, for protection, the pilots of these aeroplanes faced—often alone—hazards which most of us would never have been prepared, or indeed able, to entertain. Theirs was a rare courage. Deep penetrations into enemy territory made without company, at high altitude, and in freezing temperatures were, literally, chilling and forbidding affairs, calling for unusual resolution. Unsung, and generally unknown, their contribution to the tactical and, as the Americans would have it, 'overall strategic concept', was priceless.

The exception to prove all rules of anonymity was Adrian Warburton. He was a legend in his operational lifetime. The tales which surrounded his missions from Malta, a few apocryphal but most of them true, have improved with the years.

Warburton was a brilliant eccentric. Reconnaissance was his business, a business in which success depended on individuality, 'character', personal idiosyncrasy, accuracy and flair. Adrian offered these attributes to excess.

He was the only operational pilot I knew in the Royal Air Force who was virtually his own master. He created scope for himself. Few ever knew what he was up to or where he might fetch up next. Unpredictable and without fear, he was a doyen of photographic reconnaissance. He would have been at a loss in any other rôle.

Aerial photography, a lone occupation, was Warburton's *métier*. Slight and tall, youthfully delicate and fair, this frail man streaked into Taranto, under cover of surprise, to take photos of the Italian fleet which showed him *below the level* of the superstructure of the capital ships lying at anchor.

If Arabia had its Lawrence, Malta could boast its Warburton.

There was another photographic reconnaissance pilot of exceptional accomplishment, who was to shoulder Warburton's burdens, but who accepted none of the limelight.

Harry Coldbeck had joined us in 66 Squadron in Cornwall in the summer of 1941. A tall, fair-complexioned New Zealander, with an unruffled, placid approach to life, he possessed the imperturbable mind of a countryman. Never put out by anything, resolute but not aggressive, serious yet frequently smiling, Coldbeck was by temperament miscast in the rôle of a fighter pilot. He was made for photographic reconnaissance. He was perceptive enough to recognize this early on, and when, fortuitously, a signal reached the squadron one day asking for a volunteer for P.R.U., Harry, to our great dismay—for he was liked by all—threw his hat into the ring.

And so, by stages, he came to Malta. Here, operating from Luqa, and flying two or three sorties a week, he undertook these long and arduous missions, sometimes reaching far up the Italian mainland to the ports and cities of the industrial north, and risking interception on the long return flight by Me 109s based on Sicilian and Sardinian airfields.

Coldbeck had many close shaves because he tended to operate below the customary P.R.U. altitudes, but he made light of them. Few outside his circle of close friends ever knew of his activities, for Harry was not disposed to speak of his work. Yet his name is writ bold on the roll-call of those who set the scene for the great May victories— and thereby helped Malta to survive.

Chapter Fifteen
One genius

IT WAS now high summer 1942, and the Battle of Malta was not yet over. The June convoys, bound for Valetta from Alexandria and Gibraltar, had still to make a run for it. The crisis in the island's food and ammunition supplies remained grave. Six weeks, and no more, separated survival and disaster.

Meanwhile, Rommel could not rest. Malta was a festering thorn in the general's side as her home-based air and surface craft continued to press their attacks against his sea-borne convoys, battling their way southwards across the water to the Western Desert and his beloved Afrika Korps.

All still hung tenuously in the balance.

A few of us from 249 and 603 Squadrons were sitting on the verandah of our mess, the Palazzo Xara, a beautiful old fifteenth-century house belonging to one Baron Chappelle, in the holy city of Mdina, overlooking the battered and sandbagged airfield of Takali. The flat, parched expanse of land from St Paul's Bay in the north to Grand Harbour and Valetta in the east, and Kalafrana and Hal Far in the south, stretched away before us. It was early evening, at the end of another long, hot, dusty and highly active day—the usual quiet period before the enemy threw in his third and last attack before dusk.

Suddenly voices and movement in the room behind us disturbed the easy ebb and flow of conversation. It was some of the new batch of pilots from England who had flown in earlier in the day from the Royal Navy's now well-used carrier, *Eagle*.

The continuing losses, though relatively light considering the enemy's massive numerical superiority, had eroded the squadrons' strength. Reinforcements were now badly needed. The list of arrivals which the adjutant held in his hand was anxiously scoured for familiar or promising names.

The tendency in the past had been to send out to Malta aircrew who were not wanted in the wings and squadrons in Fighter Command. No squadron commander in 10, 11 or 12 Group in England, when asked to post three pilots to the Mediterranean theatre, could reasonably be expected to name his best men. Human nature dictated that only those whom a C.O. could most easily spare, either on grounds of their inferior flying ability or because of their lack of the social graces, would be sent.

It was understandable, but for those on the receiving end it was a different matter. We had remonstrated strongly against the process. It was neither fair to the pilots who were being posted nor to the handful of squadrons in Malta, who were pressed to the limit, fighting it out daily with Field Marshal Kesselring's cohorts from Sicily. For inexperienced or below average men to be thrown straight into the battle was to court disaster. For the squadrons on the island, and their hardened and proved members, it demonstrably increased the risks. In air combat, against odds of between eight and twelve to one, a pilot has to depend implicitly upon others for his own survival. To have to vest one's future in raw, second-class newcomers was not something the older hands cared to accept. The Australians, in their colourful and forthright language, left the senior officers in no doubt about their feelings.

The protests had not been disregarded. The flying standard and experience of the more recent arrivals from England had begun noticeably to improve. Even so, we continued to get our quota of difficult characters. I never quarrelled with this. Difficult men, properly handled, can often turn out well and become effective and rugged allies.

Out of the latest consignment of pilots the two squadrons at Takali, 249 and 603, were to get eight apiece.

The commanding officer of 249 was now Squadron Leader S. B. Grant, one of the most effective commanders in the Battle of Malta. He had taken the squadron over when his predecessor, Stan Turner, had been promoted to lead the wing. Finely trained by the Royal Air Force in peacetime, Stan Grant knew how to run and lead a squadron. He retained firm overall control but delegated detail to his two flight commanders. He was an excellent officer to serve under. Not only was he thoroughly proficient in the air, but on the ground he took the view that a flight commander was there for one purpose—to manage his flight. He left things to him. If all went well, the maximum encouragement and the minimum interference were dispensed. If things went badly, the reaction was sharp and immediate. No one could have asked for more.

Stan thus entrusted the selection of new pilots to Buck McNair and myself. He expected us to secure eight of the best for 249. We tossed with Lord David Douglas-Hamilton, the commanding officer of 603, for who should have first pick. Having won the toss, Buck and I chose our candidates with discerning care. On the list was a Canadian sergeant named G. F. Beurling from 11 Group. One member of my flight had known him in England. 'Well, well,' he exclaimed as we looked through the list, 'So they've sent us George Beurling! Flew with us in 41 Squadron. Sergeant pilot, Canadian in the Royal Air Force; good eyes, quick, aggressive. Little discipline, tended to get separated in the air. Very individualistic; a bit bolshy, but, make no mistake, he's got flair.'

I asked if he would fit into the flight. The retort was equivocal. 'Might do, but it's a risk. One thing's for sure, he'll either shoot some down or "buy it" himself.'

I thought it was worth taking the gamble. I told Buck, who wasn't keen, that I would have him.

Within two or three weeks of Beurling being posted to my flight in 249, I was given command of the squadron. I took an early opportunity of asking him to come and have a talk. There were plenty of rough edges, but as with a fine games player the abilities were instantly apparent. The question was whether he would respond to a little moulding or simply revolt when suggestions were put to him. I felt confident that if we treated him right, let him have his head in the air, he would toe most of the lines.

George Beurling was untidy, with a shock of fair, tousled hair above penetrating blue eyes. He smiled a lot and the smile came straight out of those striking eyes. His sallow complexion was in keeping with his part-Scandinavian ancestry. He was highly strung, brash and outspoken. He hadn't, I judged, had much education, but he was a practical man and had certainly made a deep study of aircraft and flying. He was fascinated by them; this was what he lived for.

He was something of a rebel, yes; but I suspected that his rebelliousness came from some mistaken feeling of inferiority. I judged that what Beurling most needed was not to be smacked down but to be encouraged. His ego mattered very much to him and, from what he told me of his treatment in England, a deliberate attempt had been made to assassinate it. I was, therefore, all the keener to bring to full fruition his manifest skills and flair. I warmed to him, and formed the impression that he was genuine and straight.

I promised Beurling I would give him my trust and he would get his chance. I said that from what I had already seen of him he had individual flying and fighting attributes far above the average on the island, and it was right in this theatre that he should have full rein. I added a caveat. If he abused this trust then he would be put on the next aircraft to the Middle East.

When I said all this those startlingly blue eyes peered incredulously at me as if to say that, after all his past experience of human relations in the Service, he didn't believe it. He was soon to find that a basis for confidence and mutual trust did exist. He never once let me down.

Shortly before the war, Beurling had decided to volunteer with a group of American pilots for service in China against the Japanese. The plan didn't work out, but, en route for San Francisco, the port of embarkation, he stopped off in Vancouver. There he had spent his last precious dollars at the local airfield learning some of the finer arts of flying under one of the most gifted aerobatic pilots in the United States. This visiting instructor had been very strict with him, stamping upon his mind the overriding importance of precision and smoothness in controlling an aircraft. Thereafter, he had had a series of daunting reverses in trying, without success, to join the Royal Canadian Air Force. In the end, he said, he had worked his passage to Britain and joined the Royal Air Force. He didn't have to. Plenty of others wouldn't have bothered.

From this first talk, and from his initial performances with the squadron, it was clear that Beurling, in the comparatively few hours he had flown, hadn't wasted his time. He had an instinctive 'feel' for an aircraft. He quickly got to know its characteristics and extremes— and the importance of doing so. He wasn't a wild pilot who went in for all sorts of hair-raising manoeuvres, throwing his aircraft all over the sky. Not at all. George Beurling was one of the most accurate pilots I ever saw. A pair of sensitive hands gave his flying a smooth-ness unusual in a wartime fighter pilot. In this he was the equal of

Douglas Bader, the only other one I saw who really could 'feel' a Spitfire on to the ground at the point of stall and use no more than a hundred or so yards of runway to bring it to rest.

This acute sensitivity told Beurling that a Spitfire was only a fine gun platform if it was flown precisely. He therefore set out to make himself the master of the aeroplane, just like a good handler, by cajolery, bribery and persuasion, stamps his authority on a gun dog. Beurling flew an aeroplane positively. He never let it fly him.

Moreover, he had also appreciated early on that no matter how good a gun platform a Spitfire might be in his hands, this could only be turned to advantage if he learned to shoot accurately. Beurling had made a study of the principles of air-to-air firing and the use of the aircraft reflector sight. Other than Wing Commander J. E. Johnson, who led the Canadians in the Kenley Wing in Fighter Command in 1943 while I had the wing at Coltishall, George Beurling was the most accurate shot I personally saw in action.

Two other attributes enabled him to capitalize his skill. First, his eyesight was quite exceptional. This gave him the edge on the rest. Time and again he would report enemy aircraft in the air four or five seconds before anyone else had seen them. Tactically, this offered a priceless advantage. In terms of positioning for an attack, it provided him with a head start over the others. Allied to his eyesight was a precise and finely trained judgment of distance. I never saw Beurling shoot haphazardly at an aircraft which was too far away. He conserved his ammunition as a miser conserves his money. He only fired when he thought he could destroy.

The sequence of his setpiece attacks was always the same. There was the first, early sighting of the target, followed by the immediate manoeuvring for position with the maximum advantage being taken of height, sun, surprise and speed. Then came the finely judged angle of attack, the concentration on closing quickly and the holding of the fire until the last moment.

Two hundred and fifty yards was the distance from which Beurling liked best to fire. A couple of short, hard bursts from there and that was usually it. He picked his targets off cleanly and decisively, swinging his sight smoothly through them as a first-class shot strokes driven partridges out of the sky. It was a fluent and calculated exercise executed positively, quickly and with aggression. It was all over in seconds. He seldom damaged or maimed. For Beurling the confirmed kill was the thing.

His desire to exterminate was first made manifest in a curious way.

One morning, soon after he had begun to operate with the squadron, we were on readiness at Takali, sitting in our dispersal hut in the south-east corner of the airfield. The remains of a slice of bully beef which had been left over from breakfast lay on the floor. Flies by the dozen kept settling upon it. As the sun rose higher in the sky and the heat gathered strength so their numbers multiplied.

Beurling pulled up a chair. He sat there, bent over this moving mass of activity, his eyes riveted on it, preparing for the kill. Every few minutes he would slowly lift his foot, taking particular care not to frighten the multitude, pause and thump! Down would go his flying boot to crush another hundred or so flies to death. Those bright blue eyes sparkled with delight at the extent of the destruction. Each time he stamped his foot to swell the total destroyed, a satisfied transatlantic voice would be heard to mutter 'the goddam screwballs!'

This routine went on rhythmically and remorselessly. The vigil, the stealthily raised foot, the pause, then the crunch and the destruction—the sequence was relentless. It was always followed by the inevitable 'the goddam screwballs!' Everything—the Me 109s, the Ju 88s, the gunners round the airfield, the Maltese—all came collectively within the ambit of the same unvarying epithet: 'The goddam screwballs!'.

So George Beurling became 'Screwball' to 249, to Malta and to the world. It was an endearing appellation, at once distinctive and well-earned. It suited him exactly. What's more, he liked it. It helped his ego. It made him feel he was now regarded as an established member of the team. No longer an ostracized sergeant pilot, he felt the gaze beginning to be focused upon him. At last he was a figure in his own right. A brilliant, individualistic eccentric for whom Malta offered just the right platform, Beurling even agreed, in the changed atmosphere, to let me put his name forward for a commission.

Screwball's total of enemy aircraft destroyed, German and Italian, now began to mount. But no one who flew with him ever questioned for an instant the strength of his claims. Beurling was an honest man. Indeed, he took honesty in his combat reports to a remarkable point.

One time, I recall, eight of us—two sections of four—had been ordered off the ground to intercept a fighter sweep which was coming in fast from Sicily to cover a German photographic reconnaissance aircraft taking pictures of the island. The admirable Woodhall, who was controlling the interception from the ground, got us off in time to enable our eight aircraft to make a quick climb, up-sun, to the south of Malta and gain sufficient height to allow us to position ourselves nicely for the pounce. It was a customarily fine piece of tactical positioning by Woody.

As the radar plotted the southerly course of the enemy fighters on the table in the underground operations room in Valetta, the controller's slow, confident, deep bass voice gave me, over the radio telephone, the news we wanted.

'Hello, Tiger leader, little jobs now approaching St Paul's Bay, angels 15,000. There are quite a lot of them. Steer three-three-zero. They are just below and ahead of you. You should see them soon.'

I acknowledged the transmission and in seconds we saw them, a couple of thousand feet below and down-sun—maybe thirty or forty 109s with a spattering of Italian Macchi 202s thrown in. They were just where we wanted them. We had all the advantages—position, height, sun, speed and surprise. It was like a quick heel from the scrum in a game of open rugby football. The ball was out on our side, being passed fast down the three-quarter back line, with each man going flat out, drawing an opposite number and trying to make an opening for the next.

The 109 pilots never saw us as we came out of the sun. It was a brief skirmish—with our aircraft, unseen until the last moment, closing right in from underneath. A series of short bursts, a quick, swinging breakaway downwards and then nose up, stick back and full throttle to gain height again over the enemy.

As I broke away from my own attack I caught a glimpse of Screwball, away on my right, pressing his attack on a 109 from what looked like no more than 150 yards. The pilot obviously had no idea what hit him. A few cannon strikes and the aircraft was falling out of control to earth, crumpled like a high pheasant hit right up in the neck—no feathers, just a clean decisive, irrevocable kill.

Screwball was the last of us to land. After he had destroyed the 109, he had then had a series of set-tos as he chased two of the enemy home. With his cannon and most of his machine gun ammunition now spent he spotted, as he returned to base, a lone Italian Macchi 202, separated from his comrades, heading north for Sicily at about 5,000 feet. Unseen, he pulled well up over his target. A quarter attack from the port side, one burst of fire and the last of his machine gun ammunition had gone. The aircraft was hit hard but Screwball was short of petrol and couldn't wait around to see the result.

He gave his report to our intelligence officer, the redoubtable John Lodge. He had, he said, destroyed a 109 and, after a series of encounters from which he could make no claim, he added that as he was returning to base he had spotted a Macchi 202, given it a burst with his machine guns and seen good strikes behind the cockpit, along the side of the engine and in the port wing. He hadn't, however, established what had happened to the aircraft so he could only claim it as damaged.

A short time later a report came through that a Macchi 202 had crashlanded on Gozo, an island just to the north of Malta. On investigation it was found that it had been hit by machine gun bullets behind the cockpit and in the port wing.

The kill was at once credited to Beurling. It couldn't have been anyone else's. When John Lodge told him the circumstances and that, although there were no bullet holes to be seen in the engine, strikes had been found behind the cockpit and along the port wing, Screwball was quite put out.

'Dammit,' he exclaimed, deadpan, 'I was certain I had hit that goddam screwball in the engine!'

*   *   *

In his first six weeks with the squadron, Beurling destroyed ten enemy aircraft. He enjoyed the fighting as a boy takes to kicking a football about. After a couple of months he asked me if he could have his tour of operational duty extended beyond the customary duration.

We tried to rest pilots, particularly those who had been on the island longest, by alternating the spells of readiness. But Screwball begged his flight commander, Raoul Daddo-Langlois, always to keep him on readiness. He never wanted to be stood down. When he was forced to take a day off he would spend it watching the combat over the island. He was a close student of tactics and fighting techniques. His criticisms were pungent and objective. He did not mind too much where they were directed.

One day in July when he was 'off', 249 had one of those textbook encounters which happen once in fifty interceptions.

Woodhall called me in the dispersal hut from the control room at headquarters. An interesting 'party', as he put it, appeared on the radar screen to be building up off Sicily. From the 'Y' messages (enemy information picked up by our listening devices) it looked as if there would be a few Italian bombers with a heavy escort of German fighters. He wanted the squadron at advanced readiness with the pilots already strapped into their aircraft. He would give the order to 'scramble' in plenty of time to let us climb away and gain height to the south of the island, to be poised, up-sun, ready, with plenty of speed, to penetrate the fighter screen and close with the bombers.

Woody read the raid perfectly. It was one of his virtuoso performances. He put 249, with its two sections of four aircraft, and one of two, in the classical position to attack, with all the advantages—except numbers—on its side.

Silhouetted against the haze of another blue and cloudless Mediterranean day, I had seen the enemy 3,000 to 4,000 feet below, approaching St Paul's Bay, with its sparkling waters, and heading south towards us, when he called up. 'Tiger leader, "big jobs" with seventy plus "little jobs" just north of the island now, flying south, angels 16. Hal Far may be the target. Come in now, and come in fast. Watch your tails. There are a lot of "little jobs" about.' He might have been in the air with us directing the show. The timing was as astute as the positioning.

My instructions to the squadron, as we turned hard to port into the attack with all the height and speed we wanted, were clear-cut and simple. Disregard the fighters, go for the three Cant Z 1007s which were now right over the middle of the island flying in a loose V formation.

Red Section—my section—would take the bomber on the port side; Blue Section, led by Raoul Daddo-Langlois, the one to starboard. Yellow Section, with Jack Rae from Auckland, New Zealand, in the lead, would cover Red and Blue Sections from the fighters as we went in, and then, if we were still disengaged, go for the leading bomber. After that, each man on to his back, and down to the deck as fast as possible. There were too many 109s about to stay and mix it.

Malta, that day, could have been Twickenham or Wembley with

60,000 or 100,000 present, and this the One Setpiece Plan Which Worked.

The squadron went straight through the fighter screen, unseen and unmolested, and closed fast with the bombers. The cannons of the section leaders struck home. The backing up of the supporting aircraft did the rest. In a few seconds all of us were diving straight for the ground with the German fighter cover spreadeagled all over the sky above us. As we pulled out at deck level and at once looked for a mate to join up with, three streaming balls of smoke and flame falling slowly from the sky to the south of the island, told the story. All three Cants had been destroyed.

249's ten aircraft were soon safe and intact on one or other of Malta's three airfields.

The whole operation might have come straight out of a Royal Air Force flying manual. It was an interception not in fifty but in 50,000. Its success was due both to Woodhall on the ground and to the finely drilled, tactical flying of the Royal Air Force's top-scoring squadron in the air.

First down at Takali and soaked through with perspiration, I got out of my aircraft and walked into our dispersal hut.

Screwball Beurling, on his day off, hair all over the place, blue eyes gleaming, was waiting for us. He was as elated as if he had just taken part in the operation himself. He had seen the whole manoeuvre from the ground. Analytically, he seemed satisfied with the squadron's performance.

'Boss,' he said preserving at least some reverence for his commanding officer, 'I couldn't fault that one.' It was the ultimate accolade.

*   *   *

On 20 May 1948, almost six years after his immortal exploits in Malta, Beurling took off with another pilot in a Canadian-built, Norseman freighter from Rome's Urbe airport. After a couple of circuits of the airfield, the aircraft appeared to catch fire as it approached the grass runway. Seconds after touching down, with flames licking the fuselage, there was a horrendous explosion and all was over.

It was an unfitting way for a genius to go.

Chapter Sixteen
Why was the mix so good?

WHY WERE the cosmopolitan squadrons in the Royal Air Force, and 249 in particular, such a success? I have pondered the question now for more than forty years, and I'm still not sure of the answer.

Between 1941 and 1945, in one way or another and at one time or another, I was given command of various units—flights, squadrons and a wing. The variety included all British, mixed British and Canadian, mixed British and Polish (with a Czech or two thrown in), mixed British and Free French, or mixed British, Norwegian, Australian and New Zealander, except in one case—249 in Malta—which was an amalgam of all except the Europeans and Scandinavians, but included some additional representatives from Rhodesia, South Africa and the United States.

As an Englishman, I always thought, probably out of patriotism—for I admit to being a besotted patriot—that I would be able to say the purely British units were, all-round, the best.

Yet, if I am frank, I can't.

I had a flight in what was virtually an all-English squadron, and I commanded a squadron, a famed auxiliary squadron, which was as English as anything could ever be in wartime. In each case the experience was unforgettable and the task as straightforward as it was agreeable, in its own undramatic way. But I could not put hand on heart and say that these English units were, operationally, more effective or more potent than the rest.

In retrospect, I have no doubt that the most colourful, the most aggressive and, above all, the most resourceful entity I saw was the mix which went to make up 249, the Gold Coast squadron, in those gruelling Mediterranean days in the spring and summer of 1942. Judged in terms of how it tackled the enemy, it was, by any test, the most skillful squadron I personally had anything to do with.

Its demeanour, spirit and discipline were of an unusual order. The pilots were relatively easy-going on the ground, but razor-sharp and opportunist in the air. It was also a most difficult unit to command. You couldn't take your eye off it for a moment. It had to be worked at all the time to get a blend of the marvellous personalities and temperaments which were there. But having once achieved that, having once harmonized all the diverse ingredients, then there was nothing else in my own experience quite to equal it.

With that stock and ability to call on—from Australia and New Zealand, from Canada and the United States, from Rhodesia and South Africa, and not least from the United Kingdom—it somehow seemed to us inevitable that it should become, in the words of the air force historians Christopher Shores and Clive Williams, '*without doubt* [my italics] the highest scoring squadron of the British Commonwealth air forces'. (*Aces High*, Christopher Shores and Clive Williams, published by Neville Spearman).

Forty years and more have done nothing to dim the picture I retain of its characters.

Take the American Harry Kelly, a pilot officer from Texas, who, like his other compatriots in the squadron, left the U.S.A. long before Pearl Harbour and the United States' entry into the war to join the air force of another country. Why did he do it? I often used to think about this, for I have always had many American friends and there hasn't been one of whom I could fairly say I didn't understand him. Yet I could never fathom what motivated this decent, deep-hearted man to chuck a good job and leave his native land when he didn't have to, and eventually to come to Malta, with its wartime flies, its smells, its bully beef, its bitter bread and its goat's butter, to fight it out—to the death—with Kesselring's Luftwaffe.

I still do not think I know the answer, nor, I believe, did my other compatriots in 249 at the time. Maybe the underlying cosmopolitanism of the United States had something to do with it. Maybe, too, 249's success itself owed something to the fact that we were ourselves such a mixed, unconventional lot.

Cross-breeding, when the basic stock is good, can produce some exceptional progeny—not according to the rules of the stud book, but to the hard, rough trials of the coverts where performance is the one measure which counts.

Turner and Beurling were, of course, the stars of our glittering firmament. But for liveliness and determined thrust they were run close by Paul Brennan, the Australian, and the two New Zealanders, Ray Hesselyn and Jack Rae. These three were like quicksilver, never still, mercurial, always looking for an opening. And usually objecting to something.

Frank Jones, the Canadian from Montreal, with eyes only a shade less acute than Beurling's, was another whose speed and sharpness in the air helped to lift the level of the squadron's flying to a point far above the average in the Royal Air Force. Jonesie often used to fly number two to me. I never felt so comfortable or so confident with anyone else.

Serious and intense, he was always expecting something awful to turn up. I quickly formed the view that, with his restless, darting movements and his consciousness of danger, he valued his own skin very highly indeed. If someone hit him he was certainly going to see who it was. He was allergic to surprise. He seemed to have eyes all over his head.

He also knew very well that flying with me put him at a disadvantage, on two counts. Because I was usually leading, he reckoned I would be painting on a broader canvas, with more emphasis on the other sections than his own tail. It increased his concern for both of us. I found this reassuring. Additionally, he recognized that for a first-class individual fighter pilot to have to stick around with the squadron commander put a restraint on his own freedom of action, and therefore on his own chances of personal success. He never once complained about it. Frank Jones was a selfless man. He sacrificed a lot to string along with me.

One morning at first light, when he and I were on readiness together with the squadron, Wing Commander W. R. Farnes, who had recently taken on the job of senior controller, rang through to our dispersal hut at Takali to say that the 'Y' service had picked up a message purporting to come from an enemy aircraft on a shipping reconnaissance south of the island.

There were no plots on the table in the operations room, which wasn't surprising as our radar wouldn't pick anything up at sea level. But he felt pretty sure something was afoot. Would we care to send a section of four aircraft to have a look? It might just be worth going out at 1,000 feet on a heading of 135° for fifteen or twenty minutes to see if anything was moving.

I had already formed a high opinion of Bill Farnes's ability as a controller. He had come to Malta with a fair measure of 11 Group experience behind him. He had a good nose for this sort of thing. My inclination was to follow up his suggestion. He wouldn't have put it if he hadn't thought it interesting.

Jonesie and I took two other Canadians with us on the sortie. 'Lint' Linton, as placid and imperturbable as Frank Jones was jumpy, and Micky Butler, another solid pilot from the prairies who had already begun to make a mark with the squadron.

It was a lovely summer dawn, warm, no wind, cloudless, with the sun easing its way up above the eastern horizon to peep over the top and see who was about. The sea was dead calm, like oil. At 1,000 feet the air was quite still, no bumps at all.

I had agreed with the controller that we would keep radio silence for the first fifteen minutes of the outward journey. Just as I was checking how much longer there was to go Jonesie's high-pitched, metallic, nasal voice broke the quiet. 'Tiger leader, two Ju 88s at eleven o'clock right down on the deck, flying east.'

Their camouflage against the sea was very effective, but Frank's good eyes had picked them up. The crews of the two aircraft had already seen the four Spitfires, 1,000 feet above, silhouetted against the early morning sky. For protection, the German pilots closed up to line abreast and went down, tight on to the water. They pushed their throttles wide open to full boost.

I told Lint to take the starboard 88 with Micky, and Jonesie and I would deal with the one to port. Our two pairs would turn into the attack from opposite sides of the 88s to draw off the cross-fire. There were no 109s to worry about, so we could take our time. I warned the other three in the section to watch the still water. Attacking an aeroplane which is flat down on a calm sea, in the face of determined return fire, was a tricky affair.

Jonesie's attack, after mine, from the left front of the portside aircraft, was a beautifully curved and smooth manoeuvre. His sequence of position, timing, angle of attack, closing speed and firing distance revealed his rare judgment. He got in very close. As he pulled his aircraft up hard left, the Ju 88, whose rear gunner had put up a resolute defence, hit the sea in a cloud of spray.

Lint Linton and Micky Butler took a little longer to dispatch the other 88, but theirs was also an accomplished and determined performance. There were no survivors from either aircraft. I was saddened by this. The Luftwaffe had resisted in the accepted tradition.

An ominous rise in the coolant temperature of my engine, the result of spirited return fire, told me to head for Hal Far, the nearest airfield on the island. I called Jonesie and then Gondar, the ground station. I guessed Bill Farnes would be waiting anxiously for news. This had been his party, his hunch, his suggestion. The credit was his.

'Hello, Gondar,' I said, 'you win, game, set, match.'

'Good show, Tiger leader. Roger. Out.'

That was all. Farnes played it, with the usual modesty of ground control, deadpan. He allowed himself no histrionics. But I did detect in his voice just a trace of elation.

He was entitled to it.

*   *   *

Three Rhodesians and, for a brief spell, a couple of South Africans gave 249 its representation from southern Africa. Between them they contributed a drive, almost a ruthlessness of purpose, which lifted the sights of others.

Of the three from the neighbourhood of Salisbury, Johnny Plagis, with his Greek ancestry, played right through the innings with a series of fluent strokes which put him in a class apart. Johnny was one of the successes of Malta; by the time he left the island for the United Kingdom, and further victories, he had a total of eleven enemy aircraft under his belt.

But while fortune smiled benignly upon Plagis, fate struck down his compatriot in 249, Douggie Leggo. Companionable and good-humoured, a gift to any squadron, Leggo was the victim of one of the very few thoroughgoing 'bounces' which the Me 109 Fs, from one of the Luftwaffe's élite squadrons in Sicily, inflicted upon us.

Douggie, flying far out on the left flank, was hit one day by a 109, in an astutely conceived manoeuvre, diving fast out of the sun from several thousand feet above. We didn't see it till too late. As Douggie's parachute floated down, a lone Messerschmitt, which had had nothing to do with the attack, fired some tracer bullets at the silk canopy. It streamed to the ground.

I had witnessed nothing so sickening in all those months of otherwise clean and hard combat until one afternoon, a week or two later, I saw a Canadian pilot, in a blind gesture of reprisal, dive on the dinghy of a ditched Ju 88 crew as it bobbed up and down on the water, ten miles south-west of Delimara Point, waiting to be picked up by Air Sea Rescue. A short burst of fire and all was over.

But Rhodesia did not have to wait long to avenge Douggie Leggo's loss. In a single-handed encounter Zulu Buchanan, a competent and dedicated pilot, gave his country, and 249, a prized victory when he picked off the German ace, Neuhoff, as he headed for home after mixing it with the squadron high up over St Paul's Bay.

Neuhoff had destroyed thirty-eight aircraft when Zulu shot him down. A revealing tale is associated with his defeat.

One of the most capable of 249's longer-serving pilots was Norman McQueen, who had himself already begun to amass a sizeable score. Good-looking, spirited and personable, Norman came from Rhyl in North Wales. One of his earlier victims in the spring of 1942 was a young Luftwaffe lieutenant named Kurt Lauinger. Lauinger was not an experienced pilot and never knew what had hit him. He baled out and was picked from the sea, a mile or two from the coast, off Grand Harbour. He was taken to hospital at Imtarfa.

There, on several occasions, Norman McQueen, Raoul Daddo-Langlois and I went to see him. He was an intelligent and agreeable man of twenty-one, full of good humour and, considering his predicament, also of spirit. McQueen was naturally interested to exchange notes with his victim.

Lauinger gave no secrets away, and most correctly and politely, put up the shutters when we turned the conversation to the strength and disposition of Kesselring's forces in Sicily.

But he was obviously fascinated by flying and, when we told him about the 'names' among the pilots we had with us on the island, was quite prepared to talk about the qualities of the good German squadron and wing leaders he had served with, their victories, their skills and their foibles.

He was also ready to give his opinion on the few Italian fighter squadrons which were now beginning to appear in small numbers in Sicily. He and his comrades obviously thought little of them. I remember when we asked him what, in particular, he thought of the

standard of the fighter pilots in the Regia Aeronautica, he picked up a
torch from the table beside him and started shining it under the bed as
if he was looking for something. Grinning away he said: 'We do not
see them. They are not anywhere. They are not, please, how do you
say, *battle happy!*'

When, one day, we were able to tell him that the great Neuhoff, for
whom he had the highest regard, had been shot down by Zulu
Buchanan from Rhodesia and was now a prisoner of war in Malta,
Lauinger couldn't believe it. He just did not think that anyone could
shoot Neuhoff down.

He wrote out a message in German (I still have it stuck into my old
log book) which he asked us to take to his hero. He would only accept
that he had been shot down and was a prisoner if a reply came back.
Neuhoff smiled when he was told the story and saw his countryman's
note. Of what he said in his reply I have no record, but it was sufficient
to destroy Kur Lauinger's belief in the aerial infallibility of man.

*   *   *

The practice of letting members of the squadron go to hospital to see
enemy pilots whom they had shot down had its uses, and certainly it
was interesting to compare notes with the other side. But an
experience I had told me that, on balance, it wasn't sensible.

After 249 had scored its 'grandstand' victory over the three Cant Z
1007s, which had so much gladdened Screwball Beurling's heart on
his day off, I took two or three of our pilots who had been engaged to
see the few survivors.

The first Italian we spoke to was the rear gunner of the bomber
which had been flying on the port side of the V formation—the
aircraft which my section had attacked. He had baled out and come
down just off the coast. When the circumstances had been explained
to him, he looked up at me from his bed. Plaintively and appealingly,
as if to cry 'why, why', he held out a heavily bandaged right arm. His
hand had been amputated. Instinctively I had to turn away. He had
been a professional musician—a violinist—in peacetime.

I resolved never to let the squadron see another of its wounded
prisoners again.

*   *   *

Buck McNair did not stay long with us, once the decisive battles were over. He had already made a massive contribution. As my opposite number in 249, Buck had proved himself a fine flight commander, forthright, direct, sometimes ruthless, yet, deep down, reasonable. The nature of our respective jobs, in the stringent conditions we were labouring under, meant that we had sometimes to find accommodations over issues which could easily have caused friction.

Buck stuck to his guns, said exactly what he thought of me, my suggestions and, come to that, my flight—and then sought out the common ground between us. In the end we never fell out. The British, just as much as the Commonwealth, contingent looked up to him. He was one of the linchpins in 249's cosmopolitan structure.

To say that McNair was, individually, a thrustful, resolute and aggressive pilot is to hide the concern, albeit at times heavily disguised, which he had for the less experienced and less successful people in his flight. They used to exasperate him and now and then he was very rough with them, but there wasn't one who wouldn't have followed him into an inferno.

In our earlier days together on the island, when 249 was right back on its heels struggling to keep alive, the 109s used sometimes to try to bounce our aircraft in the circuit at Takali as the pilots were coming in to land, out of ammunition and very short of petrol. If there was one thing which made Buck jump about, this was it. He had had a first-hand experience of it which hadn't pleased him.

It happened one day when he had a relatively inexperienced pilot flying with him. With several Messerschmitts hovering about 4,000 or 5,000 feet above, McNair told his number two to go in and land quickly while he kept up the umbrella. He only had a gallon or two left himself.

To his horror, he saw this wretched newcomer make an attempt at landing and then open flat out to go round again as he caught sight of a 109 just peeling off, as he thought, to attack. 'For Christ's sake, Blue 2,' said Buck over the R.T., 'pull the hook out and land next time. If that 109 doesn't get you, I will.'

But behind all the bluster, there lay a blend of gentleness, courage and humanity which he was able to summon when the final test came.

Almost prophetically, towards the end of his time in Malta, Buck used to confide to me that he was worried about his eyes. He was afraid they might not last him through the war as an operational pilot.

In fact, they just held. He went back to England and, after a rest, was given command of 421, a fine Canadian squadron. Later he commanded the Canadian wing in 11 Group. It was a rough passage in which he savoured both success and defeat. He was twice shot down, but escaped each time by parachute. By the end of the war he had sixteen enemy aircraft to his own guns, and a record which bears comparison with the other greats of the Dominion in the two world wars.

A quarter of a century later when, as a group captain, he came back to serve as the Canadian air attaché in London, he and his wife, Barbara, occasionally came to dine with us. Sometimes we were their guests at the spirited parties they gave in Grosvenor Square.

One day Buck told us the doctors had diagnosed leukaemia. They had indicated—because, typically, he had asked them straight out to give him a factual, direct answer—that he might have a couple of years left. It was a devastating shock to me. I kept thinking of the exploits which, with others, we had survived together in those warm, sunlit Mediterranean days of 1942 when the odds gave us so little chance. And now this. The poignancy of it was heart-rending.

But nothing in all this gay, adventurous life of endeavour so became Robert Wendell McNair as those last months when, with his wife to sustain him, he gallantly stuck as long as he could at his post in London doing his duty. When I saw him in those hard days, as he played out time, without a moment's self-pity, I felt again the buoyancy of the spirit which he had brought to us so many years before in 249.

When the end came I wrote somewhere a little piece about Buck. In it I said that nothing, in retrospect, seemed to me to fit his life better than some words Hazlitt wrote about Cavanagh, the great fives player, which I remembered Bernard Darwin had once quoted in quite another context: 'He had no affectation, no trifling. He did not throw away the game to show off an attitude or try an experiment; he was a fine, sensible, manly player who did what he could . . .'

And of his last months in Grosvenor Square, before the final curtain, we could well add with Hazlitt: 'and that was more than anyone else could even affect to do.'

*   *   *

Whatever attributes were imported into 249 from the 'old' Commonwealth and the United States—flair, opportunism and plain, untrammelled brilliance—it was the engagingly diffident, rather amateurish and self-effacing effectiveness of the few British members of the squadron which supplied the balance and the equipoise.

When my turn came to command, it was to two Englishmen of solid worth and ability that I turned for my flight commanders. Norman Lee and Raoul Daddo-Langlois, two well-educated products of the British public school system, became the linchpins in the team on whom I could always depend. They quickly gained the respect of their overseas comrades. Authority came easily to them.

Amid all the banter, the three of us had no doubts about the extent of our respective responsibilities. Maybe we showed it. 'You're the most goddam serious Englishman I've ever met,' Stan Turner said to me one evening in the mess at Mdina in one of his characteristically direct and objective asides. 'Dammit, Stan,' I replied, 'there's plenty here to be serious about.'

Perhaps it was just our realization of the parlousness of our plight in Malta at this time which provided the counter-weight for those stirringly mercurial qualities which were there.

No one typified the British contribution to a finer extent, or wrought a deeper impression with it, than our one undoubted English star, a pilot officer named Peter Nash. Nash had been a printer in Fleet Street before the war—on *The Times*, which he had joined at the age of eighteen after serving an apprenticeship elsewhere in the Street. He and I, because of our common involvement in newspapers and journalism, had found an identity of interest.

Punctilious, precise and coolly efficient, Pete Nash was the most undemonstratively successful pilot in the squadron. If the truth be told he was probably, all round, taking one day with another, the most accomplished. The squadron recognized this. He had collected an impressive total of twelve enemy aircraft in less than a couple of months when he and his number two were seen closing with half a dozen 109s and accounting for one apiece. Nothing more was heard of either of them after that.

The quality and balance of Pete Nash's flying placed him in a category which few, if any, others on the island could quite attain. Had he survived to fight through the battles of June and July, 1942, when the pendulum of aerial supremacy had begun to swing our way, he might well have been remembered among the immortals in our hall of fame.

As it was, he made an unsung English contribution to the mix of 249, every bit as polished and significant in the squadron's achievement as that provided by any of his Commonwealth contemporaries.

Perhaps, too, history will accord a paragraph to another notable English product of Bader's Tangmere wing, whose gaiety and humour used effectively to camouflage a proficiency in combat. He may, intentionally, have fooled some, but certainly not those who kept company with him in the air.

Philip Heppell came from Newcastle of a well-established Northumbrian family. His background gave him an independence of spirit which allowed him the luxury of pretending that few things on this earth, and particularly in Malta, should ever be taken seriously, least of all the opinions of senior officers. Nip Heppell was the necessary jester in 249's pack, the English antidote to the inevitable intensity which sprang from our critical circumstances.

The squadron had a rest camp at St Paul's Bay in the north of the island, an agreeable villa overlooking the sea, to which we used sometimes to repair on our occasional days off. There was a mooring attached to the villa and a boat which went with it. Now and then a few of us would row across the Bay to St Paul's Island, have a swim and a picnic and come home. It made a change from the humdrum life we led.

One afternoon Nip Heppell and I, the Canadian, Bud Connell, Jeff West, a New Zealander of infinite character, and Norman McQueen, had got halfway across the bay when a particularly heavy enemy raid was mounted on Grand Harbour, heralded by a squadron or two of 109s sweeping in fast ahead of the bombers.

The five of us had nothing on except our Service hats to keep the sun off. We made a rare crew as we kept happily on our way, taking it in turns to do the rowing.

Suddenly a section of the 109s peeled off from the rest and started to dive down towards the bay. 'For Christ's sake,' shouted Nip, 'take your hats off. They'll see we're officers.'

Chapter Seventeen
The architects depart

THE LONG, torrid summer was now almost over; a chapter in the rough, fluctuating and often turbulent Malta story was ending. Those of us who had served on the island since the early part of the year, and had lived through the crescendo of the air fighting, were ready to see new people take over. Moreover, for me, persistent and penetrating toothache, shooting pains through my head, encouraged a gathering desire to find sanctuary once again in England.

Hugh Pughe Lloyd and Woodhall, architects of the air victory of Malta, went first. For Lloyd, command of the island's air force had brought lasting acclaim. But now that the base was secure it was time for a more offensive posture. It was right that a new hand should grip the tiller.

Keith Park, whose command of 11 Group in the Battle of Britain had brought him renown and controversy, was the selected successor.

The stories of Lloyd's tenure in Malta, no doubt elaborated here and there with the years, have echoed round the Commonwealth and beyond. Which one, then, shall we take down now from the shelf, dust off, and lay once more on the table, before the final curtain falls?

The early evening of 20 April, 1942 was a significant moment. Malta's Spitfire strength, as we have seen, had just been dramatically (but, as it turned out, only temporarily) reinforced by the arrival that day, from the carrier *Wasp*, of forty-six aircraft of 601 and 603 squadrons.

Some of the new arrivals, with a leavening of combat-toughened pilots from 249, were called together, at the A.O.C.'s request, in the mess at Mdina, the holy city, which, it was claimed, the Germans would never bomb for fear of falling out with the Pope. Something important, we had been told, was going to be said.

I was standing beside the billiard table, I remember, with the

123

Australian, Paul Brennan, and the New Zealanders, Jack Rae and Ray Hesselyn, when Lloyd, flanked by Woodhall and Turner, entered the room.

The A.O.C. always had a nice sense of theatre. The long initial pause to establish authority and atmosphere . . . The serene and dignified, yet plainly pugnacious, bearing . . . The touch of aristocratic disdain . . . The roving eye, deliberately stopping here and there in the crowded room, to fix an unfamiliar face . . . The air, manufactured or otherwise, of confidence . . . The ball was well teed up, the stance according to the textbook. The ethos for the address was just right.

The words, as always, went home. No doubt at all. It was stirringly impressive stuff, given fresh meaning by the island's guns which were now, ominously, beginning to rumble once again. It was a call for maximum effort. The crisis was here. (No need to labour it—the island's guns were by now cracking and barking loudly.) We had to break the enemy in the next few weeks or he would exterminate us. (Everything was now going up—the barrages round the airfield, Grand Harbour, the lot.) Every attack had, therefore, to be pressed to the limit. The utmost determination had to be shown in closing the range. (The scream, now, of aircraft diving flat out left no doubt about the proximity of the target.)

'See the whites of their eyes before you shoot,' said Lloyd, impervious to the noise and shindig outside. 'Kill the brutes. Destroy them in the air, before they get you . . .'

The sentences were drowned by the screeching, tearing whine of a 2,000 pounder howling earthwards.

It was too much for the old warriors of 249. In a split-second, without any cue from the A.O.C., they were diving headlong for the cover of the billiard table.

It missed us—just.

As the noise subsided, the pilots, limply, tentatively, and rather sheepishly, pulled themselves up from under the table. The A.O.C., unmoved, was still standing erect. And cool.

A disdainful glance slowly traversed the room from left to right. He paused. 'You will, I think, gentlemen, understand what I mean.'

With that, he made for the door.

For Turner, the news of the advent of Keith Park as the new A.O.C. was hardly music in his ears. They had never hit it off in England.

They were even less likely to do so in the smaller confines of Malta.

We were in the mess one evening when Stan was told of Park's imminent arrival. 'Keith Park,' he said, with an air of resigned conviction, 'will have me off the island inside of a month.'

As I recall it now, it took rather less than a week.

Chapter Eighteen
Why did fate do it?

THE BUTTERY in the old Berkeley Hotel on the corner of Berkeley Street and Piccadilly had always been a favourite eating place among my generation. There, in the early autumn of 1942, soon after my return to England, I had one of those chance meetings which Fate ordains and which lead on to strange and sometimes haunting events.

My leave was almost over and I had taken a girl-friend to lunch before going, later in the afternoon, to the Air Ministry to hear whether my next posting had yet been finally confirmed. My first tour of operational flying was over. I now had to expect some less active job for the next six months before returning to squadron life. The portents were already there. I had been warned that, subject to certain formalities, I could be required to act for a spell as personal assistant to His Royal Highness, the Duke of Kent, who was a serving officer in the Royal Air Force.

The possibility posed a dilemma for me. If it came about, there would, on the one hand, be the undoubted honour which an appointment to serve a member of the Royal Family must imply. On the other, it had been made clear that this was likely to be an eighteen months' tour of duty, and I certainly did not want to become committed to being away from operational flying for so long. I recognized, however, that I would have to do as I was told.

As I walked into the Berkeley buttery I was surprised and pleased to see an old and good friend, Michael Strutt, now a flight lieutenant and an air gunner in Bomber Command. I had last seen him at Debert, in Nova Scotia, nearly eighteen months before, as we waited, week after week, for a ship to take us back to Britain, after our sojourn in Canada under the Commonwealth Air Training Scheme. Like me, he had just finished his first operational tour. A rear gunner in a Wellington squadron—as unpleasant a job as the Service then had to

126

offer—he had completed the necessary thirty missions against the enemy. He was on the point of going, as a gunnery instructor, to a training establishment in Lancashire, a prospect which he viewed with no enthusiasm whatever.

Michael and I had first met more than ten years before when he was a schoolboy at Harrow. He was an enthusiastic and good golfer, who played as well as his changeable temperament allowed. We had passed many agreeable days together in peacetime doing the rounds of the tournaments, thereby finding ourselves among friends in some lovely places. He was always a generous host, and the weekends we spent with his family—with his stepfather and mother, Lord and Lady Rosebery, either at Mentmore or at Dalmeny on the shores of the Firth of Forth, or with his father and stepmother, Lord and Lady Belper, at Kingston near Nottingham—provided me with prized memories of another age.

I confided in Michael the possibility of my next move and the apprehensions I had about it. He had no such doubts. 'My dear old boy,' he said, 'it's an excellent job. I'd jump at it.'

From there, the sequence of our thinking flowed on. He knew the Duke of Kent and many among his circle of friends, and I didn't. Surely His Royal Highness would prefer to have a P.A. whom he knew. Strutt had failed his pilot's course in Canada (if only they'd driven with him once down pre-war Piccadilly in the rush hour they'd have known he never had a chance), and, as an air gunner, he did not have the same incentive to return quickly to operational duty. The only difficulty was that he was a flight lieutenant and this was a squadron leader's establishment; but what of that?

The longer we talked the more obvious it became. Michael was a 'natural' for the job. We agreed that a word should be dropped in the right quarter. The same afternoon, Rosebery contacted the Prime Minister in Downing Street.

Within a day or two the matter was satisfactorily resolved. Strutt went to serve the Duke of Kent while I was despatched to Bentley Priory at Stanmore and to the staff of the Commander-in-Chief, Fighter Command. It seemed a much better way of handling things.

A week or two later I was in Liverpool to deliver a lecture on Malta at a nearby Royal Air Force centre. As I waited on Lime Street station for the late afternoon train to take me to London, I bought an evening paper. I was numbed by a story in the stop press. Only the barest details were given. An aircraft taking the Duke of Kent to Iceland had crashed in the north of Scotland. The Duke had been killed. The names of the other dead were there. Michael Strutt was among them.

I sat in the corner of the empty carriage gazing abstractly out of the window as the train hurried south. I did not notice the towns or the countryside; nor could I settle down to read. My mind was tortured by thoughts of that fateful lunchtime meeting only a few weeks before.

It haunts me still as I write.

*   *   *

In one single respect, life on the staff of the commander-in-chief of an operational command in wartime had a little of the House of Commons about it. We were at the centre and, unlike others outside, we knew what was going on. We could stand back and see the progress of the air war as a whole, whereas in the squadrons and wings the gaze was always fastened on the single operation and the day-to-day course of events. In the one, the concern was for strategy; in the other, for short-term, tactical gain.

I served in the humble rôle of 'squadron leader—day operations' in my four or five months at Fighter Command while Sholto Douglas presided over its affairs. Here was an officer of stature and erudition, unquestionably a 'big man'—big in mind and intellect, big in physique (he had, in appearance, much in common with Goering), big in his dominance over a large organization and big in his dealings with superiors. He was quite a buccaneer.

He also had his foibles. He was never averse to sending his aeroplane up to Stornoway in the Outer Hebrides to bring back for the mess, and his own table, a haul of fresh kippers from the latest catch. I warmly applauded the practice. There never was anything to touch those kippers from Stornoway. Anywhere.

Sholto was essentially a staff man. He backed his staff to the hilt. He had, perhaps, the best brain among the senior commanders I served in wartime, with the broad intellect of the Oxford classicist. He was, as clever people sometimes tend to be, lazy, but he drove his staff hard and placed many demands upon them. It followed that he delegated well. Like Harold Macmillan in the early days of his first adminis- tration, Sholto Douglas gave himself plenty of 'think time'. Some said 'play time'. He liked the good life. He was clear-minded on paper and could go quickly to the nerve centre of a complicated matter. Mazes were not for him. He did not flap.

I recall his reaction to a disturbing reverse he had to endure soon after the latest Spitfire IXs, with their greatly improved performance, had come into service. Initially, few squadrons were equipped with these fine aircraft. Three of them were moved one September day from 11 Group down to south Devonshire, two to the forward airfield at Bolt Head, to act as high cover for a daylight bombing attack by B-17s of the U.S. Eighth Air Force on Morlaix airfield in the Brittany peninsula. It was one of the early Fortress raids.

The fighters were operating under the aegis of 10 Group and within direct control of the Exeter sector. The wing leader was late reaching Bolt Head and did not arrive in time for the briefing. Thus he did not lead the wing.

The rendezvous with the bombers was to be at 15,000 feet in mid-Channel with the Spitfire IXs of 401, 412 and 133 squadrons flying the high cover and given plenty of operational latitude. The Met. Office had forecast varying amounts of cloud over the Channel up to 20,000 feet. The wind gradient at this height was estimated to be in the order of 35-40 m.p.h. from the south-west, i.e. off the right front as the aircraft headed towards the target. Radio silence was to be maintained on the run-in in the usual way. It was a straightforward, in-and-out operation. Nothing fancy.

In the event, things turned out very differently. There was almost unbroken cloud up to close on 20,000 feet over the Channel and the target area. Unable to make rendezvous with the bombers, 412 Squadron returned to base, soon to be followed by 401. However, 133, one of the Royal Air Force's three American Eagle Squadrons, led this day by an inexperienced English flight lieutenant named Gordon Brettell, pressed on. After a fleeting glimpse of the bombers, the leader elected to turn north, back across, as he thought, the 120-mile stretch of water for home.

Letting down through cloud on the return leg, the flight lieutenant caught a momentary sight of land. Very short of fuel and assuming it to be the Devon or Cornish mainland below, he decided to go straight down and land. Ground control at Exeter, which had long since lost R/T contact with the squadron, now picked up some faint exchanges between the pilots.

'What the hell do they think they're doing. Tell the bastards to stop shooting. Can't they see we're friendly . . .'

In fact, this was not the Cornish peninsula but still enemy-held Brittany. As the aircraft lost height, they were met by hostile flak from the ground defences around the heavily guarded port of Brest.

Apart from one aircraft,which, fortuitously, had had to turn back earlier in the operation with engine trouble, the remainder of the squadron crashlanded or bailed out around the Brittany coast, one on the island of Ouissant.

The explanation?

Horrific but simple. The wind which, at altitude, had been given to the B-17 navigators as 35-40 m.p.h. from the south-west was closer to 100 m.p.h. from a more northerly quarter i.e. behind on the outward flight. This had blown the aircraft, which were largely above cloud, miles to the south of the target area, almost to the Pyrenees. The way back, on the estimated time schedule, had taken 133 not, as they had anticipated, to the haven of the English coast but to the unfriendly territory of the Brest peninsula and into the claws of the Germans.

The loss of a dozen of the latest Spitfire IXs was an appalling catastrophe. Moreover, the disaster occurred at a weekend. Sholto Douglas, with other Service chiefs, was visiting Chequers for meetings with the Prime Minister. He had left instructions that he was only to be contacted in emergency.

We passed on the hard news. It could not have been less timely. The C-in-C's response was, perhaps, predictable. There was no comment; a few brief questions; a pause for thought; and then the instructions. He would hold a meeting in his room at 0900 hours the next morning. The A.O.C. of 10 Group, plus aides, the responsible officers from the wing and sector at Exeter, and others of his own staff, would be present.

There was no emotion; no alarm; no attempt at prejudgment. Only the clear-cut decision to hold an immediate post mortem and instructions as to who would attend. It was an impressive exercise in composure under pressure.

Chapter Nineteen
The best command of all

IF YOU were to ask a dozen senior officers in the Royal Air Force, retired or otherwise, which, of all the commands they had had in the Service, was the most pleasing, the most satisfying, the most stimulating, the chances are that each would answer the same: 'commanding a squadron in wartime.'

It was like having a private company in which you were the majority shareholder. There were certain rules which had to be observed, certain people who had to be carried with you, certain standards which had to be maintained, but having met these points it was then *your* show. What you said, what you ordered, what you wanted, went. You were the undisputed boss, the nonpareil. The wing commander flying could tell you how he wanted things done in the wing, and how he wished the squadrons to fly in it; but he couldn't meddle with the internal affairs of your unit. If he tried to, he was a fool. If he didn't like the way your squadron was performing, he had a remedy in his own hands—to have you posted. But woe betide the wing leader who, in addition to commanding a wing, also sought to command each of the two or three squadrons in it. It only made for trouble.

Being a squadron commander was a very personal thing; it was the most intimate command which patronage could bestow. In the case of a fighter squadron, the size was just right. It was big enough, important enough and, indeed, lethal enough to make you realize at once that you had a substantial responsibility on your hands which you must discharge 100 per cent. Everyone in it, from the two flight commanders down to the most junior fitter or rigger or orderly room clerk, depended directly or indirectly upon you. It was the same on the ground as in the air. All looked to the C.O. not only for discipline and leadership but also for humanity.

131

Equally, a squadron was a small enough entity to enable its commander to know everyone in it and a lot about each member's background—his family, his problems, his hopes, his fears, his strengths and his weaknesses. A wing leader's job, by comparison, was lonely and isolated.

An able C.O. of a fighter squadron could make a mark with it and lift it well above the average in the sector, in the group, in the command, in a month; under a poor commander it would slip quickly down the league table. Either way, things happened very fast. That was the devil of it. The fact was that in wartime a fighter squadron was as good or as indifferent as its commanding officer.

*   *   *

Having had 249 in Malta, I was, I suppose, lucky to be given, some eight months later, at the start of my second operational tour, command of another fighter squadron. 616, the South Yorkshire Squadron of the Royal Auxiliary Air Force, was located at Ibsley in Hampshire, in 10 Group of Fighter Command, when I took it over.

It was difficult to believe that two squadrons could be as different as 616 and 249. 616 was as English and correct and balanced as they came; 249, as diverse, rough and brilliantly unpredictable as could be. Of course, the theatre, the environment and the level and type of operational activity had something to do with it.

Ibsley, in the spring and summer of 1943, was a delightful, almost unreal, place to be stationed. Near Ringwood, on the River Avon, it had all the entrancing ingredients of the quiet English village set in lovely, unspoilt countryside. We lived in a pretty thatched cottage called Chatley Wood. On warm, sunny days, when the squadron was stood down from readiness, we used to laze about in its pleasant garden. War seemed a long way off amid the blooms and seclusion of Chatley Wood. The operations from Ibsley were nothing if not straightforward.

It was my good fortune that soon after I went to 616, I was able to arrange for L. W. Watts to join the squadron as a flight commander. Wattie had been a stalwart member of 249 in Malta. In the thick of it all, through the battle, he had collected, in his own undemonstrative way, his share of enemy aircraft. A diffident, throwaway sense of humour was embellished by the accent which Birmingham had stamped upon him; he was as dependable as they came and got on well with people.

With his flying ability and experience, allied to his special personal qualities, Wattie brought fresh strength to 616. Moreover, he and his opposite number, Phil Stewart, gave the squadron the balance it needed. It was very satisfying to me, when my time came to move on, that Wattie should have taken over the squadron. He stayed with it until it was re-equipped with Meteors—the first squadron in the Royal Air Force to enjoy the sensation of jet propulsion. Then, only a month or two before the end of the war in Europe, the grasping hand of Fate stretched out to take him away. His Meteor collided with another. I felt his loss deeply. After surviving so much, it seemed such a wasteful, ironical ending.

I left 616 on a Monday—Monday, 4 July 1943. Arthur Donaldson, the station commander and one of three remarkable brothers, all of whom achieved great distinction in the Royal Air Force, had brought me, two or three days earlier, a signal from the Air Ministry posting me to command a wing in North Africa.

The promotion was encouraging. After all that had gone before I felt I was ready for it, and I didn't doubt that I could do the job. All the same it was a daunting prospect, coming, as it did, rather less than a year after my return from Malta. I did not relish the thought of going back to the Mediterranean.

Moreover, it was a wrench to leave the squadron. We had been wonderfully happy together and, in the context of our limited opportunities, not entirely unsuccessful. Hampshire in July was at its best and Chatley Wood as agreeable a place as you could find to live. The Avon, flowing leisurely on its way, epitomized the contentment we felt with life at Ibsley. It was a halcyon period in the conflict.

The day before I departed I called the squadron together for a farewell talk. It was Sunday morning and we had a short service afterwards. It was a practice I had followed whenever operations allowed. I felt it was right that there should be a chance for all to worship together regularly. It was always voluntary, and quite informal, but as there was invariably a good response I was sure it was appreciated. On this day everyone stayed on for the service.

I made it, as ever, very simple; just a few prayers and a passage from the Bible. I read them, I remember, the first chapter of the Book of Joshua. I felt it fitted the mood. '. . . Have I not commanded thee? Be strong and of a good courage; be not afraid, neither be thou dismayed; for the Lord thy God is with thee whithersoever thou goest . . .' I finished with the spontaneous intonation: 'May God bless you all.'

616 knew that I meant it.

*   *   *

Fate was now, again, to take a hand. Having had the usual 'medical', and the overseas inoculations, I spent my embarkation leave at home, enjoying a pleasant round or two of indifferent golf with my brother Ian at Sandy Lodge, a friendly oasis in wartime, where he and I had long been members.

Two days before I was due to depart for North Africa an urgent message arrived from the Air Ministry. My posting was cancelled. Instead, I was to proceed immediately to Coltishall, the fighter station in Norfolk, to lead the wing. My relief was intense. Somewhere, I felt, a guardian angel had been watching over me.

I knew Coltishall well for, two years before, we had sometimes used it as a forward base for shipping strikes off the Dutch coast. Moreover, it was no more than ten miles or so from Filby where, for over 200 years, up to the 1920s, my father's family had always lived. Generations of my forebears had been buried in the churchyard of the little village church which lay hard by the old house. A lot of Lucas history had been enacted in East Anglia. At Coltishall I would feel an affinity with the past.

The circumstances of the last-minute switch in my arrangements were unfortunate and hardly encouraging, however. The previous wing leader, A. C. Rabagliati, born in South Africa, who had joined the Royal Air Force before the war, had just been shot down. I was needed as an instant replacement. I reported for duty the day after receiving the message, my morale noticeably improved by the promotion to wing commander.

Arriving in the mess at Coltishall about teatime, I was greeted by the station commander, Group Captain A. V. Harvey, with whom I was to establish a lifelong and enduring friendship, including a period together in the House of Commons. Harvey, a peacetime Auxiliary, with a wealth of aviation experience behind him, had founded 615, County of Surrey, Squadron, in the mid 1930s. He was in command when war broke out and was still leading it in France in 1940. I felt at once that he and I would get along.

At his side was the Senior Air Staff Officer of 12 Group, Air Commodore Lee. I did not expect this. After the introductions, Lee took over. 'Lucas, I take it you know why you've been sent here. You've come here to stop the rot.' This opening took me by surprise. I had no idea that this was the purpose of my posting.

Lee went on. 'The last three wing leaders, for one reason or another, have fallen by the wayside. This can't go on. It's time someone stayed the course. Your job here, Lucas, is to pull this wing together. I hope you'll understand that.'

I can't say I found the welcome particularly comforting. And things were made no easier when, just as I was beginning to find my feet, a section of four aircraft, on an early morning reconnaissance to the Dutch coast, failed to return. On top of this, the experienced and personable Jack Charles, C.O. of 611, was shot down off Holland. He was picked up, greatly shaken, in a brilliantly daring air-sea rescue operation under the nose of the enemy. But it was by no means a propitious start.

I could sense at once what was needed. It was much the same situation as Stan Turner had faced in Malta eighteen months before. It required similar treatment. Things had got into a rut and had now to be forced out of it.

I at once stopped the squadrons flying in line astern. Operationally, nothing but line abreast would, in future, be tolerated. I spent a day with the two squadrons instilling the principles of this form of flying. There was strong and open opposition to the change. And more, I sensed, under the surface.

At this bleak moment, the picture was, for me, transformed when I was able to arrange, with the ready help of Vere Harvey, for the introduction of two new squadron commanders, both of cast-iron, Malta experience. Johnny Plagis, the Rhodesian, was brought in to lead 64 Squadron, while one of the successes of 603 Squadron at Takali, W. A. Douglas, a patriotic Scot from Edinburgh, another peacetime Auxiliary, took charge of 611. I now had the two allies I needed.

The effect of Plagis's exceptional experience, record and authority upon the other pilots in the wing was immediate. Bill Douglas added further weight. The tricks which the three of us had learned in the fighting over the island were gradually absorbed by the two squadrons. Things now had to be done our way. If anyone didn't like it, he could be assured of fair treatment and an early and sympathetic posting.

No one asked to go. It wasn't long before Johnny Plagis, Bill Douglas and I had, amongst us, brought the standard of the Coltishall wing's operational flying up to a point where, within the scope of its equipment, it could take its place with the best of its counterparts in Fighter Command. Such was the extent of the Malta influence—and Rhodesia's and Scotland's also.

*   *   *

In the last quarter of a century and more, hundreds of thousands of words have been written extolling the deeds of the illustrious figures who, among the air forces of the Western Allies, made much of the history of the air fighting of the Second World War. The names rank beside the select few, British and German, who dominated the aerial battles over northern France and Flanders in the First World War.

But did anyone ever think to put together the story of the men—and the women—of ground control, who, normally unknown and unnamed, often made the victories and successes possible; and who frequently carried the can when things went wrong?

A few names have emerged from the mists of anonymity. Woodhall, of course, of Duxford, Tangmere and Malta; Farnes of 11 Group and the Mediterranean. But the well-known alumni were few. And, if the truth be told, the alumni in this field *were* very few. Controlling was an art. It could, in part, be acquired, but beyond the accepted and required procedures there were the special virtues of flair, intuition, sense and feel, which lifted the skilled controller above the general run.

The relationship between a wing leader or squadron commander and a first-class sector controller rests upon respect, trust and confidence. It is, in some ways, akin to the relationship which the accomplished referee can establish with opposing rugger teams.

Often there was no alternative for the wing commander flying but to play to the controller's whistle; but a decision or an order was easier to accept—and to understand—if it was underwritten by proved expertise.

At Coltishall, just as in Malta, we were specially favoured with the standard of controlling we could count on both at sector and at group. The senior controller in the operations room at Stratton Strawless was H. F. David, the British Davis Cup player and captain, who, years afterwards, was to follow another fellow officer in the Royal Air Force, Sir Louis Greig, as chairman of the All-England Lawn Tennis Club and presiding force at Wimbledon.

Herman David was a very tough cookie indeed. The views he held about controlling fighter aircraft in wartime were as unyielding and as potent—and sometimes, perhaps, as heretical—as those he expressed in peacetime about amateurism in lawn tennis. In his book there was no such animal as a world-class *amateur* in lawn tennis—or any other game. How, he would ask, could anyone play tennis all the year round and all over the world and still honestly say he—or she was an amateur? In his opinion they were all *players*—not amateurs—and Wimbledon would be nothing if the All-England Club did not throw open its courts to the professionals, to the players and to the amateurs (if there were any). He got his way. Having seen him at work at Coltishall, this never surprised me.

Herman and I did not come to terms easily. Ours was a hard-won settlement. For a while it hung uneasily suspended before falling happily into the safety net of mutual confidence where it reposed undisturbed throughout all the ups and downs we faced together. Fashioned in war, our friendship prospered with the years.

The start was unpromising. Not long after I had taken over the wing, the duty controller called me in my room one morning as I was on the point of going over to the mess for breakfast.

'I am sorry to report, sir, that four aircraft from 611, led by their squadron commander, have not returned from a reconnaissance to the Dutch coast. They took off soon after first light and are now overdue. There is no news, I'm afraid. Other aircraft have just taken off to make a search. The station commander has been told.'

As I put the receiver down, the other telephone rang. It was, as I expected, the station commander. 'There's bad news,' he said, 'I expect you have heard. Will you come to my office at ten o'clock and give me a report?'

It was a rough start. Then I remembered that on the very first day after I took over 249 in Malta we had lost four aircraft in the morning, and yet all had come right in the end. This was worse, however, because I had been told nothing of the operation beforehand. The shock was therefore all the greater.

I got dressed quickly and walked over to the mess for breakfast. Herman David was sitting at the end of a long table by himself. He had already been told.

'I'm seeing the station commander in an hour's time,' I said. 'I knew nothing about this operation. Never mind that now. But I must know the facts before I see the group captain.'

Herman, precise and alert, had all the details. He was a man who reacted sharply to adverse circumstances. I could see he was not only shaken but very annoyed. He knew I hadn't been told of the intention to send a section off, but it was not in his nature to transfer blame. He said he accepted full responsibility for the information not being passed to me by the duty controller.

The more I heard of the affair the worse it sounded. The Royal Navy had thought there might be two or three German destroyers in Den Helder, but they might already have put to sea. They wanted a reconnaissance flown. A section of four aircraft had therefore gone out to have a look.

No one knew any more. Possibly the section had got too close to Den Helder and been hit by the strong shore defences; or else, if the ships had put to sea and were being covered by numerically superior German fighters, it might have been overwhelmed. The Luftwaffe always kept an effective fighter force in Holland, and provided strong escorts for naval operations off the coast.

Whichever way one looked at it, the thing seemed wrong. Four aircraft were insufficient for a mission of this character. Had I known of the navy's request I would certainly have detailed a squadron, and possibly the wing, for the task. I told Herman I would see him after I had reported to the group captain.

I drove straight over to Vere Harvey's office from the mess. He was much disturbed and had already got the facts from the adjutant. I was forthright with my comments. It was no good glossing over the mistake. We had plainly asked for it. As the wing commander flying, this was just the sort of thing I had been sent to Coltishall to stop. I must shoulder the blame. Harvey ended the discussion abruptly. 'It's bad luck, old cock, so soon after taking over. But we can't have any more of this.' He could have said no less.

I expressed much the same sentiment to Herman David. His reaction was quite unexpected. 'I've let you down,' he said. 'You'll never have any confidence in me after this.' It was an unlikely basis on which to build an understanding.

This episode, coming as it did so soon after Jack Charles had been shot down off the Dutch coast leading 611, was an agonising reverse. Charles had been miraculously rescued from the water, but there was no denying that things were now going against us. With 120 miles of the turbulent, fast-moving North Sea between the Norfolk coast and Holland, and strong enemy defences to contend with when you got there, this was anything but an easy theatre. Even so, there could be no excuses. I knew I was right up against it.

David was still in my office talking things over when the telephone rang. It was 12 Group headquarters. 'The group controller wants you.' 'Laddie,' the voice was at once familiar, 'it's Raymond. I just wanted to say how sorry I am about these setbacks. I hope you're not blaming yourself because, from what I understand, you would be unfair to yourself if you were. It would be not only a pity but actually unhelpful to start worrying now . . .'

It was Raymond Oppenheimer, a close and enduring friend of many years' standing, whose humanity and intellect would have told him instantly of the traumas with which I was now beset. The timing of his call was typical of him.

Raymond was, by the outbreak of war, in the process of becoming to British golf very much what Herman David eventually became to national and international lawn tennis.

By a coincidence, the two were colleagues in the great Diamond Corporation of London, of which the Oppenheimer family, with their massive interests in South Africa, were the principal architects. This proved to be, for me, a most fortuitous partnership, for when this bleak initial spell at Coltishall was over, and the sun had begun to shine on our endeavours, I was able to call on Raymond's manifest arts and tact to convince Herman, one of the most sensitive of men, of the strength of my belief in his remarkable capabilities as a controller.

A combination of these two exceptional minds—Oppenheimer's at group and David's at sector—coupled with the games player's instinct for opportunity which both possessed, gave us in the wing an unusually strong home base upon which, in time, we were able to build a considerable operational success. It showed, beyond doubt, that without confidence in ground control the daylight air war could not be won.

Chapter Twenty
The great Forty-eight Forty-nine

THROUGHOUT THE last months of 1943 we were seeing almost daily at Coltishall evidence of the gathering strength of the daylight attacks of the U.S. Eighth Air Force as they began to penetrate further and further into the heart of the German fatherland. We could bear witness, too, to the murderous treatment this onslaught was receiving at the hands of Goering's steadily increasing fighter force.

Apart from seeing it all at first-hand from the limited escorting or diversionary missions which the wing was able to fly in support, there was the additional proof of shot-up Thunderbolts (P-47s) and Lightnings (P-38s), and, occasionally, of damaged Fortresses (B-17s) and Liberators (B-24s), which, at their last gasp, had found sanctuary in the haven of Coltishall as they lobbed down after struggling back across the sea. Each example bore testimony to the extent and severity of the combat which all were now having to endure.

The fights started soon after the bombers crossed into enemy territory and continued all the way in to the target. With the bombs gone, the Fortresses and Liberators, some already heavily scarred, had to brace themselves again for renewed and repeated attacks as these great sky fleets fought their way back to the coast and the North Sea.

For sustained courage, and as an example of how the impossible can be achieved by improvisation and determination, the United States' aerial offensive against Germany of 1943 and 1944 was never surpassed in any theatre of the Second World War.

*   *   *

The tale, for me, had begun the year before when I was on Sholto Douglas's staff at Fighter Command. It was then that the attacks by these vast American daylight armadas were being conceived under the

141

aegis of General Carl Spaatz and the impressively talented staff who served under him. The sweep and scope of the United States' forward thinking was breathtaking in style and character—even by their own imaginative standards.

The work we were then doing with the Americans had brought me into contact with two colonels from the U.S. Eighth Fighter Command at Bushey Hall, near Watford, J. C. Stanley and William Harkness. They were sharing a house together called Blue Shutters at neighbouring Stanmore, only a mile or so from the Fighter Command headquarters where I was stationed. The housekeeper was a gem named Mrs Alsop known to one and all as 'Mrs A'.

Bill Harkness and Jake Stanley invited me one day to join their household. It was an offer which I immediately accepted. There then began one of those easy and rare associations which, as an Anglo-American exercise, meant as much at the time to each one of the participants as it did, I believe, collectively to all three.

Jake Stanley was a stockbroker in New York City, a senior partner in the firm of Mitchell Hutchins of Wall Street, while Bill Harkness was a member of one of America's established and highly regarded families. He was not, as they say, short of a dollar.

We lived happily together, sharing the bills and dividing responsibilities. We never had a cross word. Blue Shutters became a second home during each of my two 'rest' periods on the staff at Stanmore in 1942 and again in 1944.

                              *   *   *

I used to think that the relationship between the commanding generals in the U.S. Air Force—and particularly in the Eighth Fighter Command—and the colonels and majors who actually led the formations in the air, was surprisingly close. This was helped by the fact that the generals themselves were not averse to flying on operational missions.

One of the most spirited of the Eighth's commanders was Major-General Kepner. I remember hearing him tell one evening of an incident which became a classic in the famous 56th Fighter Group.

One of the most successful of Kepner's combat pilots was Don Gentile, a captain with a commendably large number of German aircraft to his credit. He was known inevitably throughout his group as 'Gentle'. In the heat of battle and over the air this could sound uncommonly like 'general'.

Kepner was tagging along one day in a Thunderbolt behind a Fortress mission in which his pilots, including Gentile, were heavily engaged. He was by himself, listening intently to the exchanges over the radio, all the while keeping a weather eye open for a would-be attacker.

An agitated voice suddenly burst over the air. 'Break, Gentle, break! Break, goddam you!' In a flash, and scared rigid, Kepner whipped his aircraft round, hard left, pulling as tight as he could without spinning off. There wasn't a sign of the enemy anywhere.

'Then it struck me,' he said, 'they couldn't really be that rude to a general.'

*   *   *

The start of the American daylight offensive in 1943 was a tortuous affair—a mixture of obstinacy and resolve, foolishness and readiness to have a go, and a governing determination never to take no for an answer.

The initial, experimental plan, the forerunner of the great campaign which was to come, was to put up a force of 376 B-17s in a double-headed attack against the ball-bearing plants at Schweinfurt and the Messerschmitt assembly shops at Regensburg, deep inside southern Germany. Fighter cover could, in those pioneering days, well before the advent of the long-range Mustangs (P-51s) and the 'stretched' P-47 Thunderbolts, only be provided for a limited part of the way into and away from the target.

Against all British advice, and quite unmoved by Sholto Douglas's power of persuasion, the U.S. authorities elected to take the risk. When the bombers were 'naked', Spaatz and, later, General Ira C. Eaker, and their staffs, believed they could rely on their lethal, retaliatory gunpower, and the protection which the formations' cross-fire would provide, to see them through.

The bomber aircraft of the Royal Air Force had never possessed comparable defensive strength. Thus the experience which had caused the Commander-in-Chief, Bomber Command, to turn his back on the daylight air was not, in the United States' view, a sufficiently compelling factor to determine a decision. The show would go on. We feared for the carnage which must follow.

The first major mission, which took place on 17 August 1943, went much as we—but not the Americans—anticipated. There was a slaughter as soon as the B-17s lost their protective screens. The German fighter force, with all the warning it needed, but still without the experience of dealing with this sort of operation, waded into the Fortresses on the unescorted section of the outward and homeward flight. Although having their inevitable field day, they suffered heavy casualties through their inexperience.

The Coltishall wing, operating from the Tangmere Sector in 11 Group, flew what seemed, by comparison, to be a puny diversionary mission with the medium bombers of the Eighth Air Force's Support Group to a target in central France. When we returned to East Anglia that same evening, I shall never forget the gloom which descended on our squadrons as reports came in from the U.S. bomber airfields around us. The casualties of the main attacking force had approached 20 per cent. The outcome was hideous to contemplate.

Stupid or brave? Obstinate or resolute? Inexperienced or commendably determined to learn? Who were we to make an assessment? One thing was certain. The bravery of the Americans was now indisputable. It had been, for them, one hell of a baptism.

*   *   *

It may be that I was prejudiced. It may be that, with a Spitfire wing in East Anglia, in the heart of U.S. Eighth Air Force bomber and fighter country, I was better placed than most of my countrymen to recognize the scope and sweep of the Americans' daylight campaign. Or it may be that with my specially privileged relationship with two fine Eighth Fighter Command officers, and the first-hand contact this often brought me with their illustrious compatriots, I was more readily able to see the real magnitude and strength of this extraordinary enterprise. Whatever the reason, the fact is that nothing that I personally saw in the war years could ever, in my judgment, quite approximate, in terms of prolonged human endeavour, the brilliance and enduring doggedness of this wonderful United States' effort.

The U.S. Eighth Fighter and Bomber Commands in late 1943 and 1944 performed the impossible. They did what we, in the Royal Air Force, had told them they could never do—what we, with our equipment, could never have done. What's more, the Luftwaffe generals—and, indeed, the colonels who were actively mixing it in combat with the Fortresses and Liberators—had advised Hitler and Goering that it couldn't be done.

They flew in broad daylight, escorting bomber missions into every sector of Germany. There wasn't a target in the Third Reich—even in the most eastern part of the country—which was safe from their attentions. And all this was accomplished in the teeth of the strongest and most lethally equipped defensive fighter force which had ever been assembled.

The P-47 Thunderbolts and P-38 Lightnings, with their additional drop tanks, made a start possible. With these the Americans began to fly fighter missions of a duration and depth which, a couple of years before, the British and German high commands had thought to be impossible. And then in December 1943, at the end of my time at Coltishall, the advent of the P-51B Mustang, with its 1,520-h.p. Rolls-Royce engine made by Packard of America, introduced a new dimension into aerial warfare in Europe.

The Mustang was, aerodynamically, a beautiful aircraft. I had one for my personal use when, after temporarily leaving the Royal Air Force to fight the general election of 1945, I returned to command the fighter station at Bentwaters in Suffolk, during my final six months in the Service before the Americans took over the airfield. It flew close to 450 m.p.h. at 35,000 feet and handled exquisitely. Nothing could equal, let alone surpass, the qualities of our beloved Spitfire as the best hand-to-hand defensive fighter aeroplane of the war—perhaps the most perfect aircraft of its type ever made. But the new Mustang, with its capability of discharging a long-range fighter escort and support rôle, was on its own.

The groups which were equipped with this aircraft could range from their bases in East Anglia the length and breadth of Germany. Whether at high or low attitude, whether sweeping wide areas of the sky ahead and to either side of the bombers or, in poor weather, strafing at hangar-top height and against ferocious return fire from the ground the 109s and 190s parked on the airfields, the Mustang had no equal. Alongside the tough, heavy and durable Thunderbolt, a comparatively ponderous work-horse, the Mustang was an elegant Beau Brummel of an aeroplane, with a versatility which astonished us all. Its contribution to the Allied victory over Germany was undoubted.

From this unrelenting United States' bombardment it was inevitable that some outstanding pilots and leaders should emerge.

Don Blakeslee became to the Eighth what Johnnie Johnson had become, by late 1943, to Fighter Command. In their respective rôles, and in their own time, their individual performances placed them on a pedestal which was probably out of reach of any of their contemporaries. There wasn't another pair of leaders to touch them.

We rather prided ourselves in thinking that Blakeslee, a human stringbean of a man, had learned the basics of wing or, as the U.S. Air Force had it, *group* flying with us. Like his fellow-countryman, Harry Kelly, in 249 in Malta, he left America long before Pearl Harbour and the U.S. entry into the war to get into the fight against Germany. After his training with the Royal Canadian Air Force, and an operational run with the Biggin Hill wing in 11 Group of Fighter Command, Blakeslee moved on to lead 133, the third Eagle squadron in the Royal Air Force, and the last to be formed to accommodate that unique band of Americans who, in the Battle of Britain and later, in the Battle of Malta, had volunteered to fly with us and make our cause theirs.

When the time came for transfer to the U.S. Eighth Fighter Command, the three Eagle squadrons of Fighter Command formed the elements of the highly accomplished 4th Fighter Group. And the staff at 'Eighth Fighter' were generous enough to say that the success which the 4th and their fourteen other groups ultimately obtained in the air battles over Germany owed much to the experience acquired by the distinguished band of ex-Eagle pilots who had earlier made their mark in Fighter Command.

Blakeslee led his group with the finesse of a polished wing leader in the Royal Air Force. With his restless and infectious energy, he drove himself even harder than he pushed others—to the precipice of human endeavour. His example, which he kept alight for three continuous years of combat, drew his followers on after him. He didn't, as I recall it, score the victories of some of the sparkling stars among his compatriots. He did not, for instance, amass the totals of men like Hub

Zemke, the legendary leader of the 56th Fighter Group, or Don Gentile, and some others; but he gave the lead, and in this, I judge, he stood apart from his fellow men. The tactics and strategy of leadership were, for him, the vital thing. His searching mind was always looking for some new approach, some fresh concept, some variation in the conventional theme which ran through these long five-, six-, and seven-hour, daylight missions.

Blakeslee's most original contribution was a round-trip spectacular which, at the time, I remember, we could scarcely credit. This amazing act was played out in five scenes over the whole expanse of Europe. There was the collection one day by his Mustang group of several clusters of Fortresses right in the nerve centre of Germany, taking them on eastwards and putting down on an airfield in Russia. A few enemy aircraft were knocked off en route. Then there was the operation from this Russian base, with the same Fortresses, to a target in Poland and thence on to a landing in Italy. From Italy, there were two specially cooked-up sorties with the bombers, one into Yugoslavia and the other into Romania. And finally there was the flight back from southern Europe to East Anglia, with the Fortresses depositing their load on targets in eastern France on the way.

All this, mark you, in a Mustang with a single, Rolls-Royce Packard Merlin engine. If anyone had told us in 1941, when the sweeps across the Channel to short-range targets in northern France and the Low Countries with medium bombers were in full swing, that a multi-thousand mile operation of these dimensions would be flown within three years by single-engined fighters based in Britain, no one would have believed him.

When the armistice was signed on Lüneburg Heath, Blakeslee's group had accounted for slightly over 1,000 enemy aircraft over Europe for a loss in pilots of rather less than a quarter of that number.

To the British mind the extent of the achievement remains, even with the passage of time, incomprehensible. It stands as a paragon of America's belief in the Art of the Possible. And of her refreshing conviction that if convention says no, the answer most probably is yes.

Chapter Twenty-One
The corks didn't blow

THE FINAL phase of the war in Europe was now about to begin. The joint British and American staffs were already getting to grips with the planning of the Normandy landings.

As 1943 drew to a close, Vere Harvey took me aside one day in the mess at Coltishall. 'Laddie,' he said, 'I want you to know before anyone else tells you that I'm leaving here. I have been posted to the Headquarters Staff of the Allied Expeditionary Air Force at Stanmore under Leigh-Mallory. It's an air commodore's appointment and it takes effect from 1 January. We'll be doing the air planning of the invasion under Eisenhower's supreme command.'

Before I had a chance to comment, he added a rider. 'And you're going too, old cock. You've had enough and need a rest. You're also going to Stanmore, to the staff under Roderic Hill as Wing Commander Ops(i). We shall be working close to one another.'

I wasn't surprised, but the thought of leaving the wing, and all the relationships I had formed there, was dispiriting. Vere and I had, together, been able to overcome the earlier problems. Between us, we had seen the fortunes of Coltishall rise and prosper.

Under Leigh-Mallory and Roderic Hill, the work at Headquarters went on apace. One sensed at once the magnitude and scope of the task which, in a few months, was to confront the Allied forces.

Back again at Blue Shutters with Jake Stanley and Bill Harkness, we could see, between us, the extent of the problems the British and American joint staffs were having to grapple with.

It wasn't, initially, an easy ride. For one thing, the respective staffs employed dissimilar methods. Differences between the two allies began to mount as the pressures increased.

They had reached a peak early in 1944 when the Supreme Commander, General of the Army Dwight D. Eisenhower, called the staffs together at General Montgomery's headquarters at St Paul's

School in West London. It needed all Eisenhower's management skills
to quell the bickering.

The setting was a typical, stage-managed job by Montgomery. Five
or six hundred British and American officers were present. All knew
the secrets of the invasion plan. Stars and Stripes and Union Jacks, in
a galaxy of colour, were draped everywhere.

The curtain went up with Eisenhower right in the centre of the
stage, bright lights on him, that splendid rosy face, exuding co-
operation, beaming like the rising sun in the morning.

'Gentlemen,' said Montgomery, standing off to the left of the stage
and getting the timing just right, 'gentlemen, the Supreme Commander.'

It wasn't so much what Eisenhower said, or the way he said it,
which counted; rather it was the manifest sincerity, the sheer honesty
of the man's purpose, which stabbed the conscience.

A relatively commonplace, opening preamble. This great crusade
. . . The nations of the Free World who are joined together . . .
Fighting alongside one another in defence of a single cause . . . All
that. Then came the red meat.

With the passage of more than thirty years only the gist of the
words remains in the memory; but the impression is as clear as ever.

' . . . And if I hear a British or an American officer speak of an ally,
I take him to mean a Frenchman, a Belgian, a Dutchman, a Dane, a
Pole, a Norwegian—any representative of the free nations who are
fighting so valiantly at our side . . .

'I do not ever expect to hear a British officer refer to an American
officer, or an American officer refer to a British Officer, as an ally.
Gentlemen, we're closer than that; we speak the same language; we
are as one . . .'

No one in that theatre could help being deeply moved. There was
nothing else for it but to go back and get on with the work. Without
moaning.

I remember reminding Sir Miles Graham of this incident years
afterwards when my wife and I were staying with him and his wife
Lavender one weekend at Wiverton. Miles had been Montgomery's
chief of administration all through the great campaigns in North Africa
and North-West Europe, from Alamein to Berlin. He believed that
Montgomery possessed the best brain of all the Allied generals in the
Second World War.

He countered, however, with another tale about Eisenhower which showed the strength of his personality and, with it, the force of his authority as Supreme Commander.

As the Allies approached the Rhine, after the advance through France and the Low Countries, Montgomery, as all the world now knows, wanted to drive the 21st Army Group forward in a fast, left-hooking thrust round the northern flank of the German forces. There would be advantages in beating the Russians to Berlin. A detailed appreciation of the operation had been made by the staff and the conclusion reached was that success could be achieved provided the port of Antwerp could be kept open to British shipping and supplies.

The plan was represented in detail and with some force to the Supreme Commander. Eisenhower invited Montgomery to discuss the proposal at a small, ultra-high level conference in Paris. Miles Graham was present.

Montgomery developed the plan with all his customary confidence, dogmatism and conviction. When he saw that Eisenhower and the Americans were not going to accept it, and that politics rather than military considerations were dictating this attitude, he expressed himself in terms which left no doubt whatever of his opinion of their judgment and, in particular, that of the Supreme Commander.

Eisenhower, obviously inflamed, waited for Montgomery to finish. Then, turning to him and looking him straight in the eye, he said: 'Gee, Monty, you can't talk to me like that.'

Montgomery, sitting on the Supreme Commander's right, realized at once that he had gone too far. He put a light and apologetic hand on Eisenhower's arm. 'Forgive me, Supreme Commander,' he said. And immediately accepted the decision with a grace and humility which, said Miles, 'acknowledged Monty's deep and enduring respect for Ike'.

*   *   *

'D' Day had now come and gone. The Allied armies had broken out of the Normandy bridgehead and were beginning to swing leftwards in a sustained advance northwards up through France. Stanmore was taking on the appearance of a backwater. The desire to move on again and get back to flying was overwhelming.

There was resistance to my starting a third tour of operational flying. I had interviews first with Roderic Hill and then with Leigh-Mallory. Two tours, they argued, were enough; besides, I was wanted on the staff. Pilots were ten a penny; staff officers, with broad flying experience, weren't. And, anyway, at twenty-eight, they claimed, I was 'too old' for fighters. It sounded plausible enough.

What they did not know was that, after a clandestine visit to his headquarters beside the River Thames at Wallingford, I had already won over to my side the ever-resourceful Basil Embry, the most dynamic and aggressively resolute operational commander in the Royal Air Force.

His 2 Group in the 2nd Tactical Air Force was now operating, with its Mosquitos, by day and by night, all over Europe and into Scandinavia.

With his navigator, the witty and versatile Peter Clapham, a double first at Cambridge and one of the real 'characters' of the wartime Royal Air Force, always beside him, Embry himself used to take part in the hazardous low-level attacks in daylight against 'special' targets. Now he said he would take me into one of his wings provided I would go through the proper conversion course at Bicester and learn to fly Mosquitos.

To make the change I had to drop a rank and revert to squadron leader. It wasn't for long. A wing commander's vacancy was soon to occur in 138 Wing at Cambrai Epinoy in northern France for a new commanding officer for 613, the City of Manchester Squadron of the Royal Auxiliary Air Force.

Embry gave me this job, which I held from the latter part of 1944 until the surrender of the German armies the following spring.

In terms of flying hours, 613 was a highly experienced, mixed squadron. Some of the crews had had long periods of instructing in Canada. They had come to Europe for the Second Front and to get a taste of operations in the closing stages of the conflict. Yet, despite all the flying time in their log books, the casualties were severe.

Low-level operations at night, flown against defended communications targets in the vicinity of the Ruhr, behind the retreating German armies, as well as in the northern areas between Berlin and the Baltic ports, were testing affairs which demanded not only flying skill but also intuition and judgment. It was a sombre period in our operational lives.

*   *   *

Cambrai was a well-appointed airfield equipped, for those days, with all the up-to-date navigational aids. It was one of only two Royal Air Force stations on the continent with a fog dispersal installation which answered to the arresting name of Fido. We were thus able to operate in low-grade weather.

When Field Marshal von Rundstedt launched his offensive, with ten panzer and fourteen infantry divisions, through the Ardennes in the middle of December 1944, the Germans' last great attack of the war, the demands made upon the squadrons in 138 Wing were heavy. The flying conditions during these weeks were also extremely unfavourable.

With the snow had come freezing temperatures, haze and mist. Moreover, the mountainous country which Rundstedt had selected for his breakthrough made our low-level, night-time activities extremely exacting.

Basil Embry, spurred on by the demands of the hard-pressed U.S. armies under General Omar Bradley, made the most of the facilities which 138 Wing possessed at Cambrai. In one spell, over Christmas and the New Year, at the height of Rundstedt's attack, 613 operated on seven out of ten consecutive nights at the end of which, with the air and groundcrews close to exhaustion, the A.O.C. called for 'one more heave in support of the magnificent American stand in the mountains'.

I was worried about this further demand on the squadron and said so. Extreme fatigue, producing, as it does, casualness and carelessness in the air, could cause as much damage as the enemy. I asked the medical officer to come over and see the crews and maybe give them a shot or two to stimulate their reactions and counter their manifest exhaustion. He responded at once.

We went through the detailed briefing for the night's operations and those who wanted it were given a strong dose of benzedrine to help them on their way. Most accepted the artificial assistance.

My own navigator, J. W. Vick, who was now almost at the end of a long run of operational flying, refused the medication. He was, I knew, very tired and near the end of his tether, but I respected his preference. Johnny, who worked for Cadbury's in Bristol in peacetime, was a thoroughly competent navigator. He and I had built up a quiet and undemonstrative partnership based upon mutual reliance. As he had rejected the stimulant, I felt disinclined to accept it myself.

Half an hour before the scheduled time for the first aircraft to take off, with the squadron now right up on its toes and alert, the operation was cancelled. An order came through from group standing 613, and the other squadrons in the wing, down. So here was virtually the whole squadron, with its first chance for a week of a really good night's sleep, pepped up to the eyeballs and raring to go. Sleep was the last thing the pilots and navigators contemplated. Particularly the Canadians. It was daybreak before the party ended and the effects of the medication had worn off.

*   *   *

Cambrai bequeathed me a valuable legacy. Through our mess officer we had built up a close and beneficial relationship with one or two of the great French producers of champagne around Reims. It was an arrangement of which full advantage was taken. With the war in Europe over, and the general election of 1945 behind us, I was now commanding the fighter station at Bentwaters in Douglas Bader's North Weald sector in 11 Group. I had recently become engaged to the sister of Douglas's wife, Thelma. Jill and I planned to get married as soon as I could obtain my release from the Service early in 1946. Good champagne was in short supply in London. My future father-in-law did nothing to dissuade me from my suggestion that a short visit to Cambrai might serve as a useful prelude to the wedding. All was, therefore, arranged. I had the guns removed from the station commander's P-51B Mustang. We reckoned that between 175 and 200 bottles of the best vintage could now be accommodated in the empty wings and elsewhere. At a 'special' price of around 12/- (who cared about 60p in those days?) a bottle, the more the better. I flew over to Cambrai, by pre-arrangement, a week or two before the date of my demobilization from the R.A.F. to find everything in order. With the help of the mess officer and two co-operative riggers, 180 bottles of the finest stuff were fitted snugly into the empty gun compartments and other crevices of the Mustang, thus adding to the versatility of this exceptional aeroplane. The panels were safely buttoned and we were away.

The Met. forecast back across the southern North Sea to Suffolk was passable. Cloud base was 2,000 to 3,000 feet after the French coast with forward visibility two to three miles. There was quite thick, seven to ten tenths cloud up to 10,000 to 12,000 feet; but clearly there would be no question of climbing up through the overcast and going over the top. The change in pressure at the higher altitudes would have had the champagne corks popping all over the place.

All went well till about halfway across the sea. Then the cloud base began to come down. It got lower and lower until it was down to a few hundred feet above the water with forward visibility rather less than 2,000 yards. A couple of ships suddenly loomed up out of the gloom ånd flashed by. This was no place for an old hand, no matter what the cargo.

To go back to Cambrai was unthinkable; to go on at nought feet with this kind of visibility was madness. There was only one thing for it; pull up and go through the overcast hoping that the top would be lower than the forecasters anticipated. Obviously, I did not at that point want to call the ground station to disclose my identity.

Eight thousand, 10,000, 12,000 feet and still I was in fairly thick cloud. I could hardly contemplate what might now be going on under the wing panels.

At between 13,000 and 14,000 feet the cloud top was reached. Above it the sun was shining warmly out of a blue sky. By now I had given up all hope that any trace of that finest vintage champagne would remain in the bottles.

I flew well on beyond my arrival time and deep into East Anglia before I called the ground station. Weather at Bentwaters, the controller said, was adequate: 1,500 feet cloud base, visibility two to three miles. They gave me a vector for home and within minutes the Mustang was rolling safely down the runway. I taxied up to my usual parking place on the tarmac.

As the panels were unbuttoned I could scarcely bring myself to look.

To my astonished relief, all was well. The bottles were intact, with the wires still firmly securing the corks. Not one had blown.

I didn't dare to tell even my best man and lifelong friend, Charles Pretzlik, for whom I had acted, three years before, in a similar capacity when he married his lovely Susan. As a wartime Mosquito pilot, he would have known too much to have resisted the temptation, as he invited the guests to lift their glasses to the bride and bridegroom.

'Ladies and gentlemen, you do not realize how lucky you are to have anything in your glasses with which to toast . . .'

*   *   *

The last weeks and months commanding the station at Bentwaters made an agreeable valediction to my wartime years in the Royal Air Force.

It was, of course, a real personal help to me that Douglas Bader, home again now after nearly four years as a prisoner in Colditz, near Leipzig, should have been our sector commander. Soon to become my brother-in-law, he had been able to bestow some welcome family patronage in getting me this posting on my return to the Service after my defeat at the hands of Dr Edith Summerskill and the electors of West Fulham.

Douglas often used to fly over to Bentwaters from North Weald for breakfast. If any of the young squadron pilots were about at the time, I always made a point of running two or three of them over to the airfield in my car to watch him land. As an exercise in the control of an aeroplane and the use of sensitive, sympathetic hands, it was invariably a refined and accomplished performance.

A tight circuit, contained within the vicinity of the perimeter of the aerodrome; a finely judged, slow, curving approach, with the throttle cut right back and the engine popping . . . and there was the Spitfire, stalling lightly on to three points within a few yards of the start of the runway. A short landing run of no more than 200 yards—if that—a touch or two on the brakes, and all was still. A little throttle to take the aircraft along to the intersection and quickly off the runway . . . And there was the classic demonstration of the real art of flying.

To the discerning student of flying perfection, it was no coincidence that the Air Officer Commanding, 11 Group, at the time, should have possessed similar professional skills. Dermot Boyle was, by then, well on his illustrious way to the summit of the Service and to the office of Chief of the Air Staff.

Like Bader, he was a product of the Royal Air Force College at Cranwell. There, and elsewhere, the peacetime serving officers had obtained a training which, by its standards, demands and thoroughness, stood them apart from the rest.

I saw Dermot Boyle land a Mosquito, the first time he came to visit us at Bentwaters, with a style and an authority which I had not witnessed during all my previous months with 138 Wing at Cambrai. And I don't suppose for a moment he was, at the time, with all his other work, in what we would normally call regular flying practice.

The brute fact was that the first-rate, peacetime professionals in the Service, particularly those who had graduated from Cranwell, had been given the finest military flying background in the world. Golfing readers will comprehend the metaphor when I say that it was a case of Jones, Hogan, Nelson, Snead, Nicklaus and Cotton versus the Rest.

The Rest made their contribution; but it was the élite who lit the way.

4

Order! Order!

Chapter Twenty-two
Why stand?

WHY DOES a man, or a woman, enter politics?

Ask half a dozen Members of Parliament the question and as likely as not you will get six different answers.

In my case the opportunity and the decision to stand arose in an unconventional way.

With the spring of 1945 had come the strong scent of victory. Rundstedt had been repulsed in the Ardennes. The Germans' last throw had failed. Now the Allied armies were well across the Rhine, driving ever deeper into the Fatherland.

The sorties which, night after night, the fine Mosquito crews of 613 Squadron continued to fly in support of the ground forces, were directed principally against road and rail targets between Berlin and the Baltic coast. With Hitler's infantry and armour falling steadily back, we took maximum advantage of the chaos which was to be seen everywhere along the lines of communication. The last scenes of the terrible Teuton tragedy were being played out to an orchestrated crescendo of activity.

One day, just after lunch, the adjutant came into my office in the squadron's headquarters and handed me the mail from home. A typewritten envelope was among the letters. Out of curiosity I opened it first. The notepaper was familiar. It was from the editor of the *Sunday Express*. Characteristically, John Gordon came straight to the point.

'When the war ends in Europe,' he wrote, 'there is likely to be pressure for an early general election. It could come before the end of the year. Lord Beaverbrook is anxious that a nucleus of young men with broad peacetime and wartime experience should be available to stand for Parliament. You are one who comes to mind. Will you let me know what you feel about it?'

The proposition was arresting. I had never thought of the possibility of standing for Parliament before, nor, as I contemplated it, did the idea seem immediately attractive. I knew little of politics and, up to now, had had no special interest in it. Moreover, I had been out of touch with current events in Britain for much of the war, and to have to fight a parliamentary campaign on such a thin background was not particularly appealing. Nonetheless, this initiative was personally important. It could not be met negatively without thought.

I delayed replying to Gordon. During this time, in off-duty hours, I walked by myself over the flat, barren, tree-starved fields which surrounded our airfield at Cambrai. The more I thought about the proposal, the more difficult I found it to reach a conclusion.

On the other hand, the sense of service which had provided my chief motivation for the past five years of war still gripped firmly. I genuinely felt that I wanted, in some way, to continue to serve. And yet was politics the right medium? I was not then any hand at the cut and thrust of debate. I had always, from the early training I had received as a schoolboy at Stowe at the hands of J. F. Roxburgh, one of the great headmasters of all time, been able to speak adequately, but argument, repartee and use of the adroit rejoinder and the other well-known tools of political manoeuvring were a different matter. Besides, I found greater compulsion in the written than the spoken word.

I felt greatly the need to talk to someone, but there was no one in 138 Wing at Cambrai who knew the first thing about the matters which were now absorbing my thoughts. My leave was long overdue. So, instead of replying to Gordon's letter, I decided to fly back to London for two or three days to see him. There was also another more compelling reason for a brief visit to England. I wanted badly to see again a girl I had met in the house of an old friend at Sunningdale during a heaven-sent weekend on my previous leave. Love and politics, I thought, might make a good mix. They did—Jill and I were to marry two years later.

I lunched with Gordon when I got back to London. He did nothing to persuade me. 'Politics,' he said, 'is a dirty business.' However, he redirected me to Tom Blackburn who, he said, was dealing with the matter for Lord Beaverbrook.

Blackburn, who had been the manager of the *Sunday Express* during my time with the paper, now had an office in the *Evening*

Standard building in Shoe Lane, off Fleet Street. Unlike Gordon, Tom was very persuasive. Others whom he had seen were definitely going to stand when the election came. Win or lose, the experience would be valuable later on.

I was unconvinced and said so. It was left that my name would be given to the Conservative Central Office as a possible starter; it would then be up to me to pursue the matter if I wanted to. A week or two later the war in Europe was over.

Within a few days of the Armistice, the commander-in-chief of the 2nd Tactical Air Force, Air Marshal Sir Arthur Coningham, sent for me to see him in Brussels.

'Mary' Coningham had become, by the end of the war, a well-publicized figure. His command of the Desert Air Force, in support of General Montgomery's Eighth Army, had been conspicuous by its unbroken success. With his 'running mate' Air Vice-Marshal Harry Broadhurst, he had formed a partnership which, in terms of operational experience and unchecked advance, was without parallel in the Service. It began in Egypt in 1942 and finished in the heart of Germany in 1945.

Of all the great British air commanders in the European and Mediterranean theatres Coningham was, I think, the only one I had not met. The meeting was, therefore, fairly formal. After the exchange of a few pleasantries, he disclosed his hand.

'I understand you were a journalist in peacetime and worked for Lord Beaverbrook. I've got a job for you. I want you to write a history of the Tactical Air Forces covering the period from Alamein to Berlin.

'To undertake the task you will be based in Wales and you will have access to all necessary papers, records and documents. You will have the use of an aircraft and a free hand in moving about, arranging interviews and gathering whatever material you need. You will carry sole responsibility for the work and you will be on your own; but you will, of course, have a small clerical staff to help you.

'I am asking you to take this on first because of your journalistic background and the experience you have had on the Air Staff during the war. Secondly, I want you to do it because, as an operational pilot, a squadron and wing leader, having worked both by day and at night, you have a broad flying base on which to rest the job.'

I played for time. I had, I said, only taken three days' leave in the last nine months and would like to have a week in England to think quietly about the offer. Whoever did it would have to devote himself diligently to the task for a year or more. I had to consider it carefully. Coningham at once, and very fairly, concurred with my proposal.

'Take your leave,' he said, 'and come back and see me when it's over.'

Back in London I immediately telephoned Ralph Assheton, chairman of the Conservative Party, for an appointment. I was now quite clear in my mind. To fight the general election which had recently been called presented a preferable alternative to getting committed to a history of the Tactical Air Forces which might well take me eighteen months.

Assheton, who had served with distinction in Churchill's wartime coalition and who was, later, to move on to the House of Lords, to the name of Clitheroe and to an influential position in the business world, saw me the day I telephoned. In a slightly diffident, light, yet precise way he made the running. Winston Churchill didn't think an election was wise, or necessary, with the war in the Far East still being waged. But there it was, we had got one and it had to be fought. Neither party was ready for it, but we had got to make the best of it . . .

'How old are you?' Assheton's question broke abruptly into the flow of conversation. I had to think before I answered; age seemed irrelevant. 'Twenty-nine,' I replied.

'That's about right. I always think that thirty-two is about the right age for a man to enter the House of Commons. He hasn't, generally, had enough experience of life before that.

'You should be prepared to fight a difficult constituency now, and next time you can expect something better. You would then be in the House before you were thirty-five, perhaps earlier.'

This last bit brought me back to reality. In my ignorance it hadn't occurred to me that I would not be offered at least a winnable seat; a safe constituency was another matter. Such is the confidence of inexperience.

Assheton then put the position bluntly.

'You're very late coming to see me. Barring last minute changes, all the worthwhile constituencies have gone now. The best I can do for you is Limehouse against Attlee. Put up a good fight there and you will make a mark. The public gaze will be focused on the Labour leader's constituency.'

Thoughts of that history of the Tactical Air Forces began to revive. Would I really be wasting my time if I did it? I should at least have something tangible to show for it at the end of the day. In Limehouse, if adopted, I would be steamrollered by Clement Attlee. Having been obliged to leave the Royal Air Force to fight the election, I would then, if I lost, have to return to some less agreeable job in the Service—perhaps, even, in the Far East.

Assheton probably guessed something of the thoughts which were chasing one another across my mind.

'Well,' he said, with a finality and a brevity which indicated, beyond doubt, that the matter could go no further, 'you must make up your mind. It's Limehouse or nowt.'

'Limehouse it is,' I replied, 'if they will adopt me.'

'Good,' he said, and gave the impression of the satisfied salesman who has finally disposed of the last item in a sticky line of stock.

'Get down there as quickly as you can. I'll tell the chairman of the association you're coming. You will then have to face the usual procedures.'

I went home that evening to Hertfordshire to tell my family what I was up to. I hadn't been in the house an hour before the telephone rang. It was John Gordon.

'Laddie,' he said, 'I've heard about Limehouse; but I think we can do better for you than that. Jean Stickney, Lord Beaverbrook's sister, lives in Fulham. She tells me that something has happened to the candidate in West Fulham and they're looking for another.

'Edith Summerskill won the seat in a by-election just before the war, plugging the theme 'Babies before Bullets'. She'd be a good one to topple. If you let your name go forward you'll have a fight to get the nomination. If you fail, there's always Limehouse.

'If you're on, I'll tell Jean Stickney and I expect they'll want to see you.'

The West Fulham Conservative Association was hardly raring to go. I got down to the offices to find the usual kind of chaos. The absence of any noticeable organization was at once apparent.

The agent confirmed that my name had been added to the candidates' list. There would be a preliminary meeting to select a short list of three that evening. It all had to be rushed because time was now so short.

We met, incongruously, in what appeared to be the enlarged vestry of a church. There was a fairly formidable array of local talent on the selection committee. I got the impression of being confronted by a lot of rather overdressed women, all of whom wore hats. There seemed, by comparison, to be very few men.

The last three candidates on the short list at West Fulham in 1945 made an interesting trio—Messrs Erroll, Remnant and Lucas. I got the nomination and within a few weeks had been sent packing back to the Royal Air Force, comfortably disposed of by Dr Edith Summerskill with a majority of nearly 8,000.

Freddy Erroll went off to Altrincham and Sale to succeed Sir John Grigg, the War Minister, as the candidate. He won the seat by nearly 15,000 votes, and later became a cabinet minister before moving on to the quieter pastures of the House of Lords and the higher echelons of business.

Peter Remnant, a brewer, whose father had sat in the House of Commons for nearly thirty years, bided his time and then won Wokingham, where he enjoyed a majority such as those with marginal seats dream of.

Still, for the defeated candidate, there were some plusses on the other side of the account.

Chapter Twenty-Three
What did you shay your name was?

THE GENERAL election campaign of 1945 in West Fulham was a spirited and rough affair. The noise at some of the meetings surpassed all expectations. Edith Summerskill was a determined, unyielding, hard candidate. She took no notice of me—she had no need to—and ran her show in a detached and, for those days, efficient way. She was a pro at the job—and most effective with the women.

The best that could be said of the Tory campaign was that it was 'colourful'. It was neither commonplace nor dull. The inexperience of the candidate, for whom the whole process, not least question-time at the end of the evening meetings, was manifestly a nightmare, was a feature of the battle.

I was, however, lucky with my neighbours and found comfort in their ready support. Bill Astor was defending East Fulham next door. I had known him and his family since the golden summer days we all spent together as children at Sandwich Bay in the early 1920s just after the first World War.

'Always wear the same coloured suit and the same tie throughout the campaign,' Bill told me. 'Because they don't yet know you, you must make yourself easily identifiable in the constituency. Look at Winston's tall bowler, bow-tie and cigar.'

It was the first piece of political advice I had been given; and it was right.

The Astor house in Upper Grosvenor Street became a frequent meeting place in the campaign. There the political alumni gathered at lunchtime before dispersing to their various engagements and constituencies. In such company and amid such revealing talk, I recognized the paucity of my political knowledge. It was a humbling and rather unnerving experience.

'Anthony is going to say tonight in Sheffield . . . Winston thinks that the party should now . . . Rab was discussing last night the. . . Oliver said he got a very bad reception . . . Central Office are putting out a statement . . .'

I could be no more than an attentive listener, but there I was at least able to pick up points for speeches, quotes and good 'lines' to run. The comings and goings in that friendly, generous and unconventional Astor household were endless; the flow of authoritative information stimulating. Moreover, the food at lunch, which was always delicious and laid on for countless, unknown numbers, fortified us for the rest of the day. Upper Grosvenor Street became an oasis in my desert.

Bill Astor managed to arrange that in one of his afternoon campaign tours of south-west London, Winston Churchill would drive through East and West Fulham and speak shortly for both of us in Walham Green.

Bill joined the Prime Minister's car in East Fulham, and when the entourage stopped outside our committee rooms at 765 Fulham Road I hopped up into the back seat beside him.

'This is Wing Commander Lucas, sir,' said Bill. The Old Man did not notice the introduction. He was much more concerned with a group of my supporters who were surging round the car.

We moved briskly on. Churchill was standing up in the front, hand on the windscreen, cigar in his mouth, tall bowler hat raised above his head. In the slipstream I sniffed a slight aroma of brandy.

When we pulled up in Walham Green there must have been a couple of thousand people packed together waiting to hear the Prime Minister. In a few majestic and patriotic sentences in which, I noticed, he seemed to give a freshness to simple, commonplace words, he pitched the tone far above the party battle. It gave a determined and vociferous minority in the audience little chance to score.

It wasn't until he reached his peroration and his endorsement of the two National Conservative candidates that Churchill ran into trouble.

'And so, ladies and gentlemen, as we approach the end of a protracted and arduous campaign, as the nation prepares, now, to give its verdict, let me commend to you two fine young fighting candidates, each standing here in the National Conservative cause.

'First, Mr Astor—Bill Astor—who has already proved himself a vigilant representative of the people of East Fulham in the House of

Commons and, second, Wing Commander [pause] . . . er . . . Wing
Commander [longer pause] . . . er . . .'

'Lucas' prompted Bill, loudly and decisively, from behind.

'. . . and another fine, young fighting candidate, Wing Commander
[another pause] . . . er . . . [now turning to me] What did you shay
again your name was? . . .'

'Lucas, sir.'

'. . . And so, ladies and gentlemen, I invite your support for these
two fine National Conservative candidates, both of whom will serve
the interests of Fulham, and the country, faithfully and well if you
elect them to the House of Commons. With that, my friends, I say:
"Come then, let us go forward in our united strength." '

Churchill's car moved away from Walham Green leaving the
waving, cheering, booing crowd behind. We crossed the constituency
boundary and pulled up just short of Putney Bridge. As I got out, I
thanked the Prime Minister for coming to speak. A puckish beam
spread across his face.

'I congratulate you, . . . er . . . I congratulate you, . . . er . . .
Commander, on your vigorous and martial campaign.'

A tuppenny ride in a 14 bus took me back to base. And to reality.

*   *   *

Another near neighbour, to whom I was able to turn in these pressing
days, was Henry Longhurst, who was defending Acton, a seat he had
won on a Churchill ticket in a wartime by-election. His Labour
opponent was the railwayman Joe Sparks.

It didn't require much of a detour for Henry to pass 765 Fulham
Road on the way from his home in Chelsea to Acton.

Moreover, my agent, K. A. 'Ears' Lawrence, was an old and very
experienced hand at fighting elections. He regarded it as a necessary
prerequisite of any successful campaign that the agent should always
have, ready to hand in his bottom drawer, a permanently full bottle of
Gordon's. It was a philosophy with which Longhurst found no reason
whatever to differ.

One morning he came into the committee rooms rather earlier than
usual. 'I've got a good one for Sparks,' he said.

' "Vote for Longhurst and Watch Sparks Fly".'

'What did you shay your name was?'
Winston Churchill addresses the electors of Fulham—East and West—in the
General Election of 1945, Bill Astor is on the left. From the *Daily Sketch* for 3
July 1945.

'Then it was over. Val just said to me: "We're in." Then amid cheers and boos,
. . . my bearers were swallowed up in the mêlée. They dropped me perfunctorily to
earth.' Winning Brentford & Chiswick from Labour in a photo finish, February
1950. From the *Sphere,* 4 February 1950.

Under Churchill, the Tory party always had a theme. 'Make Britain Great Again' was the one we ran in Brentford & Chiswick in the 1950 General Election campaign. From the *Illustrated London News*, 9 February 1950.

'. . . And furthermore, ladies and gentlemen . . .' Winning Brentford & Chiswick for the Tories for the third time. The Chiswick Town Hall: General Election, 1955.

Jill (*second left*) and I always gathered a fine team for our Election campaigns. Our Irish setter, Red 1, ensured a few extra votes.

Ten minutes past midnight on 27 May, 1955 and the Tories in Brentford & Chiswick are home and (relatively) dry.

'There was something strangely incongruous and endearing about seeing the children scampering about this . . rather austere Elizabethan house, set in the Chilterns . . . the scene of so much political activity.' A visit with the children to Selwyn Lloyd at Chequers, summer 1960.

That evening Lord Beaverbrook came to speak for me in the Eleveden Hall. 'Henry Longhurst,' I said, 'has got a splendid slogan for Sparks in Acton—"Vote for Longhurst and Watch Sparks Fly".'

Beaverbrook's face showed no reaction.

'It won't win him any votes,' he said, deadpan.

*　　*　　*

The meetings during the campaign in West Fulham were boisterous, exceptionally noisy and relatively good-humoured. Being a London constituency, and geographically convenient, I was able to call on an all-star supporting cast of speakers which ensured that we played to packed houses. I went for colour as much as for political acumen. Our problem was that we had no hall large enough to take the audiences.

My brother-in-law to be, Douglas Bader, came and spoke and brought with him from Tangmere, where he was then stationed, a glittering array of 'names' from the Royal Air Force. The escort was badly needed. Within minutes of the start of Bader's speech a heckler was pelting the chairman with points of order. Brandishing a fat copy of King's Regulations in one hand and pointing a finger with the other, he momentarily stopped the show.

'What I want to know,' he asked, 'is what right has the speaker to be appearing on that platform tonight?

'It is forbidden [quoting page and section] in Army Orders for servicemen to take part in political meetings. How does the speaker square this with King's Regulations?'

The hostile intervention found an echo of support here and there in other parts of the hall. Had the audience not itself decided (as so often happens) that the heckler was becoming a bore and acted accordingly, he might have held things up indefinitely. One fact was quite plain. The chairman knew nothing at all about King's Regulations.

The skirmish was eventually ended by Douglas, in a customarily blunt and direct way, and to the accompaniment of deafening vocal support, saying: 'I don't know about Army Council Instructions ('that's for sure, mate'). I'm in the Royal Air Force [prolonged applause]. But I can tell you I have had official permission to speak here tonight.'

The next day, in a blaze of publicity—'Bader howled down';

'Bader on Election "ops"'—instructions went out from the government about serving officers taking part in the election. But West Fulham had got its blow in first.

*   *   *

It was not until the closing days of the campaign that we began to think we might not win.

Lord Beaverbrook came to speak for me a second and last time. True, he was by now tired, for he had been active throughout the whole election, championing the cause of his friend, Churchill. But he seemed to have lost something of the gaiety, buoyancy and bounce which had been so apparent when he first came to support me. I sensed he felt that things were beginning to run strongly against us.

The meeting was, again, a knockabout. The opposition had mounted their liveliest team of hecklers.

For a quarter of an hour or so before Beaverbrook and I arrived in the hall, Peter Remnant, who, despite being beaten for the Tory candidate's job, had sportingly stayed on in the constituency to help me, had been holding the fort, trying to keep the temperature down. Before the House of Commons, in its own ruthless way, made him liven up his voice, Peter had a rather lugubrious, doleful, almost mournful manner of delivery.

John Gordon was at the meeting. He sent me a note the next day. 'I listened to some man called Remnant starting off,' he wrote. 'I thought he was well named.'

When Beaverbrook got up to speak, our opponents had clearly made up their minds they would give him a roasting. To counter them he took a dubious risk. On the left flank of the hall a burly and determined individual in a cloth cap was keeping up an endless flow of interruptions.

'Come and sit up here, my friend,' said Lord Beaverbrook, by now exasperated. The man accepted the challenge and sat down on the platform, his cap still on his head.

'I see the signs of victory for Laddie Lucas in West Fulham,' cried Beaverbrook.

'If he wins I'll eat my hat,' retorted the heckler at his elbow.

Beaverbrook turned, lifted the cap off the fellow's head, and held it aloft.

'He's going to eat this, ladies and gentlemen,' he rasped. 'He's going to eat this.'

In the uproar which followed, I couldn't see how Lord Beaverbrook would ever get out of it. He did—just—by calling into play all the arts—the familiar distraction of the fable, the inevitable employment of the biblical reference.

'Ernest Bevin says—and I quote him—"I did as much as Churchill to win the war."

'It's the old story; the frog in the pond and the ox in the field. The frog wants to be as big as the ox, so he puffs himself up and he puffs and puffs—and he busts. So many men are ruined by attempting a greatness to which they have no claim.

'But how about the ox . . .?'

'How about the beaver in the brook?' chipped in the voice at Beaverbrook's side.

'The Bible says: "Thou shalt not muzzle the ox when he treadeth out the corn",' continued Lord Beaverbrook. 'Send Laddie Lucas to Parliament to see that Churchill is not muzzled and that Churchill treads out the corn.'

'I bet Churchill wishes he could muzzle you,' interjected the platform captive. It was his parting shot; but the legacy which was left to the unequipped candidate was hardly conducive to a quiet hearing.

The next day the *Evening Standard's* Londoner's Diary, forecasting that I would get 'a big vote from the women', reported objectively of my performance the previous evening: 'Lucas is obviously still more at home in a Spitfire than on a political platform.'

Chapter Twenty-Four
Securing the base

IT WAS Nigel Fisher who first mentioned it to me—one of those chance remarks at a dinner party which occasionally lead on to unexpected things.

Nigel, having contested Chislehurst for the Tories in 1945, had already been adopted as the candidate for Hitchin. Able, perceptive and articulate, and later to become a minister, he had a strong political background and tended to be particularly well-informed. Although he was ahead of me at Cambridge, we had known one another since our university days.

He asked me if I was going to fight West Fulham again after my defeat at the hands of Edith Summerskill. I said no, I had told the local association after the general election that it was not my intention to go on. Anyway, I added, I hadn't yet made up my mind whether I would look for another constituency. It was 1947 and I was busy making my way in commercial life.

'I rather think Brentford and Chiswick will be going,' said Nigel. 'Harold Mitchell is unlikely to stand again after being beaten by Francis Noel-Baker. He is going to live abroad.

'I am told the seat is definitely winnable. I really do think you ought to consider this very seriously if it comes up. If I hear more I'll let you know.'

He telephoned a couple of days later. The information he had was correct. Sir Harold Mitchell had decided to give up. I sent my name in at once to the constituency association and to the Conservative Central Office.

Although there were a lot of people after the seat, I never really doubted that I would get the nomination in the end.

Having fought West Fulham, only a few miles away, I had the advantage of being known in the area.

I quickly got on to the short list of three. I then had an unexpected piece of luck. Just before the final selection a local Tory stalwart named William Holliman, who dealt in watercress in Brentford Market and knew everyone and everything about the constituency, called me at my office.

He wondered if I would care to take a run round the constituency with him just to get acquainted with some of its problems. I could get questions about them at the final selection meeting. I felt at once from his voice that I had an ally.

I took up the offer immediately. The same afternoon I was sitting beside Bill Holliman in his car touring the constituency. And without a doubt when I faced the full executive committee a few days later I knew more about Brentford and Chiswick's problems than either of my two adversaries. Right or wrong, it gave me an edge.

For the next thirteen years Holliman was to be my confidant and friend. We had a clear-cut understanding both during the first three tedious and difficult years, when I was nursing the constituency, and in the subsequent decade when I was the Member. Bill would tell me straight—and without any dressing—up, exactly what was going on and what he knew was being said about me—the good and the bad. Particularly the bad.

It turned out to be one of the happiest and most valuable relationships of my political life. Plying his trade between his watercress beds in Buckinghamshire and his shop in Brentford Market, and devoting all his other moments—and more—to the local Conservative cause, I don't suppose Bill slept on average for more than three or four hours a night for years. Early or late, he was always available and always ready to lend a hand, and when things were difficult he could always find something or someone to laugh at.

I was also specially favoured in my agent, V. E. Baker. Lively and alert, Val Baker drove himself unsparingly. There were times when he overtaxed his strength in the process and had to go away for rests. He and Holliman worked together in close and happy accord. The hands of the clock meant nothing to either of them. Between them, in one way or another, they ran the shop.

I was further helped in the constituency by Reginald Howard, chairman of the constituency association for most of my time, who for many years was the editor of Gaumont British News. To Reggie

Howard's eye for news was added a remarkably acute political sense. His work as leader of Brentford and Chiswick Council, and later as mayor of the borough, gave him a special knowledge of local affairs to which he remained, until the end of his life, politically attuned. He was a good organizer and had a tidy mind. He tended, however, to place a high value on his personal dignity and, with the authority of his office to back it, he could sometimes seem pompous. He put certain people's backs up as a result, but, whatever their personal feelings, all respected his ability. For me, Reggie Howard was more than a first-rate constituency chairman; he was also a good and dependable friend. I recommended him, after years of service to the local party and the borough, for the award of an O.B.E. When he got it I do not believe there was a member of the association or the council who didn't think he deserved it—and perhaps rather more.

*   *   *

Finance is always a problem for a local party. In this we were able to enlist the support of some of the principals of the great industrial companies of Brentford, particularly those which had their head-quarters on the Great West Road. First under Arthur Hillier, chairman and managing director of the Sperry Gyroscope Company, and then, later, after Hillier's retirement, under Henry ('Leslie') Lazell, the highly successful chairman of the Beecham Group, a small and discreetly chosen committee of industrialists was set up. It transformed the financial structure of the local organization, and made it possible for the party to concentrate on the prime political function of winning elections without having the ever-present worry of finding money to pay the bills. I thought at the time, and the passage of the years only confirms me in my conviction, that the Conservative Party should have made use of Leslie Lazell's financial, organizational and marketing flair while he was still at the summit of his personal and corporate powers. He was one of the outstanding men in British business in the 1950s and 1960s.

Lazell would have made a first-rate chairman of the party, cast in the mould of Fred Woolton. There is much to be said for making an accomplished and personable businessman, who is accustomed to the executive conduct of a large organization—and to public speaking—

and who has acquired political sense and feel, chairman of the party, giving him, of course, the added authority of a seat in the House of Lords. The alternative, of selecting for this office a politician who has turned to business, does not seem to me so appealing or so effective.

In securing the base on which his political activity primarily rests, a Member must have a small and close-knit team in the constituency upon which he can fully rely. I fought and won three general elections in Brentford and Chiswick, a marginal constituency if ever there was one, during the thirteen years I carried the Tory banner there. Each time I depended for my success upon much the same hand-picked, dedicated team. I chose to go for first-hand business experience to see us through.

Our titular head, who was also president of the constituency association, was Arthur Charlton, chairman of the Brentford Soap Company. Arthur knew everyone and was liked by all. He accepted special responsibility for the conduct of our campaigns in Brentford.

Reggie Howard worked with me and my agent, Val Baker, at the centre. We took care of the overall organization of the campaigns. Jimmy Crispin, a banker, who had spent most of his life in the City, looked after the money and the fund-raising. Ron Coulthard, then with the Ford Motor Company, took charge of transport and the conveyance of voters to the poll.

Dick Avery, of Alfa-Laval, came in to the campaign headquarters at 433 High Road, Chiswick, every day, and added strength to our small administrative machine. Bill Holliman, as my personal aide, acted as general factotum and trouble-shooter. He was also responsible for intelligence and, by his multifarious local contacts, got to find out much of what the other side was doing. We usually had someone behind the enemy lines. Andrew Jardine, a business consultant, who had left the army as a lieutenant-colonel, held a watching brief over our strong wards at the eastern end of the constituency.

Then, to back all this, our vigorous Young Conservatives, led by Moira Hope-Jones, were given a roving commission and a lot of head. We used them as a sort of *corps d'élite*, probing here, thrusting there, and generally keeping our opponents on the jump. If a ward chairman called for help with his canvassing cover, the Young Conservatives were dispatched to his aid. The same day. Among them, a young man named Peter Walker, later to become a successful Cabinet Minister, was quickly making a mark.

I think it unlikely that a better constituency campaign team existed than the one we mustered in Brentford and Chiswick the elections of 1950, 1951 and 1955.

When these periodical tests were over, the team members would disperse and revert to their normal rôles within the association. There, they showed themselves to be the pillars which secured the base.

Victory in this marginal seat was always sweet, but the ejection in 1950 of the sitting Member, the personable and good-looking Francis Noel-Baker, son of Philip, by 800 odd votes gave special delight. It reversed the electors' verdict of 1945 and restored the constituency to the Conservative fold where, by tradition and history, it had rested for so many years.

Polling day and the count in the 1950 election were memorable. The ever-enthusiàstic and ebullient Val Baker reported to me after the polling booths had closed and the counting of the votes had begun in the town hall that I was 'comfortably in'. He estimated my likely majority at 4,000. Broad smiles stretched across our camp.

He further assured me that there was nothing more I could usefully do in the constituency until the counting was almost complete, which was expected to be shortly before midnight. His advice was to 'come back to the town hall about 11.30'.

For old times' sake my wife and I slipped down to the 400 in Leicester Square for dinner. Scene of many happy evenings, it seemed as good a place as any to spend the last couple of hours before the announcement of the result. Jill and I felt exhausted but confident.

Back again in Chiswick Town Hall, a profound and disturbing change of attitude had overtaken our side.

Gone was the confidence, the ebullience, of Val Baker. His face now wore a tired and disturbing pallor. In the hushed but busy hall the counting went on. Equal piles of voting papers stacked side by side began to tell their story. I was in, my supporters told me, by less than 1,000. Then I was out by a similar margin. A recount was definitely probable. One forecast followed another. Only one thing was now certain. Whichever way it went the result was going to be uncomfortably close. I began to rethink my vote of thanks to the returning officer, allowing for the worst.

Then it was over. A serious-faced official handed each candidate's agent a slip with the voting return on it. Val just said to me: 'We're in.

Relief and jubilation overtook our camp. As we walked buoyantly up the stairs to the balcony of the town hall overlooking Turnham Green, and the great concourse of electors waiting outside for the result, Francis Noel-Baker's wife nudged Jill. 'You don't know,' she said, 'what you're letting yourself in for.'

With the announcement and speeches of thanks over, we went down among our elated supporters. Two of the closest, Chuck Dales and Eric Branczik, each an anchor man in the campaign, grabbed me by the legs and lifted me aloft. I felt I was riding dangerously high. Then, amid cheers and boos, congratulations and insults, my bearers were swallowed up in the mêlée. They dropped me perfunctorily to earth.

'One moment stood he as the angels stand . . . and then he was not . . .'

Mercifully, the faithful Chiswick police stood firm.

*   *   *

Soon after I got into the House of Commons I said to 'Robbie' Robinson, the well-liked editor of the local newspaper, the *Brentford and Chiswick Times*, that I would be quite ready to contribute a non-controversial political column for the paper once a fortnight on the happenings at Westminster.

It might be called 'A Fortnight At Westminster', and I gave the undertaking that it would in no way become a platform for Tory propaganda.

Robbie had edited the paper for a great many years and had built up its circulation on the basis of a factual and informative brand of journalism which took no sides politically. Although he was beholden to the proprietor, Richard Dimbleby, and his family, whose politics, I guessed, differed from mine, he never took up a political stance. He played it straight down the middle.

At first my suggestion made him apprehensive. How could he be sure I would really be impartial? I proposed a trial run for three months to show him I meant what I said.

It turned out rather well for both of us. Robbie got, at no cost, a column which went behind the scenes at Westminster, dealt with personalities and events, and told stories about them which weren't appearing elsewhere. It became quite widely read in the borough.

For my part, I had the benefit of a platform which allowed me to keep my name regularly before the electors. Because I was true to my word and didn't give it a political slant, it helped create the impression that I was a middle-of-the-road, moderate M.P. who could see the other side's point of view and was fair.

My own supporters weren't keen on it (although they still read it) because they thought it was too pink. I knew they were wrong and took no notice. They never realised that it got me more votes than it lost. I enjoyed the job and was pleased when John Gordon told me one day he occasionally saw the stuff and thought I hadn't forgotten everything he had taught me.

The next two elections I fought in Brentford and Chiswick had their moments, and in each case my majority was increased, but neither provided the elixir and the novelty of the first. To capture is always more stimulating than to defend.

Moreover the second, in October 1951, my first defence of the constituency, was contested under the shadow of family grief. Our first child, Christopher, who was born in 1947, the year I was adopted for Brentford and Chiswick, had been seriously ill since birth. We knew there could be little hope. The burden resting upon my wife, which had been bravely endured for more than three years, was now becoming intolerable. The strain on both of us was intense.

In September, to try to refresh ourselves for the campaign which was soon to follow, we went for a holiday to Sandwich Bay, in East Kent, where, thirty-six years before, I had been born. There, two months short of his fourth birthday, Christopher's condition grew rapidly worse. The end was not long in coming. The funeral took place at St Clement's, and the child was buried in the churchyard only a short distance from my father's grave.

Jill and I, taxed with sadness, returned to London to face the rigours of the campaign. It was a sombre moment in our devoted lives. How we struggled through it neither of us then knew, but we were determined not to flinch from our duty, nor to give a moment's impression of our inner sorrow. At such moments, the Lord does not stand aside.

Chapter Twenty-Five
Private member

IT WAS half past six in the morning, towards the end of an all-night sitting, when Will Irving telephoned. The whips, he said, had just been on to him at home. There was to be a division at eight o'clock and they had insisted that he go back to the House to vote.

'So that's it, boy,' he added, 'eight o'clock is when the vote is coming and we'll have to be there. I'll see you in the lobby.'

For me it was no more than five or six minutes by car from our flat in Eaton Square to the House of Commons. For Will Irving, the Labour Member for Wood Green, chairman of the Middlesex County Council and a lifelong supporter of the moderate centre of the Socialist Party, it was a fifty-minute journey from his house in North London.

The two of us were in the habit, in my early days as an M.P., of pairing together.

Pairing is the long-established process whereby two Members, one from each of the two main parties, agree privately not to vote in a division, thus cancelling out two potential votes. It is an important part of the parliamentary system. It is based upon trust and it enables two Members on opposite sides to be absent when necessary without detriment or disadvantage to their respective parties.

There is no better way of testing the human qualities than this. I soon found that Will Irving, whom I had known before I entered the House, was a man of his word, undemonstrative, quiet and reasonable. Once a stevedore in Workington docks, he was utterly reliable and straight as, indeed, the circumstances of his early morning telephone call show.

The vote in question was on the committee stage of a Bill which had gone on all night. If there was one thing Will Irving disliked, it was having to stay in the House till the early hours if there wasn't going to be a division. He was well on into his sixties. The health of his wife, to whom he was devoted, was fast deteriorating. His own was none too good, and his work on the Middlesex County Council added greatly to his load.

The narrow parliamentary majorities of the early 1950s, and the frequent all-night sittings, did not make things any easier. Thus I was always anxious, when I could properly do so, to accommodate him. On this occasion we had left the House together at eleven o'clock.

The division at eight, to bring the sitting to a close, was quite unexpected. It would have been easy for Will to have answered his whips' call, made some excuse about having tried to contact me, returned to Westminster to vote, and left me in the cart. But that wasn't his way. He was rock-solid and dependable as a colleague and a friend. It wasn't in his nature to let you down.

I remember well his sadness when he told me, soon after his wife's death, that he was giving up the House of Commons at the end of the Parliament. He was himself then very frail. 'It's no good, boy,' he said, 'I can't keep this work up without the wife. Now that she's gone I haven't the stomach for it any more.'

Will Irving died quite a short time after he quit the House of Commons. I went to his funeral. It took place in North London where his last years were spent. For such a good and humble man, who had given so much, I expected there would be many at the service to say goodbye. I counted eleven present, including myself. I don't know who it was who said there's no gratitude in politics.

*   *   *

Wilfred Fienburgh was one of the brightest and most promising of the younger Labour Members. He sat for Islington North.

He was a journalist and worked for Lord Bernstein's Granada Television. I remember he led for the opposition one year on the Army Estimates and in the second reading debate made a first-rate speech from the dispatch box without a note. He was marked for advancement.

Wilfred and I struck up a friendship which was typical of the close relationships which are formed in the House of Commons between Members on opposite sides. We had a lot in common. There was mutual interest in journalism, not least because he had started to write (uncommonly well) for the *Sunday Express* on which I had begun my working life. Apart from this, his appointment with Granada was beginning to occupy much of his non-parliamentary time, just as G.R.A. (the Greyhound Racing Association) was occupying mine. He needed to go to Manchester from time to time, just as I did. It therefore suited our respective circumstances to be able to pair together whenever an emergency arose and the whips agreed.

It would have been hard to find two greater opposites than Wilfred Fienburgh and Will Irving. Yet with Wilfred, just as with Will, a relationship of confidence and trust was quickly established. Being young and personable and very much headed on the upward path, he was becoming more and more in demand, yet he never allowed this to affect our relationship.

Wilfred had a clever and attractive wife and a farmhouseful of children in Hertfordshire. He was also accident-prone, always falling off ladders and damaging limbs. He wrote a piece about it in the *Sunday Express*. Life for him was dangerous and hectic. And increasingly successful.

Then disaster struck. One Sunday morning I opened the newspaper before breakfast. There in the Stop Press on the front page in red typeset was a blurred headline—'M.P. Seriously Hurt'. It was Wilfred. He had had a terrible accident driving home to Hertfordshire the previous afternoon and was 'critically ill' in hospital at Hendon.

I didn't wait for breakfast. Instead I put on some clothes, got into my car and drove out to Hendon. I asked to speak to the sister and said who I was. She came, I remember, to the entrance of the hospital to meet me.

'Could I possibly see Mr Fienburgh, Sister? I have seen the story in this morning's paper.'

She didn't reply for a moment. 'You know him very well, do you?' Yes, I said, I did. I explained we were colleagues together in the House of Commons.

'I am afraid I must tell you it is no use seeing him. He will not know you. His head is irreparably injured. I fear there is no hope.'

I drove slowly back to London, heavy with melancholy. A future which promised so much was not to be.

*   *   *

I felt the loss of Wilfred Fienburgh just as acutely as I had Will Irving's a short time before. Friendships fashioned in these circumstances are unique. I could not reasonably expect to find a third member of the Labour Party with whom it would be possible to establish so close and easy a relationship.

I had already, however, a good friend in the Member for Hammersmith North, one of the tougher, more forthright and more independent-minded supporters of the Labour Party in the House. I had come to know Frank Tomney not only as a colleague in Parliament but also as the Member for the constituency in which the White City, the flagship of G.R.A.'s fleet of stadiums, was located. Frank had always taken a lively constituency interest in our activities and often came to the great international events which were held in the world-famous arena.

He was a first-rate constituency Member. He was, moreover, a resolute and effective speaker in the House of Commons, always ready to follow his conscience even if this conflicted with the official party line. In the middle 1960s, he opposed, on Second Reading, the Murder (Abolition of the Death Penalty) Bill. In so doing, he was the only member of the Labour Party in the House at the time to vote for the retention of capital punishment. In doing so I suspect he represented the views of a substantial majority of his constituents in Hammersmith. His vote may not have endeared him to some, but no one could dissuade Frank from his beliefs. He formed his judgments and stood by them.

Chance, then, and the reassuring hand of fortune, offered a third real character in the Labour Party of whom I was able to make a genuine friend, and with whom I could enjoy just the same reciprocal benefits of trust, understanding and humanity as I had earlier enjoyed with Irving and Fienburgh.

After nearly thirty years as a Member, Frank was rejected as Labour's candidate in Hammersmith. A bunch of way-out left-wingers, who had infiltrated the local Party, engineered his rejection. His uninhibited opposition to the causes of Marxism and Communism was hardly to their taste.

So much for the courage of individualism and independence in modern politics.

Chapter Twenty-Six
They have their exits

MANY OF us were surprised when Anthony Eden, on becoming Prime Minister, appointed Edward Heath to succeed Buchan-Hepburn as Chief Whip of the Tory Party and even more surprised when Harold Macmillan, having succeeded Eden, kept him in this office. No one, least of all Ted Heath himself, would claim that he was cast in the classic and historic mould of Tory chief whips.

The traditional Establishment background, hitherto regarded as a necessary prerequisite in dealing with the Tory Party in the House of Commons, from its 'red brick' representation across the board to the aristocratic, and noticeably independent, fringe, was certainly lacking in his case.

Moreover, in bearing this responsibility, both during and just after the Suez affair, when the Party was at odds with itself, the task which confronted Heath was, to say the least, formidable. His handling of it was masterly. He thus answered those who still doubted his suitability for the rôle.

With courage, directness and efficiency, and a remarkably human understanding of members' problems, he won from them absolute co-operation and loyalty and what amounted almost to subservience. He set a personal example of dedication which was a lesson for all. What is more he was so damned nice about it.

In those days you always knew where you were with Edward Heath. He communicated easily. The business and the whipping were precisely and decisively dealt with. Each Thursday evening, when the House was sitting, the programme for the subsequent week, and the whipping demands which were associated with it, were imparted and understood. There was, thereafter, a minimum of change and counter-order. Heath's style was plain, objective and straightforward, with touches of humour introduced here and there to offset the intensity of his approach. He had the job gripped tight and he ran his show like a first-rate, clear-minded executive—which, in fact, is exactly what he showed himself to be in this office.

This was an enlightened appointment—which Macmillan confirmed when he followed Eden. It is questionable whether the Tory Party ever had a tactically more able or more businesslike chief whip, or one who had a keener recognition of the difficulties of a Private Member.

I recall going to see Heath in his room one day in 1959 just after I had, sadly but irrevocably, decided that I could not stand again at the next general election but before I had disclosed this to my constituency chairman.

He listened, without surprise, to my reasons. Then he took each one in turn, dissecting it and probing about to see if a way could be found round it. He was at pains to show that every reasonable facility—and more—would be offered to enable me to continue to combine my increased and increasing business commitments with my work as an M.P. and so allow me to remain in the House.

It was essential, he said, for the party to keep as many Members as it could in the House of Commons with practical, first-hand business experience. The Prime Minister was most anxious that this should be done. Could I not consider all this afresh with my board colleagues and see whether a way might be found . . .?

When I replied that I felt the die was cast but that I hoped it might be possible for me to return to the House again later on, perhaps after another Parliament, he shook his head. When they go voluntarily they never come back.

I recount all this now, almost three decades later, to recapture something of the earlier personality and demeanour of the man who was later to reach the summit of political power and, having attained it, was then subsequently to be rejected by his party and criticized on various counts—for a lack or humanity, an inability to listen and communicate, an aloofness, an obstinate, almost arrogant disregard of others' opinions, an unyielding resolve to reject compromise and a still greater resolve never to accept an opponent's point of view. The allegations are familiar. Whatever their strength, they represent the antithesis of the attributes we came to know in the late 1950s.

Power and responsibility do strange things to those who have to wield them. Sometimes they are carried lightly with an increasing measure of humility, humanity and understanding. And ease. Authority is then gained in the process. Or, again they can affect a chosen son in quite contrary ways and precipitate a release of unfamiliar and unexpected characteristics.

It's a pity there can never be a dress rehearsal.

*   *   *

For a Private Member, the comings and goings of politics, and their constantly shifting patterns, make an absorbing study. The progression of events is like the movement and blending of colours in a brilliant evening sky. Change is ever present. To the student of human reactions, the ups and downs of ministers and leading personalities— then popular and widely acclaimed, now rounded on and often harshly, and unfairly, criticized—these twists of fortune, and their effect upon individuals, fascinate and engross. The exits and the entrances are many. A week can certainly be a long time in politics.

To the civil servants, who sustain the departments of state with infinitely more ability than popular belief accords them, the ebb and flow of ministerial life must seem perplexing. Yet, despite the kaleidoscopic character of the scene, their loyalty and dedication to their political masters, irrespective of party, remains generally constant and genuine.

I well remember an observation of Lord Woolton's soon after Winston Churchill had formed his second administration, following six years of Labour rule, and appointed him Lord President of the Council. He had asked for briefs on two separate subjects. The papers had been produced with an distinctive socialist slant about them. Such was the effect of serving, honestly and habitually, the minds of previous ministers.

'I had to remind the permanent officials that there was a new government and new doctrines,' said Woolton. 'Thereafter the briefs became impressive models of likely Conservative thought.'

*   *   *

As I look back now on my time in the House of Commons, and on the attributes—and defects—of the actors who played on the world stage, I incline to think that the qualities of judgment, ruggedness and philosophical calm, which allow a man, in the face of adversity, somehow to soldier on, count for more in politics than is generally allowed.

Selwyn Lloyd provides a good example of the value of these characteristics. His record, on the face of it, suggests a political career of steady and continuing success. Pause for a moment, and look again at the offices he held. In a quarter of a century he was progressively Minister of State at the Foreign Office, Minister of Supply, Minister of Defence, Foreign Secretary, Chancellor of the Exchequer and then, at the end of the day, when many had thought that the catalogue was complete, Speaker of the House of Commons—and an uncommonly able and well-liked one at that.

Yet I wonder whether any other minister since the Second World War had to take more knocks or contend with more reverses of a kind which would have sunk most than Lord Selwyn-Lloyd.

I count it among the favours which the House of Commons bestowed upon me that I was able to come to know him well. Once again I had golf to thank. Selwyn had been a player of ability, having learned the game in his youth in the hard Hoylake school. He was later to become captain of the Royal Liverpool Golf Club in its centenary year.

Apart from the Parliamentary Golfing Society, of which I was for several years the honorary secretary, there was another friendly and select little society called the Brigands, which I was invited to join. Toby Low, now Lord Aldington, did the organizing. Once or twice a year we all dined together and then arranged to have a meeting at Wentworth, Sunningdale or Walton Heath which for years, remained the spiritual home of parliamentary golf. These were agreeable, jolly days, and the clubs we visited were kind to us, as we were never more than ten or twelve in number and did not get in other people's way. I sometimes played with Selwyn on these and other occasions. A quiet round of golf on a Sunday, beginning at a civilized hour in the morning, when the first tee was usually empty, and returning about 4 p.m. in time for him to dispose of the red boxes and start the week prepared, offered him some relaxation from the exacting ministerial round.

His daughter, Joanna, now an accomplished actress, was born at much the same time as our son Jeremy. Our respective nannies, in whom we were specially blessed, became firm friends, taking on, inevitably, the distinguishing suffix of the family names 'Nanny Lloyd', 'Nanny Lucas'.

Later on, when Selwyn became Foreign Secretary and Chancellor, Harold Macmillan, who always preferred his own home in Sussex to the Prime Minister's country residence in Buckinghamshire, often offered him the use of Chequers. Jill and I, with our nanny and children—for by then we had another son, David—were sometimes asked for the weekend. There was something strangely incongruous and endearing about seeing the children scampering about this old, rather austere Elizabethan house set in the Chilterns which, over the years, had been the scene of so much political activity.

The highlight of a summer visit there was croquet on the lawn after lunch. Whatever endowments Chequers may have enjoyed, a smooth croquet lawn was not among them. The games, therefore, tended to follow an uneven and unusual pattern. They bore Selwyn's unmistakable stamp. Children, private secretaries, nannies, a visiting ambassador or editor, aides—all were marshalled into active participation. There was no contracting out on the score of lack of skill or size. The rules were varied to suit age, individual temperament and special situations. It was not unknown for mallets to be used for purposes other than those intended. Balls had a distracting way of disappearing, irretrievably, into the shrubbery.

One weekend when we were there, the United States' ambassador came to lunch on Sunday. Jock Whitney, whom the newspapers were rather apt to describe as 'the well-known American sportsman and racehorse owner', was a jovial and companionable man. I had golfed with him in America in pre-war days, and indeed retained a vivid recollection of playing on opposite sides to him in a bizarre professional and amateur tournament at the Seminole in Palm Beach just before Hitler walked into Austria. We had, moreover, had some contact in wartime over the work which the joint U.S. and British staffs were doing. The visits he paid to the house at Stanmore which I shared with his two agreeable U.S. Air Force compatriots still remained fresh in my memory.

When Jock Whitney put his hand to something he entered fully into the spirit of it. Croquet was clearly not His Excellency's game, nor did he accept that the rules as laid down by the British Foreign Secretary, or by the Croquet Association, should necessarily have any application for the Court of St James. When we adjourned for tea, with the ambassador perspiring freely and the children hopelessly over-tired, a ball and two hoops were missing and the lawn was in disarray.

Probably the only remaining historical record of this curious interlude in Anglo-American affairs is a nasty ink splodge in the Chequers' visitors' book beside the mark of a somewhat aggressive and impetuous three-year-old.

Chapter Twenty-Seven
We see men with their qualities and their defects

A DECADE in the House of Commons, sustained by the strange processes which go to make up a successful constituency organization, certainly provided, as Churchill had once claimed of it, 'as fine an all-round education in public affairs as any man can obtain'.

For one thing it offered an unusual opportunity for studying, at close quarters, human relations, and indeed human nature, in perhaps the most blatantly revealing circumstances of all—in the environment of power. It is there, in Parliament, 'rubbing shoulders with everyone in the lobbies and elsewhere', that one gets to know people as they really are.

Churchill made this assessment: 'We get to know something about each other when we work together in this House. We see men with their qualities and their defects.'

*　　*　　*

Thinking back, I can see I was lucky to have entered the House of Commons in a vintage year. The general election of February, 1950 produced an influx of Tory members of exceptional quality, some of whom were to emerge among the principal actors who, in the next quarter of a century, were to play their parts on the national and world stage.

Edward Heath, Iain Macleod, cruelly taken from us at the moment when his exceptional talents were most needed by the party, Reginald Maudling, Enoch Powell, Robert Carr, Harold Watkinson, Christopher Soames—these, and a number of others, were soon to make their mark on the Conservative benches.

It was a measure of the strength of the Tory Party in the House in the early 1950s that we had on the front bench a team of outstanding stature and intellectual ability, several members of which were prime ministerial material. After Churchill and Eden, there was a supporting galaxy of names which, in retrospect, makes impressive reading. Harold Macmillan; R. A. Butler; the two Olivers, Stanley and Lyttelton; Derick Heathcoat-Amory; Harry Crookshank; the three lawyers, Walter Monckton, David Maxwell Fyfe and Selwyn Lloyd; Alan Lennox-Boyd; Gwilym Lloyd-George, and others. I doubt whether, at the time, we quite realized the measure of the quality that was there.

In the House of Lords, too, there was impressive strength. The Lords Salisbury, Woolton and Home, each in his own way exceptional, provided an authoritative trinity.

For the Conservative Party at Westminster these were golden years.

No less could be said of Labour. The team which Clement Attlee collected under him when he formed his second administration in 1950 was substantially the one upon which the post-war fortunes of the Socialist Party were built—Ernest Bevin, Stafford Cripps, Herbert Morrison, Hugh Dalton, Hugh Gaitskell, Harold Wilson, Aneurin Bevan, James Callaghan, (Roy Jenkins and Anthony Crosland had still to blossom). Their names were internationally familiar, their stature unmistakable. But for several of Attlee's most senior Ministers, as indeed for the Prime Minister himself, a decade of high office lay behind. The exertions and strains of the great wartime coalition, followed by the heady years of 1945-50, had left their traces. As with the Tories in the early 1960s, with ten and more years of power behind them, exhaustion and staleness were never far away.

It is at least debatable whether the human frame was ever designed to withstand continuously for much more than five years, the physical burdens which high office places upon a cabinet minister in modern times. Only those who have seen close to the unrelenting pressures which are synonymous with present-day government can truly appreciate the nature of the load. The question must be posed: is this compatible with good administration? If, as I suspect, the answer is no, then a further question arises: what should be put in its place?

I once heard Lord Woolton, probably the most successful party chairman of the post-war era, define organization thus: 'The art of organization is the practice of delegation. Delegation for its success depends, first, on knowing what is to be done and, secondly, on finding and choosing the men and women capable of doing it.' It is debatable whether, in the context of contemporary parliamentary government, such a process is offered adequate opportunity to thrive.

Long after he had left the government to return to the private sector of industry, pausing on the way to take his seat in the House of Lords, Lord Chandos (ex-Oliver Lyttelton) expressed a view on this topic which still has significance today.

The opinion was, I recall, dispensed in rather agreeable circumstances. Each autumn Oliver used to ask me to go with him to Wentworth, one of London's best-known clubs, to watch some of the golfing alumni do battle in what was then known as the Piccadilly World Match-Play Championship.

These were delightful days on which the sun always seemed to shine. Usually there were only the two of us, attended by the good Thomas, Lord Chandos's faithful driver, who always had ready for us in the luncheon interval a delicious picnic from a nicely chosen hamper. Thinly sliced smoked salmon, a round or two of fresh brown bread and butter, cold breast of chicken and salad, fresh strawberries and cream, accompanied by an ice-cold bottle of Krug—all this, and Jack Nicklaus, Arnold Palmer and Gary Player, too. Oliver certainly knew how to do things.

This time another Lyttelton, Chandos's cousin Lord Cobham, joined us. Put Charles Cobham and Oliver Chandos together in those days, add the sparkle of fine champagne in the warm autumn sunlight, top it off with just a dash of the aforesaid Palmer, Nicklaus and Player, and there indeed you had a feast fit for the gods.

The conversation went round and round until, amid a welter of imitations (Chandos was an accomplished mimic) and stories surrounding them, we settled momentarily, and on reflection some-what incongruously, upon the advantages and shortcomings of party government.

Quoting Woolton's dictum about organization, I put it to Oliver: 'How effective, administratively, do you think government by cabinet, based upon the principle of collective responsibility, can really be today?'

'In a normal Parliament of four years or so,' he replied, 'it works—

just. But it suited much better the circumstances of forty and fifty years ago.

'Very broadly, the life of a government these days divides itself into three eighteen-month periods. In the first, having seen the books, the Cabinet makes up its mind what must be done. In the second, it does it. The third period is devoted to winning the next general election. It's the middle eighteen-month period which counts.'

Oliver Chandos, with his broad interests in business, politics, sport and the arts, remained throughout his last years an acute observer of the political scene. During the Tory Party's time in opposition in the second half of the 1960s, after its long period of power, he often used to compare the present with the post-war years of Socialist domination when he was himself an indefatigable supporter of the Conservative cause in the constituencies, going round speaking for this candidate and that.

'Under Winston,' I once heard him say, 'we always had a theme. So we did later with Anthony and Harold. The Tory Party needs a theme. Today it hasn't got one, and we lose by it as a result.'

He took each of the Party banners in turn. Churchill's 'Set the People Free'. Eden's 'A Property-Owning Democracy'—an appealing concept in the context of the middle 1950s. And then the Macmillan era, with its spirit of compromise and balance, and the 'One Nation', 'Middle Way', approach.

'Consensus politics' was the stuff of the Macmillan years. To those who wanted the Party to stand very firm on some issue I once heard him say in private: 'Firm, yes, but reasonable: that should always be our way.' This was also largely Churchill's stance in my time in the House. He felt a dampener was needed to quell the passions of post-war socialism.

Now, with Thatcherism, the centre ground has moved perceptibly to the right. Things are brisker, 'drier', if you like, more competitive. But the pendulum will swing back. It has been doing it ever since 1832 and the Reform Bill. The movements are inexorable.

One hesitates to travel far down the road of prophecy, however, for there is a lesson which one learns from having spent some years in the House of Commons and then being out of it altogether. From a seat in Parliament it is relatively easy to form worthwhile judgments and make assessments of trends and events. To attempt to do so from outside is, inevitably, to risk getting it all hopelessly wrong. You have to be in the House of Commons to know what's going on and to recognize the significance of it all. The truth is that on most counts the House is usually about six months ahead of public opinion. And ministers—the good ones—in their turn, tend, on the whole, to be ahead of the parliamentary party in anticipating needs and getting the feel of events.

No better example comes to mind than Churchill's and the Cabinet's handling, in 1954, of the controversial issue of maintaining—at an annual cost then of £50 million—80,000 British troops in the Suez Canal Zone of Egypt. The government had clearly decided it wanted to withdraw them. There were good reasons—financial, strategic and tactical—for doing so. But for an important section of the party in the House of Commons this was, in terms of a British presence in the Middle East, a sacred cow. It wasn't prepared to let the British Army's historic rôle go without a fight. Further, this was a difficult time for Churchill himself. In his advanced age he was becoming excessively autocratic and dictatorial. There were some strong backbench murmurings against him. Much lobbying was going on. The Whips, having taken soundings—a familiar process with major and controversial issues—had established that some Members had strongly held views which they were quite ready to press to the limit.

The climax was reached when the Prime Minister came, with the Minister of Defence, Field Marshal Lord Alexander of Tunis, and the Secretary of State for War, to a full private meeting of the Party in Committee Room 14 upstairs.

Alexander set out the military case. Respected and admired as a man and as an outstanding commander in wartime, he was obviously uneasy in politics and showed neither a liking nor a facility for it. His was a poor political appointment, the more so because he had been reluctant to accept it. It was a mistake of Churchill's to persuade him to take the job.

In the exchanges which followed, the government didn't come out well. Several of the interventions were forceful and hostile. How were we to maintain British prestige in the Middle East if the troops were pulled out of Egypt?

It was at such adverse moments—and, make no mistake, he was now right up against it—that Winston Churchill was at his best. His timing—he did not speak until right at the end—was, as usual, impeccable. Then, without a note, and gazing now and again out of the window and across the river, he let his mind run with a memorable flow of oratory, at once persuasive, authoritative and confident.

With one of those characteristically dogmatic and simple assertions, uttered at some risk, but with absolute conviction and a touch of obstinacy, he ended his remarks abruptly. 'Well, anyway,' he said, pugnaciously standing his ground, 'you cannot maintain prestige with folly.'

That was it. There was nothing else to be said. It was the old knock-out. In a fortnight or three weeks the decision had been forgotten. Life seemed to go on much the same.

*   *   *

The ability of a Prime Minister to handle a difficult private meeting of the party—and to make use of a favourable climate when it is there—is a test of many attributes, above all judgment. To know when and how to put the pressure on, when to coax, when to plead, when to be obstinate and unreceptive, when to give a little—these are skills which come partly from intuition and feeling, which cannot be learned, partly from experience (for history in politics repeats itself again and again), but principally from judgment.

There was none better or more adept at handling a private meeting of the party than Macmillan. Two notable instances come to mind.

The first was in January, 1957 when, having just formed his government, he met the 1922 Committee for the first time as Prime Minister on the reassembly of Parliament after the Christmas recess. He had gained the leadership not by the open electoral process which we know today but by the historic and undemonstrative procedure of the 'magic circle'. Private soundings were taken, attitudes were canvassed and, at the end of the day, a successor 'emerged'. The Queen then sent for the chosen candidate and the new appointment was confirmed.

Each method has its protagonists and its detractors. Old-fashioned and reactionary though it may now seem, I range myself unhesitatingly on the side of the 'magic circle'.

But, have no fear, it is a process which will never return.

Macmillan was undoubtedly the party's first choice, though there had been other strong candidates in the field. Still, when he faced the 1922 Committee, he knew he had been widely acclaimed, and that, even at so sombre a moment in our political life—in the immediate aftermath of the Suez reverse—he would, if he played his hand right, win the support of virtually all. Nevertheless, the balance was finely struck. It was a testing moment at the start of his administration.

Of all Harold Macmillan's performances that I personally witnessed, this was the most adroit, the most compelling, and probably the most effective.

His perception of the prevailing mood was acute. It enabled him to tune his approach exactly. He judged that what the party in the House now wanted was to get the past quickly out of mind. It did not seek to be given a programme. The time for that would come. It longed now for a call to which all could respond and which would allow the passions and divisions of the last weeks and months to be laid quietly to rest.

There were the necessary opening references. The honour, the responsibility, the challenge, the tribute to his predecessor. The past was given no more than a sentence or two. The gaze had now, immediately, to be fastened on the future. Time was short. There could be little more than eighteen months to a general election. By mentioning it early, the Prime Minister had invoked, at the outset, the most telling instrument of all in obtaining unity. Nothing concentrates the collective mind of a party more than to be reminded of the imminence of an election. And the need to win it. It is a device calculated to cement.

'I see the task,' he said, 'in three clearly-defined aims. With your help, I believe each can be achieved.'

First there was the House of Commons. We had to bring the party in the House together quickly. Without this nothing could be done. We had to dominate the House of Commons. 'I can make some contribution here, but this must depend principally upon you. I must rely on you to help me to do that.' All this might take six months to accomplish.

Then there was the party in the country. This had to be pulled together and united behind the lead given from Westminster.

'Again,' he said—and I still recall with acute vividness, despite the passage of some thirty-odd years, the gist of his words—'again, I must look to you. We shall achieve this through you and your work in the constituencies. There is no other way. Ministers can offer help with speeches and so on, but there is no substitute for the work of a Member in the constituency. Therefore, I say this must rest largely with you.' This may take another six months.

'We shall then be left with six months to get the country behind the government and the party. Here, of course, much will depend on the performance of the government during the next twelve months. But again, although I and other ministers can make our contribution, a responsibility must rest upon you in your constituencies to rally the country behind us.'

It was the fast buck. It had squarely been passed to us. How, at such a moment and with such a philosophy, could he fail to get the massive response he wanted? We were on notice. It was up to us, not so much to him and his government. It was the ultimate trick of confidence.

In the result it took no more than two or three weeks to bring the party together in the House of Commons; and very soon Macmillan, with his intellectual and political acumen, was beginning to dominate the exchanges in the Chamber. The constituencies came into line well within the timescale. The country then followed. The great overall majority at the election of 1959 confirmed the completion of Macmillan's vision of little more than two years before.

I doubt whether there can have been, in peacetime, a finer example of political and personal leadership—and of sheer efficiency of thought and performance—than Macmillan's in those first months after his arrival at 10 Downing Street.

The other example of his political astuteness and instinct for dealing with a responsive private meeting came little more than six months later.

It was the end of July and the House was rising for the long summer recess. As usual the Prime Minister came to the last meeting of the 1922 Committee. He was assured of an appreciative welcome. His stewardship over the previous six months had brought about an impressive change in the government's fortunes. It was hard to believe that this was the same party which had reached so low a point the previous December.

Macmillan had it all his own way. Even when there was a question which might be construed as being remotely critical, it was parried with a bland, urbane response which made the interrogation seem fairly pointless. He was at the top of his form.

Just as the chairman was preparing to bring things to a close, Ian Horrobin rose to ask the Prime Minister, as he put it, 'a personal question'. The background hum immediately subsided. A *personal question* to the P.M.? This was something else again. In dead silence, Horrobin put his point. The last two leaders had fallen sick in office and had resigned. It would be a disaster if there was to be a repetition of this. 'Could I, therefore, ask the Prime Minister,' he enquired, 'what he is going to do about a holiday?'

Amid the ripples of relief and amusement, Macmillan seized his chance.

'I am much obliged,' he replied, 'for the enquiry and for the concern for my health and well-being.

'I am, I am glad to say, very well. I enjoy this job. I have fine colleagues around me. They do the work. It's a great change from the days at the Treasury and the Foreign Office when the boxes kept me up until one and two o'clock in the morning.

'Now I sit up in my Vatican City and survey the world and do the thinking. It's rather like being head of a company. The executives get on with it. But they know they can always come up to the chairman if there are difficulties.

'No, I do not feel undue pressure; but I certainly take the point of the enquiry and the sense behind it. It is, indeed, my intention, as time allows, to spend some days during the recess shooting and golfing.'

The response typified the Prime Minister's delegated and detached style of leadership in the early days of his administration. It was noticeable that the longer he stayed in office, the more the pressure mounted and the more tired he became, the less inclined he was to delegate to others and the more he began to do himself.

This tends to be the occupational disease of modern prime ministers.

Chapter Twenty-Eight
Postscript to Parliament
'I want you to come and help us'

BIG BEN was striking two as I parked my car in New Palace Yard. High up over Westminster an aircraft was leaving a strong vapour trail in the sky. In the sharp and clear January atmosphere the trailing level was lower than usual. The pilot was heading north-east—on a line directly from the House of Commons to Downing Street. It all seemed strangely symbolic at the time.

It was 1957 and Harold Macmillan was forming his government. Suez was over and Eden had resigned, destroyed by ill-health and the inexorable course of events. The Conservative Party in the House, at odds with itself over the ill-starred Middle East venture, was now divided and unhappy. In the country its followers were disillusioned. It was a sombre moment in our political and national life.

I had been working in my office in Berkeley Square earlier in the day when Macmillan's private secretary telephoned. The Prime Minister wanted to see me at 2.15. The summons was not unexpected. I had felt, as one sometimes does at such times, that the offer of a job in the government might come.

I was now forty-one and had been a Member of Parliament for seven years. During this period there had been portents of possible promotion. I had been asked, first, if I would become parliamentary private secretary—dogsbody—to one of Churchill's senior ministers and then, later, if I would serve in the Whips' Office. Although I had had to decline both offers because of my business commitments, I remained on good terms with the hierarchy.

Moreover, one of my principal interests in Parliament was aviation—civil and military—and during our time in opposition in 1950-51, in Clement Attlee's second administration, Macmillan had sometimes led for us from the front bench in the debates on the Air Estimates in which, with the usual, faithful band of fifteen or twenty colleagues, I had regularly taken part.

I was not, therefore, wholly unknown to the Prime Minister, although in no sense could I claim to be a friend, still less a marked follower. I had, however, become a determined and open supporter of Macmillan for, quite apart from his personal qualities and political acumen, I felt that his intellectual and administrative powers, allied to a rare ability to speak as well as he could write, without recourse to platitude, cliché or corn, lifted him instantly above his fellow men.

As I walked across Whitehall to Downing Street, following the prophetic overhead course of the aircraft, I was gripped by frustration. Instead of a feeling of excitement and expectancy about the office which was surely to be offered, I was overwhelmed by my personal dilemma.

A few weeks before, over lunch at the Turf Club, I had been sounded by Frank Gentle and Sir Miles Graham, the chairmen (and, in Gentle's case, the chief executive) of G.R.A.'s two principal companies, about the possibility of my succeeding to the managing directorship of the group, which I had joined on leaving the Royal Air Force ten years before. If I accepted, the magnitude of the job would necessitate my retirement from politics at the end of the present Parliament, which might still have two years or so to run. I was then assistant managing director. Apart from my earnings from business, I had no sizable means of my own.

The G.R.A. offer, at once stimulating and challenging, had come right out of the blue. I had not expected it. The prospect of heading up the management of one of Britain's most publicized and controversial companies in the leisure and entertainment field was, to say the least, exciting. This was a group in the public gaze. Its news tended to go on to the front page. The benefits which the appointment would bring to my personal and family circumstances were obvious.

All the same, to have to give up the House of Commons, after all that had gone before, would be a great wrench. I had become absorbed with it all. The friendships I had made there meant a great deal to me.

But once all this was set in perspective, reality dictated the way. I therefore told Gentle and Graham, within the week which was allowed for the decision, that I would let my name go forward to the board and that, if my appointment was confirmed, I would sign a ten-year contract with the company. Ethically speaking, therefore, I was on the hook. The appointment was to be effective from 1 June. I began at once to plan for the day.

And now, as I walked along Downing Street towards Number Ten, past the inquisitive waiting crowd and the flashing cameras, a massive personal problem intruded. The opportunity to serve in a government—and under a Prime Minister to whom one was instinctively drawn—would not recur. What if I was to risk it all and say yes to whatever ministerial offer was now imminent?

The possibility was compelling, the thought tormenting.

Reality again took possession. How, without private means, could a man live and keep and educate a family on a junior ministerial salary which, in those days, was £1,500 a year? It wasn't on; and certainly not when I contemplated the prospect, within a couple of years' time, at the age of forty-three, of being without office, without a seat in Parliament and without a job. And yet . . . and yet . . . the chance of ministerial office beckoned . . .

The Prime Minister, spruce in a dark blue suit and Brigade of Guards tie, was sitting alone in the cabinet room, erect and alert, as I entered. Outstretched arms and hands, with their long, slender fingers, rested on a large writing pad in front of him. The distinguished, greying hair had been freshly dressed. Only the familiar drooping eyelids of the mandarin gave a glimpse of tiredness.

Macmillan motioned me to the chair beside him. Impassive, he paused before he spoke. You could tell the touch of theatre.

'I want you to come and help us. I have seen something of you in the little work we have done together in the House and I hope that you will now accept office in the government.'

Then, picking up a piece of paper from the pad and holding it close to his eyes, he added: 'I want you to go and help Geordie Ward at the Air Ministry as Under-Secretary. You would work well together. Your experience of the Air Force will tell both in the Ministry and in the House of Commons.'

Only then did Macmillan turn and look at me.

I gave my answer and the explanation for it.

'Prime Minister,' I said, 'the fact is that with a family to keep and two sons soon to educate, I just cannot afford to give up all my business interests and accept your offer. It is a mortifying experience, for there is nothing I would sooner do than take this job and serve you. But I cannot honestly contemplate it.'

Macmillan shook his head. 'I so well understand. You have been forthright and, I think, rightly realistic. I run into this problem all too often. It always seems to be the good people who are affected. I'm very sorry; I had hoped to have you in the government.

'Now go away, make your fortune, and come back here in ten years' time.'

It was all over in less than ten minutes.

As I walked away from 10 Downing Street, I noticed neither the quizzical crowd, the reporters, the photographers, nor the questions I was asked. The complexities of life wrapped themselves round me like a cocoon.

By now the vapour trail had vanished from the sky.

*   *   *

I played out the last months of my time in the House of Commons as best as I could, combining my work as the newly appointed managing director of G.R.A. with my parliamentary duties. The pressures were considerable but I knew they could not last for more than a year or so.

Nearly ten years as an M.P. had demanded sacrifices and some privations; they had also bestowed privileges and compensations. In retrospect, it was an experience which I would not willingly have forgone. The satisfaction which came from feeling that one was trying to do something for one's fellow men was an enlivening incentive.

Throughout my time in Parliament I had made a habit of seeing constituents by appointment every other Friday evening in a room in Chiswick Town Hall. I never had an open 'surgery', which is the more common practice. I took the view that if someone wanted to see 'the Member' badly enough he or she would always arrange a time. It added authority to the procedure and increased its importance. I felt this justified the administrative work it entailed.

The executive committee of the local Conservative Association wanted me to have these interviews at the Conservative Party's headquarters on account of the publicity this would bring. I opposed this. I felt it might be embarrassing to constituents who were of another political persuasion. I preferred the neutrality of the town hall. Once elected, I was determined to be impartial and to act—and be seen to act—as the cliché has it, 'without fear or favour in the common interest of all.'

Each appointment was allotted twenty minutes and I always made it a rule to be alone. It involved me in clerical chores, but above all I wanted this to be a personal service and for each constituent to feel able to speak privately and in strict confidence to me. It became a process which, despite its demands, I found greatly rewarding.

The problems which were raised in these talks often fell well outside the usual scope of a Member's responsibility; I tried never to shuffle them off on this account. The pleasure one got from seeing them through far outweighed the effort which this entailed.

Of all the hundreds of cases I dealt with—the successful ones and the failures—one remains embedded in my memory.

One Friday evening an unlikely-looking central European name appeared on the appointments list. Against it my agent had written two words: 'Family matter.' It was soon after the great uprising in Hungary. The hideous newspaper photographs of Soviet tanks in the streets of Budapest pulverizing the local population were still fresh in my mind.

Two Hungarians, father and son, came into the room. They were engineers by trade. Their story, told in scarcely recognizable English, was poignant and frightening. They had escaped, at great risk, over the border into Austria, making for England. There they had waited—the son for his wife and young child, the father for his wife, at a pre-arranged destination. A dangerous plan of escape, involving other relatives, had been prepared. The deadline for the arrival of the three other members of the family had come and gone. Cast down, father and son had made their way to England, there to wait and to hope.

Months had passed and still there had been no news. Then a letter reached the father from his wife. In halting words he translated it to me. It was a heart-rending plea to him to devise some means which might at least offer a hope that the family could one day be re-united. It was sufficient to make me feel that I would not rest until a last, final effort had been made somehow to obtain a passage for mother, wife and child to England.

My good friend, Jack Profumo, was then an under-secretary at the

Foreign Office. Here was a first-rate minister, efficient, punctilious, helpful and human. I put the case to him. He offered no promise, no real hope of success; all he could say was that every effort would be made to help. I passed the news on by letter. Father and son made another appointment to see me. It was only to express thanks—personally. They were much moved by the attempts which the Foreign Office were making.

I heard no more for well over a year. Then one evening, on the list of constituents wanting to see me, the now-familiar Hungarian name reappeared. Father and son came together. They sat down opposite me at the table, stiff and correct, just as they had done more than twelve months before. This time emotion seized them. They found it difficult to speak. But words didn't matter. The tears told the story. Mother, wife and child were here.

5

Changing
Balance Sheets

Chapter Twenty-Nine
You must spend money to make money

IT WAS against a background of newspapers, the Royal Air Force and a first excursion into politics, that I decided, on leaving the Service after the war, to embark upon a civilian career with the Greyhound Racing Association. Known to one and all as G.R.A., this securely established and highly publicized company operated in the sports promotion and entertainment field.

My introduction to the organisation owed much to the encouragement of one of its two founders, Brigadier-General Alfred Cecil Critchley, a member of that select group of Canadians who settled in Britain in the inter-war years to make their mark upon the country's commercial and industrial life.

General Critchley, 'Critch' to his friends and 'General' to everyone else, was a formidable character, energetic, restless, always fully charged and (whether he actually felt like it or not) exuding confidence, fitness and high spirits. He worked hard, played hard and lived his life to the full, sixteen hours of every waking day.

Born in Calgary, Alberta, in 1890, he was twenty-eight by the time the Armistice was signed in 1918 and had become the youngest brigadier-general in the Canadian Army, a substantial figure in his own right, with an exceptional and well-decorated war record behind him. Within a decade of the ending of the Great War he had, in partnership with an engaging American named Charles Munn, established greyhound racing in Britain by means of a brilliantly conceived promotional exercise which began at Belle Vue, Manchester, on 24 July 1926. That was the effective start of G.R.A.— not to be confused with the National Greyhound Racing Club, later the sport's governing body.

Over the next remarkable years, the company, sustained by he popularity and financial success of its greyhound racing activities, quickly became one of the leading entertainment groups in Britain. Offering its equity to the public, G.R.A. saw its shares become a hit on the London Stock Exchange—not, perhaps, a currency for widows and orphans (although a few of them didn't do so badly out of it) but a nice speculation in the halcyon days for some.

Within a very few years of the opening at Belle Vue, the organization had spread its interests countrywide. London, Birmingham, Manchester, Edinburgh . . . G.R.A.'s stadiums in these cities (the total of racecourses was soon to rise to nine) became synonymous with enterprise, immaculate presentation, imaginative and aggressive promotion, lively publicity and large crowds.

The White City in London, built initially for the Olympic Games in 1908, and later to become virtually derelict, was taken over in 1927 and turned into an arena famous across the world as a home of international sport—of athletics, of boxing, of show jumping and the rest. But its name and prestige, like that of G.R.A., its parent company, rested upon the success of its greyhound racing and the money which was made out of it.

The first thirty-seven meetings at Belle Vue in 1926 had played to total attendances of upwards of 333,000. But when, later, the business at White City rose to its initial peak, the crowd never fell below 40,000 in an uninterrupted stretch of fifty meetings.

The Greyhound Derby, the principal classic race in the greyhound racing calendar, developed over the years into one of the major events in British sport. The roar from the packed stadium on Final night became a legend. Mounting steadily to a striking crescendo as the electric hare approached the starting traps, and held at that pitch throughout the pulsating seconds of the 525 yards' race, it was never exceeded at Wembley, Hampden or Cardiff Arms Park.

Four greyhounds, Mick The Miller, Patricia's Hope, Mile Bush Pride and Pigalle Wonder, the first two with two Derby victories apiece to their credit, became, in their respective reigns, favourites in millions of British homes, and drew immense crowds to the White City for the annual greyhound racing fiesta. People travelled the length of the country and from Scotland, Ireland and Wales to see them run. They were the personalities of their times.

Critchley, to whom so much of this achievement was directly and indirectly due, was an outstanding publicist. He employed all the tricks to keep his own name and that of the company before the public. He regarded this as one of his first responsibilities, and an essential ingredient in G.R.A.'s success.

He always paid close attention to his business entertaining.

It embraced, among others, editors, managing directors of the newspaper groups and columnists. In London, away from G.R.A.'s premises, it was done mostly at the Savoy.

When he was in the United States, which was not infrequently—it was five days there and five days back by boat in those days—he maintained the same frequent dialogue with the sports columnists on the New York papers—Joe Williams, Bill Coram, Richards Vidmer, Dan Parker and the rest. They came to the Ritz-Carlton to see him.

New promotions, coming attractions, provocative arguments and controversial ideas flew all over the place in a sort of dizzy, fast-moving, newsreel of events. He had both a good news sense and a flair for creating talking points.

You got the feeling with Critch in those days that he was pushing things along hard because time was running out. There seemed to be an urgency to construct and create and build. New events were always happening—or about to happen. Everything was done in style in a big way and only the best would do; furnishings in the executive offices, the company's notepaper, his Rolls-Royce, his well-fitted caravans, his silk shirts, his suits, his hand-made shoes—it was the best or not at all.

'You've got to spend money to make money,' he used to say.

He spent plenty; and, at that time, he also made it.

He struck the famous G.R.A. motif with the heads of three greyhounds, racing neck and neck together; he gave the company its colours, blue and yellow, and got the manufacturers to make him up some special golf balls with blue and yellow dots painted on them. He ordered a supply of striped golf umbrellas in the same colours.

He discovered that the letters 'G.R.A.' were the motor registration serial for an area in the north of England, so he acquired GRA 1 to 37 and put them on the company's cars and vans. He carried GRA 1 on his own Rolls-Royce. He had cufflinks fashioned in coloured enamel, with the three greyhound heads on either side, and distributed them to his friends.

When he ran for Parliament a third time (he won Twickenham in a by-election) he drove round the constituency on polling day in a four-in-hand, dressed in grey top hat and tail coat; he held the seat for the Conservatives with an increased majority against the run of the tide.

He looked after the staff in the company and knew most of them personally and by name. They were on their toes; morale was high, discipline was good. Their loyalty was undoubted. He made G.R.A. count for much in their lives.

With the success of greyhound racing inevitably there came criticism. And, from one or two familiar quarters, hostility.

Legislation was passed through Parliament. The Betting and Lotteries Act of 1934 gave the new sport its charter and set a pattern by which it has been rigorously controlled ever since. It makes the more recent betting and gambling laws look lax by comparison.

In the early 1930s, when the government was taking the 1934 Bill through the House of Commons, the then Home Secretary, Joynson-Hicks, one day made some predictably disparaging (and, as it turned out, ill-judged) remarks about greyhound racing at the dispatch box. Moore-Brabazon, the member for Wallasey, who had been a director of G.R.A. since the company's early days, was in his place in the Chamber. Declaring his interest in the usual way, he asked the Home Secretary whether he had ever watched the sport. A negative answer gave Brab the chance to lay it out on a plate.

In view of his Rt Hon. Friend's reply, had he called for, and received, a report from the police? Again the answer was no. The rest of the exchanges left Joynson-Hicks running for cover with the undertaking that a police report would be sought and laid on the table for the House to see.

An adroit Member of Parliament, acting openly, with proper discretion and judgment, and possessing at first-hand all the facts, can make pulp of a minister who hasn't taken the trouble to brief himself on a specialized topic.

When the report was eventually published, the police gave greyhound racing a clean bill of health and commended its organization and control. In fact, over the fifty years of its existence, the relationship between the industry and the police has always been frank, trusting and based upon mutual confidence and respect. Much of this is due to the seeds which Critch sowed early on. And to the disciplines he himself imposed.

'Greyhound racing,' I once heard him say to a group of news-papermen in New York, 'is the easiest sport in the world to run crooked; it's also the easiest sport to run straight. It's not in the interest of the promoter to run it crooked; the public will soon sense it, lose confidence and stay away. It's then the hell of a job to get them back.'

*   *   *

There were no half measures with Critch. His friends were devoted to him and would rally passionately to his defence; his enemies regarded him as a bounder.

After taking charge, as an air commodore, of the pre-flying training of all Royal Air Force aircrew for the first three years of the Second World War, he became director-general of British Overseas Airways. When this controversial appointment was being considered by the Government, Brendan Bracken, then a member of the Cabinet, strongly supported the nomination. Pressed by the Prime Minister, Brendan had to admit that Critch was rather apt to go at things 'like a bull in a china shop.'

'Two bulls in a china shop', retorted Churchill.

We had some great days together, not least with Johnny, Critch's eldest son by an earlier marriage, a fine, hard young Canadian with many of his father's characteristics and qualities. He volunteered for the Scots Guards in London at the outbreak of war and was killed fighting Rommel in the Western Desert. This was a grievous blow to Critch, the more so because Johnny was a close companion who shared many of his father's interests.

But, given time, life tends to find its compensations. It was thus a special joy to him, in the cruel years of blindness which overtook him towards the end of his life, that Jeepie (Bruce), the son of his successful marriage with Diana Fishwick, should by then have been knocking at the door which was ultimately to lead to the highest international honours that golf has to offer. It made an absorbing and enriching interest as twilight turned into night.

Judge a man by his friends, and a master by his servants, and you could only find in Critch's favour. Allen, his chauffeur, and George, his valet, would have followed him through hell-fire; and when George died he extracted from Fred Robson, the golf professional at the club at Addington, near London, a marvellously loyal and kind little character called 'Tich' who was Fred's caddie, factotum and Man Friday. Tich began caddying for Critch, and later became his valet. The transition was a tortuous affair, but Critch, with uncharacteristic patience, persevered with the training. It succeeded wonderfully—for both.

Tich had an unobtrusively friendly manner and a humour which, mostly, he kept to himself. Critch used to tell the story of a golf match he lost when everything seemed to go wrong for him and monstrously right for his opponent. As they walked disconsolately back to the clubhouse together from some distant point out on the course, Tich broke the silence.

'D'yer know,' he said, 'if we'd 'ave done a 'ole in one today we'd 'ave lost it.'

I shall always carry with me one enduring and cherished memory of this remarkable Canadian. The social clubs of London compete in a golf tournament each year for the Bath Club Cup. It is played at Woking by foursomes, with pairs representing the respective clubs. Humphrey Legge, who was then, I think, the chairman of the golf Committee, asked me one day in the Bath Club, towards the end of the 1940s, if I would pick a partner and play for the club in the competition that summer. I hadn't given up playing in tournaments by then, so I said I would.

'Who do you want to play with?' he asked.

'Critch,' I said.

'Good heavens! ' Humphrey's comment was understandable. Critch was then nearly sixty and long past his best; besides we had a number of other good players in the club. But I was anxious to ask him; he had always been a first-rate foursomes partner and was still a fierce competitor. Moreover, because we got on so well together, I knew it would appeal to him to have a go—particularly if he was told that others in the club thought he was too old and past it.

Critch threw himself headlong into the spirit of the thing; he practised as he hadn't practised since pre-war days. I don't suppose he ever tried harder to win any competition in his life. The nearer we got to the end, the keener and more competitive he became. I could see he was aching to win. The spectre of failure began to hang over my game like an early morning nightmare.

Having won the semi-final in the morning of the last day, we walked briskly on to the first tee together after lunch for the final against the Guards Club. Critch's tail was right up. 'Goddam it,' he said, 'we'll win this match if it's the last thing you and I do.'

It wasn't, perhaps, the easiest base from which to start.

The outcome is of little interest now. What matters is that whereas I, trying like the very devil, missed several holeable putts in the round, Critch rattled them in from all over the place with that upright and abrupt rapping stroke which either sent them bolting into the hole, or (for his partner) several ghastly feet past. He finished the game off with another determined ten-footer on the seventeenth green.

A few years afterwards, very soon after he had gone blind, I made, over lunch, some sympathetic remark about his ill luck.

'Never mind,' he said, brushing it shortly aside, 'I can still see Humphrey Legge's face that day we won at Woking.

'He had laid me 10-1 before the tournament. I took it in tenners.'

Chapter Thirty
Cloth cap or top hat?

THE AFTERMATH of war, with its unreal and short-lived economic climate, brought boom days to greyhound racing, the like of which its founders could never have contemplated even in their wildest moments of fantasy. Attendances, and the betting turnover on the totalizator, escalated. The profits of the promoting companies nudged the roof. Dividends on equity capital followed the upward trend. Greyhound racing quickly became the second largest spectator sport in Britain after football—a distinction which it has retained over the years.

G.R.A.'s London headquarters, when I joined in 1946, were still at 70 Pall Mall. Another two years were to elapse before we moved to larger premises at 20 Berkeley Square, where the staff could be accommodated under one roof. Pall Mall was familiar territory. As an undergraduate in my last year at Cambridge, I had spent a vacation at work there (unpaid) at General Critchley's invitation. Then, in 1942, soon after I had returned from the Mediterranean and Malta, Critch had offered me a seat on the board of the White City Stadium, one of G.R.A.'s subsidiary companies.

'There will be a place for you in G.R.A. after the war', he said, 'if you feel like joining us when you leave the Service. A directorship of the White City now could be a convenient stepping stone.'

And so began an association which was to last for the next thirty-four years, until my retirement from the company at the end of 1976. In the interim I became first, in 1946, assistant to the administrative director—a sort of dogsbody to the two principal executives. Then, in the mid-1950s, I moved on to be assistant managing director before being appointed managing director in 1957. I was to hold this office for eight years, until my election as chairman of the company in 1965.

Greyhound racing's remarkable rise in Britain had one important by-product. The profits generated by the larger promoting companies enabled them to use their stadiums and arenas for a variety of other sports and activities. The success of G.R.A.'s racing programmes indirectly made possible the staging of a series of great international events at London's White City.

There was the unforgettable October evening in 1954 when the red-headed Christopher Chataway challenged and, in one last, desperate throw of courage, finally beat off the great Vladimir Kuts over 5,000 metres in front of a stamping, yelling crowd of more than 50,000 in one of the most thrilling foot races ever run in Britain.

On another summer's evening in the same stadium a few seasons later, four runners, with Britain's Derek Ibbotson at their head, miraculously for those days, each ran a sub-four minute mile as the hands of the time clock, exposing the significance of the performance, lifted a massive, chanting audience to its feet in spontaneous recognition. Ibbotson's world record of 3 mins 57.2 secs that Friday night injected hope and heart into a new generation of British athletes.

It was at the White City, too, on an evening in July 1948, that London's own Freddie Mills, throwing a torrent of punches, hammered the American, Gus Lesnevich, into defeat to bring the Light-Heavyweight championship of the world to Britain for the first time since 1903. This fight was staged before another 50,000 gate, the largest post-war crowd ever to witness an act of pugilism in the capital.

Under the floodlights of the same arena, and in front of Her Majesty Queen Elizabeth II and 30,000 of her dutiful subjects, Harry Llewellyn rode Foxhunter—the favourite showjumping pair of them all—to win their third King George V Cup in the Royal International Horse Show: one of the great moments of sport, which B.B.C. Television took live into four million captivated British homes.

Then, over on the other side of London, in Harringay's indoor arena, the Russians brought perfection and elegance to the circus with two remarkable three-week runs which transformed the big top from sweat and stink and sawdust into a polished, theatrical production, beside which Britain's familiar counterparts looked a drab and unimaginative second-best. Tom Arnold, with the redoubtable Clem Butson at his side, staged his winter ice shows and Jack Hylton presented symphonies to the masses. Jack Solomons, with no more

A master pilot with his two nephews. Group Captain Sir Douglas Bader with Jeremy and David Lucas at Albufeira, Portugal, August 1965.

After the ball . . . with Dixie (Major R. L.) Alexander, stalwart of the U.S. 8th, 12th and 15th Air Forces in World War II, and former U.S. Eagle Squadron pilot; at the Churchill, Portman Square, September 1990. Dixie had flown over with other surviving 'Eagles' for the fiftieth anniversary of the Battle of Britain.

My wife—to whom I and our devoted family owe so much. Jill Addison and I met at Thatch Cottage, Sunningdale, then the home of an old friend, Francis Ricardo, on 25 February, 1945 while I was still commanding No. 613 (Mosquito) Squadron in France. Victory then intervened and on 22 May, 1946 we were married at the Grosvenor Chapel with the Royal Air Force offering strong support.

For my wife Jill, there was a variety of duties. Presenting the White City Stadium cup at the Royal International Horse Show, July 1967.

Managing Director G.R.A. Property Trust, 1957-65,
Chairman, 1965-1975.

'The aftermath of war, with its unreal and short-lived economic climate, brought boom days to greyhound racing, the like of which its founders could never have contemplated. . . .'
Highly trained greyhounds racing flat out touch nearly forty miles per hour.
(Photograph by courtesy of the British Greyhound Racing Federation.)

'I took it in tenners'.
With Critch—Brigadier-General A. C. Critchley—co-founder of the Greyhound
Racing Association and a former director-general of British Overseas Airways,
summer 1948.

Sports Council, Northern Ireland, 1977. (*Left to right*): Jimmy Hill, Laddie Lucas, Lieutenant-General Sir James Wilson.

than the mutual trust of our respective words as a contract, promoted his monthly boxing programmes in a sustained sequence of success which, for the consistency of its support, can find few parallels in the history of the Noble Art. The Horse of the Year Show became an annual sell-out and, together with the Royal International Horse Show at the White City and with the backing of television, gave a fillip to the horse in Britain from which so much equestrian activity has since flowed.

The Ford Motor Company, with the tough and resilient Patrick Hennessy at its head, launched its Three Graces—the Zodiac, the Zephyr and the Consul—with a cleverly conceived week's display which for the first time took the limelight away from the traditional Motor Show at Olympia. Through the impact of its originality and timing, Ford scored a walloping sales success.

The scene then changed as a fair-haired and personable young preacher from the United States named Billy Graham, with the confidence of God in his heart, set a record in evangelism in Britain which for duration and the strength of its support, is never likely to be equalled.

Apart from one critical (and hushed-up) crunch period at the start of the second week, when his standard bearers and devoted adherents had to work overtime to marshal the troops, Graham played (there is nothing irreverent in the word) to packed congregations over which Solomons, Arnold, Hylton and others must have cast envious eyes.

Graham was an impresario in his own right. He knew all the tricks of presentation and promotion. He gathered around him, for his nightly spectaculars, a well-drilled and eminently attractive cast, at the centre of which was a young, predominantly female choir, neatly and appealingly dressed in white blouses and navy blue skirts, to lend a freshness to the proceedings exactly in keeping with the star's own special appeal. Here and there, the presence of a negro participant showed that he was well ahead of the game.

In person, I found Graham an honest, direct and unaffected man. He was utterly devoted to his task, no doubt of that. His was 'A Crusade'—and he meant it to be nothing else. He never gave failure a thought—even in private.

He had a pair of young and very bright American professionals to advise him. One, a lawyer, who conducted the negotiations for the three months'—*yes, three months'*—hire of the arena, would have been a match for any of his counterparts in show business.

A flat, basic rent of £10,000 for the period, plus all the trappings, was, we thought, in the money values of those days, pushing it a bit. It was accepted instantly and without demur. At once the thought nagged: 'Why didn't we double it?'

When the agreement had been signed and the documents exchanged, I took Graham's lawyer to one side.

'Do you honestly think,' I asked, 'that Dr Graham will be able to fill Harringay, all 10,000 or 11,000 seats of it, for three months on end? I tell you, there's no entertainment in London—ice shows, circuses and the rest—which could.'

The answer was positive, confident and serious, and delivered with a penetratingly straight eye.

'The Lord will give His answer.'

He did.

*   *   *

Later on, and probably five years ahead of its time, G.R.A. saw the potential which golf, properly presented and promoted, possessed as a participant sport with mass-appeal. Stimulated and provoked by the growing use of television, and the idolizing of the dollar millionaires—Palmer, Nicklaus and Player—the game was beginning to attract a new public whose pockets, in the past, had allowed them to do no more than sniff tentatively at the fringes of the game.

Led by the realistic and progressive Yorkshire mind of John Jacobs, Britain's Dr Golf, we pioneered the concept of the 70 to 150-acre, comprehensive golf centre, with floodlit driving range, nine-hole mini and conventional length courses, instructors, well-stocked shop, bar, restaurant and facilities for the family. Here a beginner could be taken, without inhibition, through all stages of the game, and the average player could flourish.

The opening acts of the operation met their difficulties, but we set a pattern which, considering its now proved trading success, should, in the next quarter of a century, provide the blueprint for public golf. With land and capital at a premium, there is no other way of offering so much, in golfing, social and family terms, for a comparable investment.

*   *   *

However, as other sectors of Britain's commercial life have found to their cost, financial success, politics and the Treasury do not make comfortable or enduring bedfellows.

With the country returning to more normal living, the boomtide of greyhound racing was on the turn anyway when Hugh Dalton, in his short stay at the Exchequer, slapped a ten per cent pool betting duty on the greyhound totalizator—alone. Horserace betting went free. The cloth cap of the White City patron was taxed while the grey toppers of Ascot escaped. It was a curious piece of Socialist philosophy. The cry went up from the tribunes: 'One law for the rich and another for the poor.'

For seventeen long years, greyhound racing, alone in the racing field, carried this discriminatory impost. The sport's lifeblood was draining away. It wasn't until Reginald Maudling, during his sojourn at the Treasury, had the knowledge and the guts—for reductions in betting taxes are never politically popular—to tackle the problem, that the duty was cut to five per cent. That was, at least, a lifeline.

Not many months later, after R. A. Butler, in a burst of reforming zeal, had replaced the prostitutes with betting shops in the High Street and, with the establishment of commercial bingo and casinos, had brought hard gambling to Britain for the first time, James Callaghan, rightly, redressed the balance of betting taxation by going for an equitable two and a half per cent duty right across the board. By this time, however, Butler's 1960 Betting and Gaming Act, which was to set loose an unprecedented nationwide gambling spree, with a turnover running not into hundreds of millions but thousands of millions—billions—was beginning to deal greyhound racing some lethal blows.

Chapter Thirty-One
Attack and assassination

HIGH SUMMER, 1963, was important for G.R.A. By now the new laws were biting deep and affecting the company's results. It was a combination of factors which made the competition at once so fierce and so unfair. The rules which governed the operation of betting shops, casinos and commercial bingo halls were liberal by comparison with the circumscribing controls with which, thirty years before, Parliament had strung up the greyhound racing industry.

Licensed betting offices could operate throughout the day, every day of the week except Sunday, all the year round. So, effectively, could bingo halls. Gaming, too, enjoyed exceptional latitude, the casinos being allowed to remain open through the night as well as during the day. By comparison greyhound racing, which had been bypassed by Butler's legislation, remained in a straitjacket. It was obliged to face its competitors with one hand tied behind its back.

At this time, while the gambling free-for-all was gathering momentum, greyhound racecourses could only be operated twice a week—104 meetings a year. All tracks in the same licensing area had to hold their meetings on the same days and compete against one another. If a race meeting was lost because of weather or some other technical reason, it could not later be replaced. No more than eight races could be run in any one race programme. The duration of a meeting was limited.

The percentage which a promoter could retain from the totalizator turnover, his principal source of revenue, to 'defray expenses', was set by Parliament in 1934 at six per cent. It was still six per cent thirty years later, in Butler's time. If six per cent was right in 1934, with rising costs it certainly wasn't still right in 1963.

Unlike in the United States, where a totalizator monopoly exists on the racecourse, the operator of a greyhound stadium in Britain has by

216

law to provide 'reasonable facilities' for bookmaking on his track. But the 'rent' which a bookmaker pays for his right to stand is limited to five times the admission price of the enclosure in which he sets up his pitch. If the entrance fee was ten shillings (anyone remember what that used to be worth, by the way?) in 1963, his 'rent' for standing at a single meeting was fifty bob, or £260 for the 104 meetings in the year, irrespective of the size of his turnover. In addition to this, the greyhound racing totalizator, unlike its horse race counterpart, could not take bets off-course. It was strictly an on-course operation.

Another, and most telling, factor also militated against the sport. The amount of money available for betting on horses and dogs had remained relatively steady over the years. Generally, there was only so much cash about for the various betting activities. But when new gambling opportunities were created, as they were by Butler, the existing outlets were bound to suffer. The betting offices provided an immediate counter-attraction for the cash which had, hitherto, been finding its way on to the greyhound racecourses. Greyhound punters were fair game for weaning on to horse or dog betting in the shops. By 1977 off-course betting on greyhounds was running at an astonishing £350 million annually.

Yet again, unlike horse racing, the greyhound racing industry was not accorded by Parliament a statutory levy on its off-course betting turnover to counter the flight of money away from the tracks into the shops—despite the fact that it was supplying the medium, at its own expense and its own risk, on which the growing volume of betting was being done.

To add to the problem, the women, who for years had enjoyed a night out at the dogs, now found a new appeal in the plush comfort of the bingo halls which were springing up all over the country.

For close on forty years, ever since its start, greyhound racing had never had to contend with such alternatives; nor would it have flinched from having to do so now had the competition been fair. But it wasn't. Almost overnight, a chill draught had begun to penetrate right through the industry.

At this bleak moment, and getting his timing exactly right, Oliver Jessel, using his Jessel Securities as the vehicle, turned his attentions to G.R.A. His aim was to obtain control of the company by first getting control of the board. His offensive was to have a profound effect upon the future of the group. Things were never to be the same again.

*   *   *

Jessel, thirty-four at the time and Rugby-educated, was already establishing himself as a name in the City of London. He was certainly not standing still. Only progress of an aggressively acquisitive kind would satisfy the commercial talents and instincts which were quickly becoming manifest.

As things turned out, he failed to win control of G.R.A. by a short head, principally because he went for board rather than equity dominion. His cash resources at the time may well have dictated his tactics. Had his raid come four or five years later, with all the experience and success which the interim would have brought him, I find it difficult to see how he could have failed.

In the event, with the aid of our accomplished trinity of advisers—Daniel Meinertzhagen of Lazards, Rupert Nicholson of Peats, and H. W. (David) Higginson of Herbert Smith, between them merchant banker, accountant and solicitor of quality—coupled with the loyalty of G.R.A.'s small shareholders, who made up seventy per cent of the company's register, the line held firm. Just.

But Jessel, for whom I had, as G.R.A's managing director at the time of the battle, developed a lively regard, both personally and commercially, had tossed a telling chunk of stone into the company's pool. The ripples were not long in reaching the shore. We now had to act with all speed. There was an imminent danger that the attacker, having failed once, would try a second time. New defences had to be fashioned.

For several years some of us in the greyhound racing industry had watched, with increasing respect, the performance of a well-run, progressive, family-controlled company in south-east London called Catford Stadium Ltd. The principal founder, Frank Sutton, had died in late middle age. Now the cares of office had fallen unexpectedly early on his son, an only child, who, after school at Westminster, had already learned much of the practical side of operating a greyhound company with Brighton and Hove Stadium Ltd, of which he was later to become managing director. There he had done, in turn, most of the jobs in the business.

At Catford, John Sutton, then in his late twenties, had brought a freshness and an originality to the promotion of the sport. He had flair, courage and a propensity for attracting the public gaze which set him apart from his contemporaries. He was a dominant shareholder in his company.

Sutton had hit the bull's eye at Catford by introducing, against all advice (not least, legal), a Tote Jackpot pool. Offering the attraction of a potentially large dividend for a small stake, it was an instant success. The Horserace Totalizator Board later cribbed the idea, and G.R.A. went for its own Quinela pool. It took strength and imagination to scoop the market. It put him ahead of his competitors.

I, therefore, proposed to Sutton that, with the temporary withdrawal of Jessel, an opportunity was now at hand, which would not recur, of a merger between our two companies on a shares-and-cash basis. If such a plan went through, with the issue of new G.R.A. shares to friendly hands, he would be left with a strong individual shareholding in G.R.A. which would thereby be fortified. At his age (he was still just under thirty), he would have considerable scope for the future. But time was short; Jessel must be expected to raid again soon.

The deal, master-minded for the company by Lazards, and by Warburgs for Catford, was accomplished in six hectic weeks, give or take a few days. Two million new G.R.A. shares passed into trusted hands and the group obtained the services of indisputably the brightest and most fertile of the younger minds in the strange world of greyhound racing. The company, now reinforced, braced itself for Jessel's next move.

It never came.

A dozen or so years later, in the aftermath of the appalling collapse of the Heath-Barber economic strategy, Oliver Jessel invited John Sutton and myself to lunch at the Garrick Club. It was a sombre moment in our respective lives. G.R.A. was, by then, itself struggling to hold its head above water, but Jessel Securities, after a meteoric rise, had succumbed in the holocaust. As usual, the assassins were now busying about their work.

I was glad to be able to remind Oliver of a couple of sentences Patrick Sergeant had written in his column in the *Daily Mail* only a day or two before. It struck me that, not perhaps for the first time, Patrick had got it about right.

'There are too many people,' he wrote, 'who, never having made anything in their lives, cannot forgive the mistakes of others. Anyone can make a mistake, but a fool makes it twice.' (*Daily Mail*, 12 December 1975.)

Chapter Thirty-Two
Las Vegas looked over its shoulder . . .

WITH JESSEL behind us, it was plain, as we moved into the second half of the 1960s, that the conventional and long accepted policies of G.R.A. could not endure. Change had to come.

Britain was now on its way to capturing the title of the Gambling Centre of the World. Las Vegas looked over its shoulder and saw a shadow creeping up behind. Greyhound racing was becoming an isolated activity in this new environment, isolated by the legal anachronisms under which it had been forced to labour. Too many inadequately appointed racecourses were chasing too few customers.

Against this background, it was clear that the number of tracks in the country would have to be drastically reduced if the sport was to survive in strength. And G.R.A. would have to modernize those which were ultimately to remain in order to compete with the comforts and attractions of the finely furnished, slap-up places of entertainment which were now to be found in town and city centres.

There was another consideration which was greatly concerning shareholders. The massive property boom in Britain was riding high. Land values were escalating as favourable changes of use were obtained. Stockholders, egged on by stories in the financial press, became restless and pressed boards to seek variations in planning consents to realize the potential—imaginary or otherwise—in their stadiums.

There was no way in which a board of directors of a company like G.R.A. could turn a blind eye to these new conditions—and remain in office—while greyhound racing attendances were slumping. With its extensive freehold properties, the pressures on G.R.A. to take on the rôle of developer began to mount rapidly.

By this time, in 1965, top management changes had taken place within the company. John Sutton, now G.R.A.'s largest, non-corporate shareholder, and strongly established after the Catford merger, had succeeded me as managing director. Sir Miles Graham, the chairman, who had played a notable rôle during Jessel's attack, and had served the group for more than thirty years before retiring, became president. I had succeeded him in the chair. These dispositions were to remain in being for the next nine, hectic years.

*   *   *

When we declared our new policy, the support of shareholders and financial press alike was immediate and undoubted. The board would rationalize its greyhound interests and reduce the number of its racecourses. The ultimate target was to retain four, or perhaps five stadiums in London, and one in each of the principal provincial cities. These would be modernized to a high standard. The surplus properties thrown up by the rationalisation would either be sold or redeveloped in order to finance the modernizing process.

To give expression to this new policy, and to gain the means whereby it could be implemented, we had first to obtain control of the nerve centres of the sport in those areas where G.R.A. wished to consolidate. To reduce the overall number of tracks we had to make acquisitions which would, in their turn, pave the way for the reductions. To have set about it in any other way would have handed some part of the reduced business on a plate to our competitors.

We pressed ahead with our plan throughout the second half of the 1960s with a series of takeovers, mergers and purchases. By the early 1970s we were within sight of the final goal.

One hurdle blocked the forward march.

On the periphery of the north-eastern sector of London lay two dominating stadiums—Harringay, which belonged to G.R.A., and Walthamstow, a family-controlled business, which had been founded in the inter-war years by Billy Chandler, the bookmaker. Charles Chandler, of the next generation, now ruled the company. His son, also Charles, still in his twenties, worked with him on the board.

The valuable 24-acre site at Harringay, comprising the stadium and former indoor arena, was ripe either for refurbishing (at an unacceptable cost) or for redevelopment. It was, in the jargon of the times, 'an interesting situation'. The Greater London Council had shown some sympathy for the idea of a total redevelopment (including some local authority housing) or, alternatively, a mixed development, embracing a new and much smaller stadium, tailored to suit latter-day greyhound racing needs.

To deal with the project comprehensively—for racing as well as for development—it was most desirable that Walthamstow should first be absorbed by G.R.A. If a complete redevelopment was to take place at Harringay, the greyhound business could then be substantially transferred to Walthamstow, a well-equipped, well-patronized and successful stadium on which significant sums had been, and were being, spent. Here, indeed, was a natural solution. An opportunity was fashioned for G.R.A. to acquire a thirty-two per cent stake in Walthamstow at a cost of some £235,000 or £2 a share—a very competitive price.

When John Sutton and I discussed the proposal with Charles Chandler, who enjoyed the formidable title of governing director, and who effectively dictated the Company's affairs, two cardinal points found ready acceptance with both parties. With the acquisition of the holding,

   (i) Chandler's son, Charles, would join the board of G.R.A. as an executive and work under Sutton, the group managing director, while still retaining his directorship of Walthamstow, and,

   (ii) As soon as the circumstances were propitious, the two companies would be merged.

When the deal was put to the G.R.A. board, Verner Wylie, a managing director of Lazards, and an intellectually able and perceptive merchant banker, expressed his doubts about the wisdom of allowing the proposed merger to rest upon the word of one man. It should be obtained in writing. Strange things, he said, could happen in families.

Chandler would not have such a written undertaking; he felt an understanding reached in good faith across the table was sufficient. Besides, his son would be joining the board of G.R.A., while still continuing as a director of Walthamstow, so an intimate relationship would exist between the two companies.

On this basis the stake was acquired. The young Chandler joined G.R.A. and, in due course, became managing director of the grey-hound racing and leisure division under Sutton, the group managing director. All the while for the next six years, his father, with a series of equivocal delaying moves, and using the strength of his individual position, parried one attempt after another to bring the two companies together. This deliberate resistance by Chandler was later to lead to argument, embarrassment, acrimony and mistrust, and, later still, and indirectly, to a recourse to the courts.

Looking back now with all the advantages of hindsight, I incline to think, on balance, that having seen his son safely on to the board of G.R.A., and with (at one time) a million or so G.R.A. shares in the Walthamstow locker, he never had the slightest intention of allowing a merger to take place.

Wylie was thus proved right; and we, manifestly, were wrong.

*   *   *

Meanwhile, the greyhound racing industry, fighting for its life after Butler, turned its hand to winning a few piecemeal amendments to some of the more unreasonable and outmoded parts of the existing law by which the sport remained gripped. To get Parliamentary approval for changes in betting legislation is always a delicate business. The House of Commons tends to be allergic to gambling in most of its forms. Hot potatoes are not normally picked up with enthusiasm.

By and large, the relationship between the greyhound racing hierarchy and ministers, the departments of state and members of Parliament was now good. There was an altogether better understanding among the Executive of betting and gambling affairs than there had been in other days.

Much of this was due to the lead given by Lord Ward, for many years president of the National Greyhound Racing Society, then, in effect, the industry's trade association. An old friend from our days together in the House of Commons, Geordie Ward had been a successful Secretary of State for Air. Behind an engagingly disarming, aristocratic exterior, there lay a resourceful and resolute mind—and intuitive judgment. With the industry's secretary, Fred Underhill, a human encyclopaedia of greyhound racing knowledge, at his side, Geordie achieved much for the sport. And left his own indelible mark upon it.

In its important parliamentary work, the industry—and G.R.A.— had another signal asset in the balance sheet. For most of the time since Critchley had first founded the Greyhound Racing Association, there had been a member of Parliament on the company's board. Critch, who was more attuned than most to these things, realized early on that in the controversial area of entertainment and betting sound political judgment counted for much.

Brabazon of Tara, except during the period when he was serving in Winston Churchill's wartime cabinet, was a G.R.A. director for some thirty years. Then, after Brab's demise, and after I had myself left the House of Commons, Sir Tufton Beamish (later Lord Chelwood), for twenty-nine years the member for Lewes, and for quite a lot of that time vice-chairman of the 1922 Committee, joined us.

Apart from his extensive political experience, Tufton had, like Brab before him, a quick grasp of business and, with it, the ability to cut through irrelevant detail and go straight to the sensitive centre of a problem. With his other directorships, he brought to G.R.A., and to the industry, in a non-executive rôle, an objective mind and a rare sense of balance.

It was not perhaps surprising that, thanks notably to the support it could always count on from its friends on both sides of the House of Commons and the House of Lords, the greyhound racing industry was able to achieve in the 1960s and early 1970s unexpected success in gaining acceptance of some vital changes in the legislation which covered the sport.

Taken together, the impact of these changes was immediate and, in one case, immeasurable. In 1963 we obtained the statutory right, hitherto denied, to replace, up to a maximum of four in a year, those days of racing which, for one reason or another, had been lost. Eight years later, in 1971, a further concession was won, which increased by twenty-six, from 104 to 130, the number of days on which racing could take place in any one licensing year. In addition to this, tracks were enabled to select the race days of their individual choice, rather than having to accept set days on which all in a licensing area were obliged to race in direct competition with each other.

But most significant of all was the variation, secured in 1969, which transferred from Parliament (where it had rested since 1934) to the Home Secretary the right to determine what percentage of a track's totalizator turnover the operator should be allowed to retain for his own benefit.

Immediately this change was on the statute book, a reasoned submission was put to James Callaghan, Home Secretary at the time, arguing the case for a rise in the percentage from six per cent, where it had stood for almost forty years, to twelve and a half per cent. With the industry's total annual totalizator turnover running at around £61 million, such an increase would have an impressive effect on its fortunes. Callaghan, well advised by his permanent officials, accepted our case, set the new level at twelve and a half per cent, and thereby saved the industry from collapse and a number of racecourses and companies from extinction.

Under the same statutory provision, Roy Jenkins, Callaghan's successor as Home Secretary, in answer to another cry from the National Greyhound Racing Club, granted, in September 1975, a further increase of two and a half per cent, thus pitching the new limit at fifteen per cent. It produced another most timely injection of funds into the industry.

For G.R.A., with an annual group turnover from its twelve totalizators of upwards of £20 million, the ability to increase its revenue from this source, without extra cost, by up to two and a half per cent was indeed (as I saw it described elsewhere) a 'windfall'. It had a timely and significant effect on the group's earnings both in 1975/76 and in 1976/77. It came, moreover, as a further reminder of the advantages which can accrue from having ready to hand, sound political advice, and of the importance of keeping parliamentary and departmental contacts in what Dr Johnson might well have described as 'constant repair'.

*   *   *

For some time now, since we had been pushing ahead with the rationalization of the group's greyhound racing interests, we had been becoming increasingly aware that the White City was, for present and future needs, too big; it was outdated, and lacking the comforts demanded by the public as we moved towards the last quarter of the twentieth century.

The stadium had served its purpose with huge success. Licensed at one time to hold 75,000, it had become the acknowledged centre of greyhound racing, the linchpin of the industry. Earning, by now, upwards of half a million pounds' worth of profits annually, the international arena was the rock upon which G.R.A.'s fortunes principally rested. We could not, therefore, sit back inactive and let the place gradually run down. The problem, as we looked into the future, would not go away.

But how, with escalating building costs and the need to service loan finance, could we justify the heavy investment required to replace it (as we wanted) with a compact, multi-purpose, specially tailored and appointed arena? The answer, as we thought about it, became plain—only as part of a comprehensive redevelopment of the entire site. With the company's double-headed policy of rationalized greyhound racing and property development such a concept would fit naturally into the pattern.

Fortuitously, at this key moment, we were able to establish a solid relationship with Stock Conversion and Investment Trust, one of the best managed and most financially secure groups in the property sector. Headed by the able, astute and exceptionally qualified Robert Clark (he had become both a solicitor and a barrister early in life), whose interests spread wide into property, entertainment, television and elsewhere, and Joseph Levy, whose name was synonymous with property, this was a company which really knew its business.

Within days of our first meeting, an option agreement had been negotiated on the White City under which Stock Conversion could, in certain circumstances, acquire from G.R.A. the whole of the sixteen and a half acres for redevelopment. The plan, which put a £2 million price tag on the asset, provided, among other things, for the building on part of the site of the new, compact arena which we sought. Equipped for greyhound racing and participant leisure pursuits, with all the modern aids and comforts, it would be the first of its kind in Britain. Fifteen minutes by road from the heart of London's West End, it could hardly miss.

G.R.A. was to have a twenty-five per cent participation in the equity of the proposed development. Peter Levy, a partner in D.E. & J. Levy, the estate agents, and son of Joe, now joined the board and became G.R.A.'s adviser on property. Planning consent was obtained for the overall redevelopment. It included provision for an hotel, a warehouse building, a conference centre and, of course, the new multi-purpose stadium, which was to occupy no more than four and a half acres of the total complex. With partners of such standing, it was just the base we wanted from which to venture into the then bright and summoning world of property. The deal won G.R.A. many bouquets from the City.

Chapter Thirty-Three
Raising the wind

THE 1970s opened briskly for G.R.A. Events were moving on apace. One had the feeling that things were running our way and that we were approaching the time when the first fruits of our new policies would be ripening. Markets were buoyant; rumour and speculation, in tune with the times, abounded; G.R.A.'s share price moved up with the rest.

At this point in the journey, it had become clear both to the board and to Warburgs, the company's financial advisers, that the group must now take steps to strengthen its base and seek long-term finance to sustain the advance.

For some while, we had enjoyed the services of one of the most resourceful and agile minds in the merchant banking business. Now well into his sixties, Frank Smith had carved a reputation for himself in the City of London as a shrewd, tough and resilient operator in the take-over field who fought the contest hard, employing all the arts in the process. At S. G Warburg, he had become something of a legend.

Frank Smith had begun his working life as a bookmaker's runner at Wimbledon Stadium, and was never afraid to say so. For my money, defending or attacking, he ranked among the first three or four exponents of the corporate art. He made some of his counterparts elsewhere look just what they were—Third Division players.

I saw his expertise and master-mind at work on a number of occasions, but only once when he was on the 'other side'. That was quite enough. One felt instinctively with him that unless you got up pretty early in the morning, he would, in that picturesque transatlantic phrase, 'skin the bark off you'.

On the other hand, if you were up against an aggressive foe, in a no-holds-barred situation, Frank was the man to have at your side. I suspect he was close to being the best defender in the business. Anyway, he was far and away the nimblest performer I ever saw.

Working with him on our affairs, and taking care of much of the detail, was J. R. S. Boas, then one of Warburg's younger directors, a man of feeling and judgment whose placid and benign exterior disguised an acute negotiating mind.

Hard-won experience tells me that when you have brushed aside all the carefully-nurtured mystique, a merchant bank is as good or as indifferent as the director or directors you are dealing with—no better, and no worse. As a pair in support, Frank Smith and Bob Boas suited us nicely at G.R.A.

*   *   *

It was Warburgs who set up for the group at the end of 1970 the £18.5 million long-term financing arrangement with the I.C.I. Pension Fund (Pension Funds Securities Ltd, to give them their full title) headed, then, by the ubiquitous and personable Norman Freeman.

The overall sum was cut two ways. £6.5 million, carrying interest at ten per cent, was specifically earmarked for the Company's rationalization plans—for acquisitions and for modernizing the stadiums which were to remain. The balance of £12 million was sale and lease-back finance to victual the property development programme. This money carried interest at seven per cent and each development was to be dealt with and approved separately and treated strictly on its merits.

Tied into the package was an option which gave the Pension Fund of Britain's largest industrial company the right to take up 2.7 million G.R.A. shares (roughly ten per cent of the Company's equity) at 62½p. Freeman declined our invitation to put a director on the board; but we were now 'in it together'. A spirit of partnership animated the deal.

There was enthusiasm on both sides for the outcome. Once again, the City and the financial press gave us favourable mention. G.R.A.'s share price was now on course for the stratospheric 160p it was later to nudge at the height of the market, and all seemed right with the world.

'The broad and sunlit uplands' now beckoned from beyond.

*   *   *

The agreement with Stock Conversion, coupled with the new association with the Pension Fund, and the long-term finance by which the group was now underpinned, gave G.R.A. an altogether stronger and more impressive base upon which to rest the work which lay ahead.

When a tide starts flowing for you, the currents swing in behind. Good things like bad seldom come singly.

The Heath administration, with its powerful European slant, was now in office. Very soon, the long-discussed Channel Tunnel project, dressed up in new clothes and openly supported by the Government, came into play. As plans for the rail link from the Kentish coast were laid, British Rail, with Richard Marsh at its head, gave clear-cut backing for the siting of the rail terminal in West London. White City was the specific choice. With all the arguments in favour of this location—rail junctions, motorways and the rest—there was small doubt that this preference would prevail.

With the additional land which the Company had recently acquired adjacent to the existing stadium site, we now controlled 35 acres in this key area. The Pension Fund manager had himself spotted the potential which this zone held for G.R.A. 'Never forget', Freeman said to John Sutton and myself one day over lunch at the Carlton Club, 'that in all your plans the first aim of the Company must be the successful development of the White City. That must always be your point of concentration.'

However, the intention of locating the rail terminal at the White City, although offering glittering promise for the future, meant that the total area was put into limbo while the interested authorities had their say and all the customary procedures were followed.

Until British Rail's plans, and the scheme for the associated road network which was to complement them, had been crystallized and agreed, and the whole approved by the departments responsible, no detailed planning applications concerning the affected neighbourhood could be dealt with. Irksome and intensely frustrating though this was, there was nothing for it but to be patient. We therefore bided our time.

*   *   *

Elsewhere in the group, both on the development and on the racing sides, we continued to push ahead with our programme.

The earlier purchase of Charlton stadium in south-east London from the London Stadiums group was followed by a successful planning application to develop the site for office and warehouse use. This was to become the first and, as it turned out, the only development we were to undertake with the I.C.I. Pension Fund under the £18.5 million financing arrangement. Freeman, with the trustees, had given it the go-ahead. It proved to be a success.

With the closure of Charlton, G.R.A. was able to rationalize greyhound racing in this south-eastern sector of the capital. With racing finished at New Cross as well as Charlton, the business of these two racecourses passed principally to Catford. It was the first real manifestation of the policy to which we had set our hand.

Other examples followed. In Birmingham, a few miles down the road from G.R.A.'s stadium at Hall Green, lay the smaller, competing racecourse at Kings Heath. We bought this, closed the track and with Bryant Holdings, the Midlands building group, saw the site successfully developed for housing.

G.R.A.'s competitor in this part of Birmingham was thus removed, and the way opened for a major modernization scheme at Hall Green. Here also, on a small acreage of surplus land, a warehouse development was undertaken. This stadium is now one of the best appointed and most successful racecourses in the provinces.

North of the Border, in Glasgow, G.R.A. applied a similar policy of acquisition and disposal. Here, another warehouse development on residual land followed the Hall Green pattern.

$$*\qquad*\qquad*$$

While we were still marking time with plans for the White City development, two further mergers were achieved. The first was with Wimbledon Stadium Ltd—Wimbledon being one of the three most profitable and best-run stadiums in the country and a linchpin in the group's rationalization scheme for London. The second was with the Midlands-based construction and development group, Kay-Bevan Ltd.

Set up by Warburgs, and with G.R.A.'s share price standing at around 144p, these two deals, worth together some £6 million, went through in double-harness. The acquisition of Kay-Bevan, designed to give the group an in-house builder to aid its development programme, found general acceptance as another logical step in the process of broadening the base of G.R.A.

*   *   *

As 1973 drew to a close, early signs of a break in the spell of fine weather which the company had been enjoying began to appear.

The delays over the planning of the Channel Tunnel which, a year ago, we had accepted with equanimity and understanding, now became unsettling. National decisions affecting aspects of the project were being postponed; uncertainty increased. Over the site of the proposed terminal at the White City, and the Company's thirty-five acres which embraced it, a blight had descended.

Instead of being by now, as we had expected, in the throes of the group's principal development, we were unable to make a move.

*   *   *

In December, another event took the property sector's breath away. Anthony Barber, at the Treasury, in an outbreak of political zeal, dealt development, which had anyway started to go over the hill, a pulverizing blow. The so-called tax on first lettings—a tax on development gains, arising, among other things, from the letting of a newly-constructed building—which was later to lead to crisis and collapse, was unwrapped in all its finery. It was an ill-thought out measure designed to draw the rich developers' blood. Wisdom and judgment seemed to have been surrendered to ignorance and political expediency.

It required no streak of genius to see that by the early spring of 1974, property development was likely to remain in the doldrums for several years. Once a political football has started to be booted about in the air it takes a long time to trap it and keep it on the ground. The advent of a new Wilson administration did nothing to dispel the belief that the property sector would be kept out in the cold for some time.

The affairs of G.R.A. were now finely balanced. Considerable strides had been made with acquisitions and with the rationalization and stadium modernization programme. Several important steps remained to be taken; but much of the work was now complete. The

fruits were yet to come. On the other hand, the development programme was still young and very much in embryo. Planning consents
had been obtained for a number of projects, but only the warehouse
and office development at Charlton, in London, and the warehouse
developments at our stadiums at Hall Green, in Birmingham, and
Shawfield, in Glasgow, were strongly under way. These must clearly
be pressed ahead and finished despite the blight which had now
descended upon the property scene.

Against this background the group still had considerable resources
available from the £18.5 million financing arrangement entered into
with the I.C.I. Pension Fund three years before. Of the £6.5 million
facility inside the package which carried interest at ten per cent and
which was earmarked for acquisitions, rationalization and stadium
modernization, some £1.4 million still remained. Of the £12 million of
seven per cent 'sale and lease-back' finance for development, no more
than £1.2 million had been used—on the Charlton project. £10.8
million or so was, therefore, intact under this heading. Thus, out of the
all-embracing £18.5 million, a healthy £12 million plus still nestled in
the locker. It made a comforting bulwark for the group as the economic
blizzard began to tear on towards its climax.

Faced with such prospects, the question now for G.R.A. was how to
maintain the forward impulse after the encouraging outcome of 1973
when the group's trading profits reached a record £2.6 million. This
result, achieved in the face of a Middle East war together with the
associated rise in oil prices, a miners' strike and a three-day working
week, brought special satisfaction to the management.

After the merger the previous year, it was rewarding to find the
building, civil engineering, car sales and steel stockholding side of Kay-
Bevan, headed now by the practical and determined Leslie Bevan, a
down-to-earth construction man, who also farmed in Herefordshire,
contributing close to £800,000 worth of trading profits to the group's total.

Greyhound racing was also doing well. With a turnover of some
£6.5 million, the racing activities were earning profits in excess of
£1 million annually. These could be expected to be pushed up in the
next year or two as the effects of rationalization and modernization
worked through. But more than this was clearly going to be needed.

In times of depression, inflation and money shortage, betting and
gambling usually prosper. The punting public, with hope springing

eternal, reckon there must be a chance of making up on the horses, dogs, pools, gaming machines and tables what they're losing elsewhere.

The gambling spree, ignited by Butler fourteen years before, was still blazing away. The big multiple bookmaking concerns, with their gaming and their bingo, certainly weren't feeling the draught.

During the early months of 1974 several discussions took place with Freeman and his associates at the Pension Fund. They could see the picture as clearly as we did. Because of the closeness of our relationship it was as important for the Fund as it was for the company that the impetus of G.R.A.'s advance should be maintained so that the existing programme might be sustained. Development was out; but the curiously assorted world of gambling and betting was very much in. There was no doubt on either side about the direction in which G.R.A. should be pointed. At the same time, Freeman saw, with us, that there was no way, in the present circumstances, that G.R.A. could increase its borrowings with the Fund for long, without suitable and effective mitigating arrangements being made.

An opportunity now fortuitously arose to acquire a twenty-seven per cent equity stake in the soundly-managed and successful Coral Leisure Group. Here, timed to the moment, was the chance we wanted to strengthen the group's betting and leisure arm. If betting and gaming were going to stand up well—as we felt confident they would in this dreadful national climate—this was the field where we should find growth and profits.

Giltspur Ltd, an industrial holding company of which Maxwell Joseph was head, owned the stake and wanted to dispose of it. Coral was aware of Giltspur's wish to sell. Open and forthright talks had taken place between the parties about G.R.A.'s possible purchase of the holding. The afffinity between Coral and G.R.A. was immediately apparent to the two companies. Moreover, Coral's profits, which were running strongly at around £5 million, put together with our freehold assets, would make a good mix.

In Nicholas Coral, the group had, for its executive head, a thinking, conservative and balanced leader. He had had the high distinction of having gained, at the end of his three years at Peterhouse, a Double First in mathematics. Had the tugs of the family business not claimed him, Nicholas would have become an academic—at Oxford rather than at Cambridge, his alma mater, the scene of his success. Such a background is rare in bookmaking, probably even unique.

There was a disposition on the part of both boards to see the two companies merged together as soon as circumstances allowed. There wasn't a doubt on either side that the two would be capable of working in harmony. It was a natural union.

The plan was put to Norman Freeman at the I.C.I. Pension Fund. Freeman, who had an unusually alert eye for this sort of chance, at once saw the industrial sense and logic of the move both for his pensioners and our shareholders. The trustees would be ready to vary the existing financial arrangements to enable the stake to be bought. £5 million of the £5.7 million needed would be provided on the clear understanding—and only on the understanding—that the purchase was to be regarded as a first step in the ultimate fusion of the two groups.

Beyond this, it was abundantly recognized that to enable G.R.A. to contain its interest payments after buying the shares, it would be essential for the company's debt to be reduced. The group would not be in a position to service a further £5 million or so of borrowing for more than a very limited period. To this end Freeman indicated that the Fund would be quite prepared to consider taking a parcel of G.R.A.'s properties to minimize the additional debt.

Underpinning it all was a final fall-back position—a 'fail safe', to use the jargon of the thermonuclear age—with the £7 million balance which still remained within the original £18.5 million financing arrangement. No new developments were proposed, so this sum could be available to be brought into play to underpin any acceptable deal in the leisure, betting and gambling field upon which the Group's gaze was now fastened.

Such, then, was the understanding we reached with Freeman and his colleagues; and such was the clear basis upon which the 27 per cent stake in Coral was to be acquired. It would not have been possible to proceed without it.

*   *   *

A change now became necessary in our financial advisers. For G.R.A., this was a monumental misfortune. Warburgs, with whom we had enjoyed a happy and beneficial relationship, were advisers to Maxwell Joseph, and Giltspur was one of his companies. A conflict of interest would have arisen if the merchant bank had continued to act for G.R.A. in the purchase of the Coral shares from Giltspur with Joseph in the chair. We were, therefore, obliged at this critical moment to go to another bank to arrange the acquisition.

The I.C.I. Pension Fund encouraged the selection of Keyser Ullmann. This, remember, was the spring of 1974, and although we did not know it, Keysers were then at the threshold of their massive troubles. A year or so later, they were to reach a nadir in their fortunes—but not before we had parted company.

The Coral deal, completed quickly, was finalized in Giltspur's offices off Grosvenor Street on 25 March, with advisers and bankers present. With the Budget the next day, there was pressure to have everything buttoned up by midnight. Final confirmation of I.C.I.'s approval and support had been given that same afternoon, while we were at Giltspur, in a telephone call from Freeman to John Sutton.

Freeman, who was then meeting with his trustees, was quite definite. He wanted to confirm again that there was no doubt about the principle upon which the arrangement would rest. The Fund was ready to provide the finance, as already discussed and agreed, subject to the one overriding proviso that the purchase of the shares was to be recognized as a prelude to a merger between Coral and G.R.A. Otherwise there could be no deal. At the same time, it was appreciated there would subsequently be a need to take a package of G.R.A.'s properties to relieve the Company of the burden of heavier interest payments which would otherwise accrue from the new loan. The confirmation reaffirmed the position which had earlier been established between the Fund and G.R.A.

After all the discussions, prolonged, intricate and detailed, of the past weeks, John Sutton was able instantly to give the Fund manager the assurances he sought. All was thus agreed. On this plain, straight and mutually co-operative understanding the deal went through.

Chapter Thirty-Four
Coral reef

PETER LEVY, on behalf of G.R.A. now submitted to Freeman and his people at I.C.I. a list of completed and let properties. This package represented a comprehensive selection from G.R.A.'s and Kay-Bevan's portfolios. In subsequent exchanges, specific properties in the schedule were earmarked as being the ones most suitable for attention.

Meanwhile an event now took place which, although we regretted it on personal grounds, seemed to have no special significance at the time, but was, in the result, to have critical consequences for G.R.A. Asking one day at the Fund about the progress being made with the property portfolio, John Sutton was told that Norman Freeman was taking an early retirement and the matter must now await the arrival of his successor.

Freeman's place was taken by a recruit from the Church Commissioners, one Alwyne Conlong. It would have been hard to find two more complete opposites. Their personalities and working methods were worlds apart. Freeman, who had managed the Fund for the greater part of two decades, had a quick, traversing mind and a good eye for an opportunity or special situation. He played an expansive hand. By contrast, Conlong, short of stature, balding and bespectacled, was precise, incisive and, on the face of it, pretty tart.

If you had an interview with him (it was never particularly easy to get one), he made full notes on a pad which he kept in front of him and from which he seldom raised his eyes. When the discussion was over, the pages were neatly clipped together and stacked away into their allotted slot. A month later, a quick reference to the record would always enable him to remind you of what you had said at the previous meeting. If he wrote a letter, the number of words was restricted to the minimum, the sentences to rather less. He eschewed histrionics.

Anyone who was close to things could see what had happened.

1974 wasn't the 1960s or the very early 70s. I.C.I. now wanted someone to go round with a brace and give each nut a turn. Or maybe two. Conlong slipped unceremoniously and unobtrusively into the rôle.

With the new manager in the saddle, and the autumn now upon us, we waited anxiously for word about the important issue of the properties. After what seemed like an eternity—in fact, it was about five months—the letter came, crisp as toast melba. The properties offered had been considered but would not fit into the Pension Fund's portfolio. That was it; nothing more. It was a far cry from the spirit of co-operation and partnership which had encouraged G.R.A. on its way less than four years before; and it was still no more than six months since the clinching of the Coral purchase.

With the Fund's refusal to take the package of properties, another instance of the hardening relationship arose. We wished to arrange finance for the warehouse developments at Hall Green and Shawfield. The request was rejected. Instead we were recommended to go round the corner to Trade Development Bank. There, the money was provided—but at seventeen per cent instead of the seven per cent which would have applied under the £18.5 million umbrella with the Fund.

Two snowfalls may not make a winter, but the climate was changing. Fast. Looking back, it had become obvious to me as we went along that despite I.C.I.'s preparedness to back the Coral plan, it was their refusal to take the package of properties on the basis of the understanding we felt we had reached with their former Fund manager at the time of the Coral purchase, which contributed significantly to the failure of the mission.

Had they been prepared to accept the parcel and so strengthen G.R.A.'s balance sheet, and then continued to support the merger the story, in my judgment, might well have been different, for their pensioners and for the Company.

But they weren't. And that, for the time being, was that.

Chapter Thirty-Five
The wings of a man's life

NINETEEN SEVENTY-FIVE dawned bleakly. The property sector was already shattered. Sales, except for the primest of prime developments in the city centres, were drying up. Forced selling was, anyway, splintering the market. Prices, in some cases, weren't even matching security values. External forces were at work, effectively dominating events.

A winter of national discontent was followed by a spring of economic severity. Words like Dunkirk started to fly about as the year wore on. At G.R.A., time was not on our side. As we wrestled, like others in the property field, through these tortuous days, with short-term expedients and answers, the words which Humphrey Gilbert once wrote to the first Queen Elizabeth, exhorting her to press on with her policy took on a new reality:

'Haste, madam, for the wings of a man's life are plumed with the feathers of death.'

The hatches were battened down, but, in the face of the economic hurricane, it now became, for many companies, a question of whether the ship could ride the seas.

*　　*　　*

We turned again to the Pension Fund and to their trustees. The fact was now inescapable. After all that was behind us, it was they, and they alone, who held the key to G.R.A.'s future.

In the first half of the year, the group managing director, in extensive correspondence with the Fund manager (General Manager—Investments, to give him his full title) had dealt frankly and directly with the situation with which G.R.A. was now struggling. To read again the letters which passed between them is to revive afresh the

239

tensions which we—and others in the financial and property sectors—were living with in those days.

John Sutton recurred successively to three practical courses which remained open.

In February, he put it to the Fund manager that we should now revert to the original concept of a Coral-G.R.A. merger—the primary purpose of the acquisition of the Coral shares. To do this, the managing director proposed that the balance of £7 million which remained under the £18½ million arrangement should be brought into play.

In making his proposal, Sutton had referred to the undertaking which Norman Freeman had asked him to give on 25 March 1974, less than twelve months previously while we were finalizing the Coral deal in Giltspur's offices and while Freeman was with the trustees.

In rejecting the proposition, Conlong, who had not, of course, been present during the earlier discussions, contended that a third variation of the original agreement would be straining credulity, or words to that effect.

If this was, for us, an unexpected rejoinder, the interpretation which the Fund manager now put on his predecessor's vital telephone conversation with Sutton on 25 March 1974 fairly took our breath away. Referring to the managing director being asked to give the assurance that the purchase of the twenty-seven per cent stake would not be regarded as an investment but as a prelude to a merger between Coral and G.R.A., he asserted that Freeman must have sought the undertaking personally and verbally, as it hadn't been asked for by the trustees.

So there we were. Whatever, we wondered, had been going on at the Pension Fund of Britain's largest industrial company. New brooms may sweep clean but. . . . It seemed extraordinary to us that without such an assurance and an understanding about possible measures to reduce the level of G.R.A.'s borrowing after the acquisition, the trustees could have sanctioned the deal in the first place. Moreover, Conlong's understanding of what had taken place was made the more perplexing because there had never been any doubt in the minds of those of us who had dealt with Freeman that he was representing to us the circumstances correctly. The passage of time has not altered this conviction.

With his customary persistence, Sutton returned early in May to the issue of the properties. The proposition was that the trustees might look again at a list of the group's commercial properties which had been prepared and priced for G.R.A. by its property consultants, Jones Lang Wootton, with a view to the Fund acquiring them.

The properties, as John pointed out, had a total income of roundly £407,000 which, at a price of £3.499 million, placed on them by Jones Lang, would produce a yield for the Fund in the order of 11.7 per cent.

The answer, ultimately, was the same. No.

Dispirited and disappointed, the managing director, in the name of the board, and with the utmost reluctance, now put to the Fund manager the only other possibility which was left—the disposal of the Coral holding, purchased for £5.7 million no more than sixteen months before. The trustees were holding the shares as security for £2 million. The thought was awful because of the great potential which this stake offered G.R.A. but there it was. It had come to this.

The answer? No.

We asked if we could sell half the stake. Still no.

We put it to the Pension Fund that if they would reconsider their attitude, we would be prepared to repay, out of the sale, more than the £2 million for which the stake was secured. Again, no. The Russians had never used their 'niet' with greater consistency or purpose. I began to wonder whether G.R.A. was being made the 'fall guy' for some of Conlong's predecessor's more bizarre investments with which the new manager was himself now having to grapple.

Nevertheless, the board felt it right to have one more try to see whether the trustees would vary their attitude. As chairman of the company, I, therefore, made a final appeal to the Fund manager. The text of my letter was approved by the board. In this, I recall being aided by Graham Corbett, a thoroughly able accountant and one of Peat Marwick's partners, a stout and punctilious ally in rough times, and by John White, another solid Peats' man.

In these testing and traumatic days, Peats, like the National Westminster Bank, stood four-square behind client and customer of nearly half a century's standing. Indeed, in the quiet night hours, I often used to reflect how lucky I had been in my eighteen years, first, as managing director, and then, later as chairman, to have had people of the calibre of Whatmore, Nicholson and Corbett of Peats, and

Gordon Reeve and Ron Hodson of the National Westminster, to work with. These, together with David Higginson, the senior partner of Herbert Smith, for many years the group's solicitor-extraordinary, made, for me, a valued galaxy of counsellors.

With my letter I attached a copy of the correspondence which, at our request, Peats had written to the directors immediately before, summarizing the group's financial position. We all felt it right that the situation should be put straightly and bluntly.

I indicated that the existing cash shortfall was projected to rise to £2.339 million by the end of the year (31 December 1975). I pointed out that the only course now open to us was the disposal of the Coral holding. If the Pension Fund blocked the sale, the board would then have to consider whether it was right for the Company to continue trading. At the same time, I made it plain that the group was trading profitably before paying loan interest, with the profits from its greyhound racing and leisure activities keeping up well. The current trading of Kay-Bevan suggested that we should be able to look to them for better results in the present financial year. Overall, I showed that it was the heavy interest charges which were continuing to absorb profits and cash flow. It was this which was breaking the group's back.

Once more, I.C.I. refused permission to sell.

*   *   *

We were now into August. From my days in the House of Commons I remembered that August seldom used to pass without a crisis occurring somewhere in the world, keeping ministers at their desks. Barings, having taken over as G.R.A.'s financial advisers after our short-lived and ill-starred spell with Keysers, made contact (after some difficulty) with Conlong. I recall the merchant bank reporting that the Fund manager was just off on three weeks' holiday, leaving specific instructions that no action was to be taken on G.R.A. until his return.

*   *   *

Barings now proceeded to make their own assessment of the group's position. The situation had not been made any easier for us in the summer by the Pension Fund starting, with their solicitors, vigorously to probe and prod about with the title deeds of the properties which they were holding as security against the £10.7 million of loans.

Having reached this stage in the story, the trustees argued with some justification that everything must be scrutinized and tested. Nothing must remain unchecked. The steel-capped toe of the boot was now well in. We interpreted this action as a deliberate and manifestly obvious attempt to find imperfections in the deeds to break the existing 20-year agreement and the association between us. If this was their purpose, they succeeded wonderfully. Two defects were uncovered. We hurried, with our lawyers, to remedy them.

Taken separately, Barings reported to us, they were relatively insignificant; but, taken together, they produced a situation where the Pension Fund held a position of great strength.

Another matter compounded our problems. G.R.A. had already exercised its right to require the Pension Fund to buy the company's interest in the development at Charlton. On the exchange of contracts and completion—and the receipt of the cash—depended, as things stood, our ability to pay the Fund the interest due to them. Easy to see here how the need for exceptional vigilance and scrutiny could extend the process. The sale, for £315,000 net, did not go through till October, roundly a month later.

The screw was now turned right up tight. One more twist and the thread would break. The Pension Fund gave us till 30 September to remedy the defects. They also demanded a supplementary agreement which would remove from G.R.A. its ability (exercisable after 1 January 1976) to sell the Coral shares. Had we been able to do so, we would have paid the Fund the £2 million to which they were entitled, and kept the balance (£1.5 million, at least) in the group.

In other words, the Fund, having refused to allow us to sell the stake, were now implacable in their determination to maintain their veto indefinitely. If we could not meet their stringent deadline, they had the ability, at 14 days' notice, to call the total loan, now £10.7 million, thus busting G.R.A.

What, then, to do? At least it was reassuring now to find Barings substantially recommending the action which we ourselves had felt to be right. To allow G.R.A. to continue its historic and successful rôle as a greyhound racing and leisure group, they made three principal proposals:

1. The immediate sale and lease-back of the White City for £2 million which, in November 1975, Robert Clark was quite ready to advocate with his Stock Conversion colleagues.
2. The sale of G.R.A. Developments' property portfolio to produce, within twelve months, a cash surplus of £600,000 over outstanding loans.
3. The sale of the Coral shares, now the jewel in G.R.A.'s balance sheet.

To give time for this action to be followed—and for the Company to survive—it was now essential to obtain the creditors' agreement to a short standstill period during which impending debt payments could be withheld without the danger of foreclosure. Interest due would be temporarily rolled up and added to the capital sum.

The merchant bank, therefore, came to the question of how to deal with the Pension Fund, by far the largest creditor, to persuade them to become a party to this moratorium, and refrain from exercising their rights over their security. On this score, two of Barings' observations, in the context of what was to follow, are of special interest:

1. They believed it would be necessary for the Pension Fund to be able to convert their outstanding loans into the equity of the group—perhaps to the extent of a majority stake.
2. They expected the Fund would impose conditions about the management and direction of the Company.

I had now reached a personal conclusion. After more than 30 years with G.R.A., I had little more than twelve months to go to the date of my retirement on 31 December 1976, at the end of the year in which the Company—and greyhound racing—were celebrating their fiftieth anniversary.

If the Pension Fund was going to require management changes, I was determined to do whatever I could to preserve the chances of G.R.A.'s ablest executives, particularly those with the flair and aggression for promoting greyhound racing, from which all but a small fraction of the group's trading profits in the future would come. Younger executives of ability, drive and experience, in this sector of leisure and entertainment, are very few. We had them. Much better, then, if the trustees wanted their sacrificial goat, as Barings were rightly suggesting they would, that I, rather than others, should go. 'The cemeteries of France,' I often reminded my colleagues in these days, 'are full of indispensable men.'

When we came, with the merchant bank, to the inevitable creditors' meetings to seek support for a moratorium, I made my position clear. If change in the management was the price to be paid to I.C.I. and others among the principal creditors for their support, then, subject to their wishing it, to the provisions of my contract, and to a moratorium being obtained, I would go, sad though this would be for me. I was ready to give a lead.

The creditors, however, did not want this—as Barings confirmed to G.R.A. in writing at the end of September. Rather, they wanted the board to be strengthened with a new managing director and a new finance director from outside the group. The financial advisers, however, made it quite clear to me at this time that the Pension Fund, who were now calling the tune, would want a chief executive who would work closely with them and pursue their interests. In such a situation, they said, the shareholders didn't count.

I did not wish to remain chairman of the Company in such circumstances.

In the event, I agreed to act as executive vice-chairman for the last few months, not least because I was now engaged, as chairman of the National Greyhound Racing Club's drafting committee, together with other colleagues, in preparing the industry's 30,000-word submission to the Royal Commission on Gambling. As this was a task of first-class importance, and as we had already thrown ourselves fully into the work, I wanted to see it through.

It was satisfying to make this valedictory contribution to the industry I had served so happily for more than thirty years.

Chapter Thirty-Six
Fluttering in the dove-cote

FIRST THINGS first. The prime need now was to obtain, for the whole group, the moratorium without which, all recognized, G.R.A. could not survive. Meetings were held with creditors during October with this end in view.

Only three-quarters of the battle was, in the end, won. On 23 October 1975, there was agreement from G.R.A.'s creditors for the major part of the group. Barclays did not, however, grant Kay-Bevan the same concession. A receiver was therefore appointed at the sub-group. This was, I felt, not only a very great pity (events were to prove it), but also probably quite unnecessary.

Barings, I thought, played a disappointing hand. It seemed to me that their mistake lay in assuming too soon that the moratorium was in the bag. If I.C.I., the National Westminster and, perhaps, the Inland Revenue were in line, was it really likely that Barclays would step out of it? A senior executive of the National Westminster, who knew what was going on, told me later that, had it all been played another way, with a shade more perceptiveness and sensitivity, and with a readiness to make use of indirect and behind-the-scenes persuasion, the result might have been different. As my informant was then himself in the thick of sorting out, with Barclays, victims of the so-called fringe-banking collapse, he was well placed to judge.

Anyway, G.R.A.'s own creditors held firm and provided the breathing space which we needed. And so we passed into the unreal, twilight world of quasi-receivership with which G.R.A. was wholly unfamiliar. Much, however, was to be learned from the events which followed.

*   *   *

A statement to G.R.A.'s shareholders on 20 November explained the

246

Company's problems. It was signed by the new chairman and chief executive, E. J. Aaronson, an accountant. Found for the group by Barings, he was favoured by the Pension Fund as he had been associated with Cork, Gully, the accountants, in the run-down of the collapsed Lyon Group in which the Fund had been significantly involved. Board changes were now announced—including my appointment as executive vice-chairman with responsibility for greyhound racing and leisure. Four consequential moves were also detailed.

John Sutton, the former managing director, was to become group assistant managing director, a post which he at once accepted with his customary grace and spirit. Brian Franks and John Cearns were to cease to be deputy chairmen, but would remain as directors. Peter Levy, who had earlier offered his resignation quite voluntarily, now left the board.

At this point, events took a most curious turn. Hardly was the ink dry on the shareholders' circular, when, on 4 December, there was a great fluttering in the dove-cote. Birds and feathers started to fly all over the place. A falcon had descended.

Executive directors were urged to tear up their service contracts. The new chairman reported that he had consulted Herbert Smith, the company's solicitors, who had advised that these should be surrendered. In place there should be temporary arrangements on a monthly basis. My own advisers took a quite different view. Questioned, Herbert Smith later confirmed that the contracts were valid.

Amid all the confusion, John Sutton, ostensibly to save money, was fired on the spot by the chairman, without notice and without compensation. John Cearns was, among other things, offered the chance of an 'early retirement' on 31 December.

Fashioned by the chairman, with Barings close at hand, it was, of course, designed as a master coup, sharp, decisive, and all over in hours. One morning of the long knives—and tomorrow, ah, tomorrow would be another day. In the result, it struck me as a massive miscue. Relations were irreparably harmed; the board was utterly split, with only the finance director at this stage marching in step with the chairman—an incongruous spectacle since it was only a month or so since he had been named for removal by the creditors.

On the other side were ranged the remaining six active directors, including Lord Chelwood, who was becoming increasingly vigilant and objective, probing, questioning and challenging any action which might appear not to be conceived in the best interests of the Company, its staff or members. There was, moreover, a ridiculous situation where the former managing director, the company's largest individual shareholder with some 400,000 shares, having been summarily dismissed from his newly-created post of group assistant managing director by the chairman, couldn't be fired from the board because a majority of the directors—all of whom were shareholders—wouldn't have it.

*   *   *

A plan had, by this time, been prepared by the chairman and his advisers which would replace G.R.A.'s informal moratorium when it expired and pave the way for the introduction of a Scheme of Arrangement to which all creditors, if they agreed, would be legally bound. During this period, debts could not be called. It would, therefore, be the means by which G.R.A. could be allowed to recover.

In essence, the intention of the plan, and, subsequently, of the Scheme, was to arrange for the orderly disposal of assets which could be dispensed with to realise cash; and to group together those companies which would earn profits and generate cashflow.

*   *   *

A signal mistake in human relations was now made. The plan was shown to some of the creditors before the Board had had a chance to see it. The directors who, in general, supported the principle of the Scheme, had not been offered an opportunity to discuss its detail before it was circulated. It did not, therefore, carry the board's stamp.

The significance of this became more apparent when we ultimately got our eyes on it. No immediate sale of the Coral stake was contemplated, nor was it intended that a sale and lease-back of the White City should be tried with Stock Conversion despite their earlier indication that they would be prepared to consider it. By this time, of course, Kay-Bevan had already been lost to us.

All this flew straight in the face of the principal elements of advice which Barings, at some cost in fees, had given the board only three months before. Now, it seemed, the rapid disposal of saleable assets, and a swift and sizeable reduction in the overall debt—and, therefore, in interest charges—was no longer to be the governing priority.

In the circumstances, the majority of the board, of which I was one, insisted that I should attend and be able to speak at the meeting to be held at Barings' offices on 22 December at which the creditors' support for the plan would be sought.

When I spoke, and I have my speaking notes before me as I write (a wily old politician's long-established habit), I dwelt, among other things, upon the board changes and the illogical and ill-conceived attempt to dismiss John Sutton from the group.

I told the creditors the story of John's coming into the Company from Catford, via the merger, eleven years before, of his flair for promoting greyhound racing, and how, as a competitor, he had been a constant thorn in our side, particularly in south-east London.

'What sort of logic is it', I asked, 'when G.R.A.'s future is going to depend substantially upon the success of its greyhound racing, now to be getting rid of the ablest and most experienced of the younger executives in the industry?

'Let John Sutton go and other good men will follow to join our competitors.'

I must admit I did not expect my words to be vindicated so soon.

*   *   *

An unhappy atmosphere now permeated the Company as things moved on to a climax. It was clearly necessary at this late hour to support the concept of the Scheme, although there were others in the City, merchant bankers among them, who felt this to be a clumsy, complicated and dreadfully expensive way of handling things. It was a paradise for the professionals and their high fees.

An attempt was made by the majority of us on the board at another difficult meeting on 14 January 1976 to get our detailed alternatives to the plan accepted. Although we put and carried our proposals, they met unyielding resistance from the chairman. To overcome the impasse Barings, very fairly I thought, invited us to submit our views in writing, on the understanding that they would be seen and considered by the principal creditors.

In a closely-argued and detailed statement (I recall it took three of us much of a week-end to draft), we put our proposals 'for . . . restructuring . . . the management of the Company and for achieving economies which all accept to be essential.' We contended, that the savings we should be making would exceed those proposed by the chairman. Out of a host of points, the principal variations to the plan were these:

1. The Coral stake should be sold. That company's forthcoming announcement of profits, and possible rights issue, could well offer a favourable opportunity for this. An impressive saving in interest charges would thereby accrue.

2. Making it clear that there was a readiness on the part of a majority of the directors to give a lead and accept sizeable reductions in salary, we came to the management changes.

    (a) As the new chairman and chief executive was an accountant and was himself directing the financial affairs of the group, the finance director, as requested by the creditors, should go with appropriate compensation.

    (b) The company secretary, who had recently been co-opted to the board, should leave the company on 31 March 1976, the date on which he had himself earlier elected to retire after more than a quarter of a century with the group.

    (c) The chairman and managing director of Wimbledon Stadium, John Cearns, who had successfully thwarted the attempt to retire him early, should become managing director of the greyhound racing and leisure division of the group. He had a lifetime's experience behind him and proved ability in this field.

    (d) It was not logical, right, or in the interest of the group that the former managing director should leave the company. If the chairman and certain creditors insisted that John Sutton should relinquish the post to which he had just been appointed, then his exceptional flair and knowledge should be retained. We proposed, therefore, that he should become a consultant.

3. We also touched on a rather delicate matter. The early

re-establishment of good relations within the board was, we felt, a prime need. Herbert Smith, in addition to acting as G.R.A.'s solicitors, also acted for a company called Equity Recoveries, of which G.R.A.'s new chairman was the controlling shareholder, and which provided his services for the group. The chairman of Equity Recoveries was a partner of Herbert Smith—a very senior one. The company secretary was also a partner.

Although we were well aware of these circumstances and had accepted them—indeed, I had been required to sign a letter to this effect—we felt it reasonable, in the emotive atmosphere which prevailed, to invite the partners in question not to become involved in any negotiations which might directly or indirectly affect G.R.A. directors.

With this submission now in Barings' and the principal creditors' hands, we awaited with interest the meeting which was to follow.

Chapter Thirty-Seven
The battle of Leadenhall Street

THE BOARD met the principal creditors at Barings' offices on the afternoon of 21 January. In addition to the I.C.I. Pension Fund, the Inland Revenue and the Kay-Bevan receiver, the National Westminster Bank, Stock Conversion and Giltspur had their representatives present. This was later to form the composition of the creditors' committee.

The meeting was a typically heavy affair. Leadenhall Street, I thought, had been well named. This was obviously to be the show-down and was being dressed up accordingly, with all due pomp and solemnity. Did I get a whiff of intimidation, just a sniff of the old heave-ho? The bigger guns of I.C.I., in the form of Conlong, flanked by his usual bevy of advisers, were marshalled on the opposite side of the table, close to the centre. I noticed that the Fund manager seemed to be on the alert, as if waiting for something unexpectedly tricky to turn up. Barings' representatives, serious as a pair of vergers who had just discovered that the collection was missing, made everything ready.

The discussion was slow to get into its stride, hesitant at first, but soon things began to hum. Spirited, and, I suspect, for the Establishment, embarrassing support for our alternative proposals came from Stock Conversion. National Westminster, with the Revenue, preserved a sound neutrality throughout, counselling moderation, and warning against anything precipitate or rash being done. It was a model stance. The Kay-Bevan receiver and Giltspur, an unsecured creditor, predictably, fell quietly in behind the official position.

Conlong, by comparison, was unequivocal. Brushing the alternatives aside, he laid his one card down on the table face up. Accept the chairman's and the advisers' plan, or risk the withdrawal of

252

the Pension Fund's support. He gave the majority of the board till between 12 noon and 1 o'clock the next day at the latest to decide.

Those of us who supported the variations, which the Fund manager would have nothing to do with, now withdrew for private reflection. The moment of truth was near. That was obvious. Views were mixed to begin with. But as the discussion developed, the risk of putting our detailed alternatives to the touch, seemed to grow. It might well be too great, sensibly, to accept. We were ourselves all shareholders, with two of our number very large ones—unlike the three directors toeing the party line outside, who held no shares at all. There was no question but that, in our case, the interests of the shareholders were being given full weight.

I myself remained convinced that we should stand firm, and meet Conlong's challenge head on. I argued that it was unlikely that the Pension Fund of Britain's largest industrial concern would knock the working man's sport of greyhound racing (never mind the property) on the head under the arc lights of the public's gaze, less than eighteen months after Norman Freeman and the trustees had backed G.R.A. 100 per cent, and to the tune of £5 million, in buying the Coral stake. The logic, quite apart from the ethics, would be difficult to justify, to say the least. Beyond this, I felt that if I.C.I. were bent on destroying G.R.A., then their purpose should be made plain for all to see.

This was a minority view. Most of my colleagues thought the danger of taking on the Pension Fund was, on balance, too great. If we failed, there would be a heavy accountability for those who had forced the issue. They may well have been right. As always, I at once respected their judgment.

The price of acceptance was very high. Whatever slant was given to the story, the fact was that two independent, forthright and widely experienced, non-executive directors, who were costing the company no more than £1500 a year a piece (and they were prepared to reduce this by £500 each) were forced off the board by the chairman's casting vote.

Of the three executive directors among the supporters of the alternative proposals, the one who, among the younger generation, possessed unrivalled flair for the promotion of greyhound racing, was dismissed. The other two—John Cearns and myself—were stripped of central executive power.

Another, Charles Chandler, absent on holiday from the fray, survived. I thought of him, stretching languidly for a mint julep in the shade of a West Indian palm.

And therefore, at the kinges court, my brother,
Ech man for him-self, ther is non other.

Transcending in importance the decisions affecting individuals, however, was the change in the authority governing the direction of the Company. A resolution was passed which effectively took power away from the board and vested it in a small committee of management. While its minutes were to be circulated to all directors, the committee's resolutions and proceedings were not to be subject to ratification or approval of the full board.

So the Pension Fund, by their threat of liquidation, had effectively forced an elected majority of the board to capitulate—and this, despite the assurance which I had personally sought and obtained at an earlier board meeting that the statutory duties of the directors remained, in these circumstances, unimpaired. I.C.I. had won the day, game, set and match. The Fund were riding high—for the time being. Soon to get the chance to lay claim to all the proceeds of the Coral stake, and, in addition, the ability to acquire, by a complicated process of convertible loan notes, up to 46 per cent of the equity of G.R.A., they certainly hadn't been wasting their time. The chairman, and those who were advising him, must have been thankful for the muscle the trustees had given them.

And yet . . . and yet . . . As the guns were stilled, and the dead and wounded were recovered from the field, I had the feeling that Pyrrhus and Asculum might not be so very far away.

The first consequence of the upheaval, which I personally felt should have been avoided, was the formation of a G.R.A. shareholders' association. Lord Chelwood, immediately after being forced to resign from the board, had made a telling and objective statement to *The Times* in which he urged the shareholders to unite. He performed an important service thereby, giving the members a wise lead.

The challenge was taken up by a thorough-going, determined, forty-two-year-old Yorkshire solicitor from Huddersfield, named John Briggs. A bland, squire-like, slightly diffident exterior, hid a purposeful, rugged, buccaneering spirit. A substantial shareholder, Briggs accepted the chairmanship of the association.

He had arrived on the scene too late to muster sufficient shareholder strength to obtain amendments to the Scheme which, in its first stages, was to last for two years after receiving the formal approval of shareholders and creditors and being given the legal backing of the High Court.

The whole thing was to be managed by an all-powerful creditors' committee of which I.C.I., in the shape of their Pension Fund manager, would be the dominant member. The committee would be chaired by a scheme manager who, in this case, would also be G.R.A.'s chairman and chief executive. In the event of a dispute arising between the board of G.R.A. and the scheme manager, the will of the scheme manager would prevail.

A year later, at G.R.A.'s 1977 annual meeting, Briggs led the members in open revolt against the board in a deftly-organized and acutely-timed attack. At the previous general meeting a resolution, designed to give shareholders their own representation on the board, had been put from the floor and carried, on a show of hands, by an overwhelming majority. This had been rejected by the chairman calling for a poll and using, as he was fully entitled to do, the proxies of members who could not possibly have known beforehand that their votes would be employed to deny them this representation.

Now the shareholders' association was resolved to turn the tables. In a hard-hitting circular, chairman Briggs turned his guns on the I.C.I. Penson Fund which, he declared, had got G.R.A. 'by the throat'. Rousing the members, the Huddersfield solicitor went on: 'No major moves can be made without its consent. Not content with this stranglehold, it has now obtained the legal right to acquire, by a system of loan notes, up to forty-six per cent of the equity of G.R.A., nearly half your company. . . .'

As counsel for the association had earlier said in the High Court, when objecting to the Scheme of Arrangement, by seeing the Company's capital reduced, shareholders were going to lose approximately ninety per cent of the value of their shares, while the Pension Fund could end up with forty-six per cent of the equity which would guarantee them control.

Raising the cry: 'The Shareholders Still Count . . . You Have

Nothing To Lose But Your Chains', Briggs took on the board from scratch. He rallied the holders of eight million G.R.A. shares to his side, removed one director, got himself elected in his place, and left the board and Barings who, in the final week, had chucked everything into the ring in a last, desperate attempt to stave off defeat, sprawling all over the canvas. Conlong was seen to be applying the second's towel.

I remember thinking at the time that, in earlier days, Frank Smith and Warburgs would have played things rather differently.

*   *   *

A side issue of real significance now followed in the aftermath of the shareholders' meeting.

Within a fortnight, and with the board and its advisers still smarting under Briggs' victory and all the pressures and manoeuvrings which had preceded it, the Coral stake was sold.

The story behind the sale was intriguing. Coral were manifestly anxious to see G.R.A.'s twenty-seven per cent holding in their company split up. The acquisition of so large a stake by an unwanted predator would have been acutely embarrassing, and Coral and their advisors knew that G.R.A. and Barings were at the climax of their battle with Briggs and his supporters and were desperately canvassing votes. They, therefore, reserved the moment of sharpest pressure for their approach.

'Let the holding now be broken up and spread in separate parcels around the City,' they said in effect, 'and we will vote our G.R.A. shares (they held close to half a million in the Company) with the Board.'

The bait was grabbed. The shares were parcelled up into small packages and placed with the various institutions at 145p a share—a discount of 5p on the market price or roundly £6.3 million in total. Yet Briggs still won the day! To make matters worse, less than six months later, Coral's shares, after a massive rise, touched 286p. The twenty-seven per cent stake would then have been worth more than £15 million gross, against the £5.7 million which G.R.A., with I.C.I.'s full support, had paid for it three years earlier—or sufficient to repay the whole of the Company's secured debt.

No wonder that, afterwards, word was put about that the I.C.I. Pension Fund had, at the crucial moment, forced the sale of the Coral holding. In fact, the Fund had done no such thing. They had simply acquiesced with G.R.A. in its disposal—a very different matter.

*   *   *

In his book, *The Gathering Storm,* Churchill called the 1939-45 conflict the 'Unnecessary War'. 'There never was a war,' he wrote, 'more easy to stop than that which has wrecked what was left of the world from the previous struggle.' Looking back now in another context, it is plain to see how easy it would have been to avert the convulsions which shook G.R.A. in the months between late 1974 and early 1976 and left such havoc in their train. Had the I.C.I. Pension Fund then been prepared to sustain the company as we felt entitled to expect, they could have done so at a stroke. The union which was sought would have been achieved, an enlarged and highly profitable entity established and a short-lived crisis would have passed.

Others were standing firm in the holocaust. As the Governor of the Bank of England, speaking of the financial sector's traumas in those days, told a Select Committee of the House of Commons on 18 January, 1978: 'Had the rapidly escalating crisis of confidence passed to the banking system proper . . . had a major bank defaulted, I do not know where we would have stopped in the course of collapse.' Many of the larger property companies were technically insolvent at the time. But, succoured by the banks and the institutions, the majority survived.

G.R.A. Property Trust was, however, in a quite different category. The group had a relatively small property content. Underpinning it was a strong and successful, cash-generating greyhound racing and leisure business, earning profits of more than £1 million annually, with a proved, fifty-year operational record behind it. It seemed to me unnecessary and strangely out of character for I.C.I. to disregard both future promise and past performance.

Several years later, one of the industrial giant's favourite sons put the whole episode into perspective. 'It was a great pity,' he said to me, 'you didn't appeal over the heads of the Pension Fund to the whole board of I.C.I. The attitude might well have been different. . . .'

It was what Lord Chelwood had argued so vehemently for at the time.

Chapter Thirty-Eight
Full circle

THOSE WHO have seen professional accountants and solicitors at work, operating the closed-shop principle in companies where insolvency is alleged to exist, will have observed some familiar traits.

Debts are highlighted. Values of assets, down to the charlady's mop, are written down to lower basement levels. It is the essential prerequisite of an exercise which, after years of 'diligent and patient application,' will have for its goal 'progress and achievement in the eventual restoration of financial stability.' Yet the paper reductions in debt, which often appear to run into maximized millions frequently bear small relation to the actual sums paid out in cash.

Little is performed simply or directly or without recourse to further (expensive) advice. Short cuts to recovery are eschewed . . . More profitable, by far, in terms of continuing fees and expenses, to opt for the long road home.

> 'For there is good news yet to hear and fine things to be seen
> Before we go to Paradise by way of Kensal Green.'

Rupert Nicholson, at Rolls Royce, was a notable exception in his profession.

Experience tells me that what is needed, above all, is *impartial* supervision and scrutiny, and *full* disclosure and periodical reporting to *all* the parties concerned.

If ever there was an area of Britain's corporate life where further attention was needed to achieve fairness and justice for all it is in the dark Satanic depths where liquidators, receivers, operators of schemes of arrangement and the like, who trade in company gloom, make their considerable livings and have their being.

To be fair, however, recent legislation affecting Administration has gone a long way to meeting these objectives. Previous laws governing insolvency were so diverse and complicated, and left so many grey areas, that few, except the professionals, could ever understand them.

*   *   *

G.R.A.'s Scheme of Arrangement, which was costing a bomb to administer, dragged on for six years. It's a fair guess that, with a more fertile and resilient approach, and a disposition to sell valuable freehold stadiums instead of holding on to every one of them as the heroine clings to the last ledge of the precipice, it could well have been ended in half the time.

As it was, the company was placed in a straightjacket with next to no money being spent on profit-earning assets which could thus only be run down. Morale fell with the then fall in greyhound racing attendances. While the Home Secretary increased yet again the percentage retention which the tracks were allowed, by law, to deduct from the totalisator—the prime source of the group's revenue—the actual turnover, which for years had more than kept pace with inflation, began inevitably to turn the other way.

It was a dispiriting juncture for the discontented shareholders who could see little hope for the future of the company.

Then, one day in 1980, A Strange Thing Happened On The Way To The Forum. The men at the I.C.I. Pension fund, sniffing rumour in the air, thought they could identify an informal approach to G.R.A., and its advisers, from the acquisitive (and now late) Keith Wickenden, Tory member of Parliament and the then chairman of European Ferries. Playing an unfamiliar opportunist hand, the trustees switched their convertible loan stock in G.R.A. into the company's shares.

At a nominal 5p a share, it at once gave them a dominant twenty-six per cent stake in the group while, at the same time, confronting existing shareholders with a massive dilution of their equity. In a twinkling, what had originally been intended by G.R.A.'s chairman and his advisers to be a nice, comforting bulwark in the storm now became a menacing spring-board for attack and control—not, assuredly, in the hands of I.C.I. who only wanted 'out' at a price, but in the possession of a predator to whom they might well sell. All at once, the holding became the key to control of the group.

It was in June, 1983, seven years after the famous battle of Leadenhall Street, that the fortunes of the company were set once more upon an upward path. Few ever knew (or still know) that it was the outcome of persistent and dogged scheming by three or four influential and resolute individuals, operating in unison with G.R.A.'s former managing director, the brilliantly resourceful John Sutton, who were dedicated to putting things right.

A powerful consortium of interests, headed by Isidore Kerman, as nimble and intellectually able a solicitor as ever graced London's West End, now entered the stage. It was backed by a brace of McAlpines, Sir Donald Gosling, synonymous with National Car Parks, the ubiquitous Frank Sanderson, former chairman of Bovis and man of many parts, and one or two others whose presence, had it been known, would have raised a few eyebrows.

This all-star cast bought I.C.I.'s twenty-six per cent stake in G.R.A. for roundly £2 million or 17$1/2$p a share. The irony of it was that the trustees of the Pension Fund should have thought that they had made a good deal. No doubt they had been listening to the scheme manager's oft-repeated opinion that G.R.A. was then unlikely ever to be worth much more than 15p a share.

Waiting off-stage was a South African group, controlled from Johannesburg. It had been quietly amassing a telling eleven per cent holding in the company. Much of it was acquired at prices at or below 15p a share. Sensing that a consortium of such calibre would not be buying a twenty-six per cent stake in the group without a purpose the South Africans, with a spring in their gait, put their full weight behind the call for an immediate change both in the chair and in the direction of the company.

The palace revolution was deft, swift and effective. Kerman, himself a very substantial shareholder in G.R.A., took the chair in place of Aaronson, the former scheme manager, who at once exited from the group.

Taking their profits, the Johannesburg interests sold out, and other advisers took Barings' and Herbert Smith's place.

Within less than six months of Kerman taking the chair, G.R.A.'s share price had touched 80p and the company was headed once more on its correct and familiar, two-pronged course of sharply-rationalized and modernized greyhound racing on the one hand and property development and disposals on the other. It was a play-back of the policy being pursued in the 1960s and early 1970s.

The nightmare was over. The wheel which Conlong and his I.C.I. trustees had set spinning in 1974 and '75 had turned full circle. When Kerman eventually did the deal which brought G.R.A. sailing under the Wembley Group's banner, the company's share price had been nudging 150p—a far cry from the levels at which some had claimed the group was 'fully valued'.

*   *   *

I had never before found much enjoyment at scoring points at others' expense. An eye for an eye and a tooth for a tooth had not, hitherto seemed a particularly fruitful doctrine. In this case, however, I had to confess to a feeling of requited pleasure at the course of events which had changed again—and irrevocably—the central direction of G.R.A. as 1983 merged into 1984. Justice had, I thought, not only been done, it had also been seen to be done.

Moreover, a dash or two of piquancy was added to the coup. The principal architect—this one courageous, hidden mastermind, John Sutton, who, eight years before and subsequently, had been the butt of so much denigration and malice, was totally unsuspected by those whose removal he had so skillfully and effectively planned. Having himself made another fortune in the meantime, he was entitled to a celestial grin.

The wheels of God may have ground slowly, but the grind had been exceeding sure.

*   *   *

I had long resolved that when my time to retire from the company eventually come round I would turn again to writing. I had looked forward expectantly to the prospect. Most of us become conditioned by the circumstances of our early working life. For my part, I had thoroughly enjoyed my few pre-war years with Express Newspapers in Fleet Street whose training was to bring so many benefits in its train. Indeed, I have no doubt that, without the subsequent intervention of the holocaust which was, in time, to engulf the world, I would never have been persuaded to turn away from my original profession. But war changes lives.

However, not even in my moments of fantasy could I have visualized the extent which authorship would illuminate the 'retirement' years. Certainly I would not have been able to find a more effective antidote or therapy for the convulsions which I.C.I.'s unexpected decision in 1975 to turn their back on G.R.A., had set in train.

Nor, if I am honest, could I fairly say I had ever envisaged that, within thirteen years—between 1977 and 1990—I would complete and publish eight substantial books which in the event would take my name as an author to distant parts of the globe.

It is, as I write, a little more than fifty years since I walked out of the *Express* building in Fleet Street for the last time to play an airman's part in Hitler's war. Returning again to the typewriter after such an interim I recall some words of Churchill's:

Happy is the man whose work is his play.

Index